English Structure Practices

English Structure Practices

Keith S. Folse
Intensive English Language Institute
Spring Hill College
Mobile, Alabama

Ann Arbor   The University of Michigan Press

*To my family and friends who have been
with me throughout this endeavor, but
especially to my parents.*

Copyright © by the University of Michigan 1983
All rights reserved
ISBN 0-472-08034-2
Library of Congress Catalog Card No. 82-50725
Published in the United States of America by
The University of Michigan Press
Manufactured in the United States of America
⊗ Printed on acid-free paper

2004   2003   2002   2001   17   16   15   14

Contents

Contents

Acknowledgments

Many people have contributed to the preparation of this book. I want to thank Deborah Bilberry for reading parts of the manuscript and making valuable suggestions. I would like to thank Carolyn Sayago for her ideas in revising several exercises and for her help in proofing the manuscript. I would also like to express my gratitude to Dorothy Hirs and Linda Paul, who used these exercises in their classes and offered their comments and suggestions. I am also indebted to Judi Prickett for her considerable advice and assistance in proofing the text.

Friends and colleagues play an important part in the success of a writing endeavour. Therefore, I would like to extend special thanks to two former colleagues who have been extremely important in the writing of this text. I wish to express my sincere thanks to Kay Baldwin for continually urging me to have my material published. I owe a great debt to Rosemary Woullard, who consistently used and advocated my material. They have been a constant source of motivation with their ideas and encouragement.

Finally, I offer a very special word of gratitude to my parents. Their support, encouragement, and counsel have guided me to this level of achievement.

Acknowledgments

To the Teacher

The exercises in this workbook were developed to provide written reinforcement of the grammatical patterns found in *English Sentence Structure* (Robert Krohn and the Staff of the English Language Institute [Ann Arbor: The University of Michigan Press, 1971]). Although the exercises were written to correspond to the lesson sequence in *English Sentence Structure*, they may be used as an independent set of supplementary/reinforcement materials or in conjunction with other structure texts.

Each lesson consists of a chapter outline and vocabulary list, various structure exercises, and two review test exercises. Though the vocabulary list is intended primarily as a reference guide for the students' sake, it may be actively employed in the classroom at the teacher's discretion. The structure exercises require the students to perform various tasks, such as underlining, circling, or selecting the correct answer in a multiple-choice format. The exercises have been graded so that the cognitive level for a given structure gradually increases exercise by exercise. The first of the two review tests requires the students to supply original answers by different methods, such as filling in the blanks or writing a new sentence. The second review test, on the other hand, contains ten multiple-choice questions. Since these review exercises are of two completely different types, they allow all students an opportunity to demonstrate their knowledge without interference caused by the type of question or test. For further practice, this workbook features six comprehension tests, each of which consists of fifty multiple-choice items. These tests correspond to lesson 10 (review of lessons 1–9), lesson 20 (review of lessons 11–19), and lesson 30 (review of lessons 21–29) of *English Sentence Structure*.

At the end of the workbook, there is a section which contains the answers for all exercises in this text. These answers are provided so that students may check to see if their answers are correct. It is supposed that students will use the answer key after they have actually done the exercises. It is further hoped that students will use the answer key to detect their mistakes and then return to the exercise to discover the source of their error. The answer key also makes it possible for students engaged in independent study to use this workbook.

The written exercises in this workbook are short enough to be done in a small amount of time, yet they are thorough enough to provide sufficient practice for the structure in question. These exercises may be done in class or as homework. Furthermore, they may be checked quickly either individually or as a group.

For the most part, the exercises in this workbook follow exactly the structures presented in *English Sentence Structure*. In fact, the page numbers on which the given structure can be found in the Krohn text are given in parentheses with each exercise. Teachers will want to note one digression in particular. This workbook, unlike *English Sentence Structure*, makes an active distinction between "who" and "whom." This digression primarily affects lessons 4 and 9 and, to a lesser extent, lessons 5, 11, and 16.

Lesson 1

A. *Be: am, are, is*

    Statements and questions: It is green. Is it green?
    Contractions: It's green. It isn't green.
    Short answers: Yes, it is. No, it isn't.

B. Singular and plural noun phrases

Vocabulary List

a	comb	noun	small
adjective	contraction	now	statement
am	doctor	old	student
an	dog	open	table
and	door	pen	teacher
answer	easy	pencil	the
architect	green	plural	they
are	happy	pronoun	thirsty
be	he	question	tired
black	heavy	read	today
blue	hungry	red	verb
book	I	right	vowel
businessman	is	room	warm
busy	it	she	watch
chair	key	shirt	we
change	large	shoe	window
circle	late	sick	write
class	lawyer	singular	wrong
closed	long	sleepy	you
cold	new		

Exercise 1 (A.1–3, pp. 1–4)
Write the forms of *be* on the line. Follow the examples.

I   __am__   we   __are__

you _____   you _____

he   _____

she _____   they _____

it   _____

Lesson 1

Exercise 2 (A.1–4, pp. 1–5)
Select the correct form of *be*. Underline the correct answer.

   We (am, is, <u>are</u>) happy.

 1. Mary (am, is, are) busy.
 2. They (am, is, are) hungry.
 3. The students (am, is, are) in class.
 4. You (am, is, are) from South America.
 5. Mr. Lee and Mr. Wong (am, is, are) Chinese.
 6. The teacher (am, is, are) busy.
 7. Jane and John (am, is, are) sick today.
 8. I (am, is, are) sleepy.
 9. You and I (am, is, are) friends.
10. The girls (am, is, are) tired.

Exercise 3 (A.1–4, pp. 1–5)
Write the correct form of *be* on the line.

   We __are__ happy.

 1. You _____ tired now.   6. The watch _____ on the table.

 2. It _____ 10 A.M.   7. John and I _____ students.

 3. I _____ fifteen years old.   8. Pam _____ thirsty.

 4. Pedro _____ from Mexico.   9. Mark _____ a student.

 5. Pedro _____ Mexican.   10. Paul and Mark _____ in class.

Exercise 4 (A.1–4, pp. 1–5)
Select the correct form of *be*. Underline the answer.

(Am, Is, <u>Are</u>) we happy?

1. (Am, Is, Are) the window open?
2. (Am, Is, Are) we late?
3. (Am, Is, Are) John twenty years old?
4. (Am, Is, Are) she here now?
5. (Am, Is, Are) Bill and Mary hungry?

6. (Am, Is, Are) you cold?
7. (Am, Is, Are) they sick today?
8. (Am, Is, Arc) the watch new?
9. (Am, Is, Are) you and Paul students?
10. (Am, Is, Are) Jill tall?

Exercise 5 (A.1–4, pp. 1–5)
Write the correct form of *be* on the line.

_____Are_____ we happy?

1. _____ the boys sick?
2. _____ the pencil long?
3. _____ I wrong?
4. _____ you thirsty now?
5. _____ he cold?

6. _____ the grammar book green?
7. _____ Pat in class?
8. _____ Pat and Matt in class?
9. _____ the keys on the table?
10. _____ you tired?

Exercise 6 (A.1–4, pp. 1–5)
Change the statement into a question.

The table is heavy. _____Is the table heavy?_____

1. The dogs are hungry. _____

2. The pen is new. _____

3. My key is on the table. _____

4. They are from Honduras. _____

3

5. You are sick today. _____

6. It is cold in the room. _____

7. The green books are heavy. _____

8. Bill is thirsty. _____

9. I am right. _____

10. We are wrong. _____

Exercise 7 (A.1–4, pp. 1–5)
Write the correct pronoun.

John   = <u>he</u>

the book   = <u>it</u>

1. the table	= _____		11. the teacher	= _____
2. the tables	= _____		12. the teachers	= _____
3. the boy	= _____		13. the student	= _____
4. the boys	= _____		14. the students	= _____
5. John	= _____		15. the cat	= _____
6. John and I	= _____		16. Paul and Mark	= _____
7. Mary and I	= _____		17. Mr. Smith	= _____
8. you and I	= _____		18. Miss Brown	= _____
9. Mary	= _____		19. Mrs. Jones	= _____
10. Mary and John	= _____		20. the tables and the chairs	= _____

Exercise 8 (A.1–4, pp. 1–5)
Write a pronoun for the noun phrase.

The man is old.

_____He_____ is old.

1. *My grammar book* is green.

   _____ is green.

2. *Mary and I* are hungry now.

   _____ are hungry now.

3. Are *the students* busy?

   Are _____ busy?

4. *The table and chairs* are small.

   _____ are small.

5. *Mary and John* are happy.

   _____ are happy.

6. Is *the man* from Canada?

   Is _____ from Canada?

7. Is *the pen* on the table?

   Is _____ on the table?

8. *You and John* are thirsty.

   _____ are thirsty.

9. *Mrs. Jones* is a teacher.

   _____ is a teacher.

10. Are *the books* heavy?

    Are _____ heavy?

Exercise 9 (A.1–4, pp. 1–5)
Is it a statement? Is it a question? Write *S* on the line if the sentence is a statement or *Q* if it is a question. Add the correct punctuation (period . for a statement and question mark *?* for a question).

____S____ I am right.

____Q____ Am I right?

____Q____ Are the boys in class?

1. _____ Bill is a student

2. _____ It is 10 A.M. now

3. _____ Are we hungry

4. _____ We are hungry

5. _____ Am I correct

6. _____ Is Maria from Mexico

7. _____ Joe is late for class

8. _____ Is Joe late for class

9. _____ She is Chinese

10. _____ Are Mark and Paul busy in class

Exercise 10 (A.3, p. 4)
Write the correct contraction.

he + is = **he's**

1. it + is = _____
2. I + am = _____
3. she + is = _____
4. they + are = _____
5. you + are = _____

6. Mike + is = _____
7. the key + is = _____
8. the boy + is = _____
9. he + is = _____
10. we + are = _____

Exercise 11 (A.3–4, pp. 4–5)
Write the word in parentheses and the correct form of *be* on the line. Practice contractions.

(we) **We're** hungry.

(Joe) **Joe's** a good student.

1. (he) _____ thirsty.
2. (they) _____ cold.
3. (I) _____ a student.
4. (she) _____ a teacher.
5. (it) _____ easy.
6. (they) _____ from Japan.
7. (they) _____ Japanese.
8. (we) _____ late.
9. (Mary) _____ twenty years old.
10. (I) _____ happy.
11. (you) _____ sick.
12. (she) _____ sleepy.
13. (it) _____ blue.

14. (they) _____ right.
15. (John) _____ hungry at noon.
16. (you) _____ a lawyer.
17. (I) _____ late for class.
18. (we) _____ wrong.
19. (you) _____ happy today.
20. (he) _____ tired.
21. (Mary) _____ from Mexico.
22. (the book) _____ green.
23. (it) _____ a grammar book.
24. (I) _____ in the room.
25. (the key) _____ small.

Exercise 12   (A.5, p. 6)
Answer the questions with an affirmative short answer.

Is the book green?

__Yes, it is.__

1. Are the students busy?

_____

2. Is Mr. Miller in the room?

_____

3. Are we late for class?

_____

4. Is Joseph a student?

_____

5. Are you in the United States?

_____

6. Am I late?

_____

7. Is the key small?

_____

8. Are the books heavy?

_____

9. Is Anne from England?

_____

10. Are you hungry?

_____

Exercise 13   (A.6, pp. 7–8)
Answer the questions with a negative short answer.

Is the book green?

__No, it isn't.__

1. Are the boys sick?

_____

2. Is Mr. Smith in the class?

_____

3. Are we hungry?

_____

4. Is Maria a doctor?

_____

5. Are you in China now?

_____

6. Are we on page twenty?

_____

7. Is the answer correct?

_____

8. Are the answers correct?

_____

9. Is the book heavy?

_____

10. Am I wrong?

_____

Lesson 1

Exercise 14 (A.5–6, pp. 6–8)
Change the statements into questions. Write an affirmative short answer and a negative short answer.

The chair is black.

___Is the chair black?___

___Yes, it is.___

___No, it isn't.___

1. You are hungry.

_____

_____

_____

2. The boys are cold.

_____

_____

_____

3. I am a good student.

_____

_____

_____

4. They are late for class.

_____

_____

_____

5. The books are on the table.

_____

_____

_____

Exercise 15 (A.7, p. 8)
Answer the questions with a negative short answer. Then give a true answer.

Is the boy wrong?

No, _he isn't. He's right._____ .

1. Is the grammar book red?

    No, _____ .

2. Are the windows open?

    No, _____ .

3. Are you a doctor?

    No, _____ .

4. Is Mary from Japan?

    No, _____ .

5. Is English difficult?

    No, _____ .

Exercise 16 (B.1, p. 9)
Write *a* or *an* on the line. If *a* or *an* is not possible, draw a line.

I am __a__ teacher.

It's __an__ apple tree.

They are __—__ doctors.

1. We are _____ students.

2. He is _____ engineer.

3. Joe and Matt are _____ friends.

4. It is _____ book.

5. Mr. Smith is _____ teacher.

6. Is it _____ grammar book?

7. You are _____ student here.

8. You are _____ students here.

9. He is _____ architect.

10. Are they _____ lawyers?

Exercise 17   (B.2, p. 10)
Change the statement from singular to plural.

The girl is beautiful. ___The girls are beautiful.___

1. The boy is hungry. _____

2. He is sick now. _____

3. I am busy in class. _____

4. The shoe is black. _____

5. Is the book closed? _____

6. Am I late for class? _____

7. He is a teacher. _____

8. You are a student. _____

9. The cat is black. _____

10. He is a good student. _____

Exercise 18: Review Test
A. Write the correct form of *be* on the line.

1. I _____ tired now.

2. It _____ 10 A.M.

3. We _____ not tired.

4. Mrs. Smith and you _____ hungry.

5. Mary and John _____ busy.

6. _____ you very thirsty?

B. Write the plural of the sentence. Use contractions.

1. I'm here. _____

2. You're a student. _____

3. He's busy now. _____

4. It's a book. _____

C. Write a question. Give a short answer.

1. The books are green.

    _____

    Yes, _____ .

2. The watch is new.

    _____

    No, _____ .

3. You are tall.

    _____

    Yes, _____ .

D. Write *a* or *an* on the line. If *a* or *an* is not possible, draw a line.

1. My father is _____ lawyer.

2. My father is _____ good lawyer.

3. I'm _____ architect.

4. I'm _____ hungry.

5. Are they _____ students?

Exercise 19: Review Test
Choose the correct answer. Put a circle around the letter of the answer.

1. "Is John happy?"
   "Yes, _____ ."
   a) he is
   b) John's
   c) is he
   d) is thirsty

2. "Are you thirsty?"
   "No, _____ ."
   a) I'm
   b) you aren't
   c) I'm not
   d) I amn't

3. Mr. Allen is _____ .
   a) teacher
   b) engineer
   c) hungry
   d) a hungry

4. "Are the books open?"
   "No, the books aren't open. _____ ."
   a) It's closed.
   b) It's open.
   c) They're closed.
   d) They're open.

5. "Are you from Africa?"

   "No, _____ ."

   a) we are

   b) we aren't

   c) you're

   d) you aren't

6. "Are the girls hungry now?"

   "Yes, _____ ."

   a) they're

   b) we're

   c) they are

   d) we are

7. "Are they teachers?"

   "No, they aren't teachers. Mary is a student, and John and Bill _____ ."

   a) is an architect

   b) are an architect

   c) is architects

   d) are architects

8. My grammar book is on the table. _____ green.

   a) They're

   b) I am

   c) It's

   d) He's

9. The red pencils are on the black chair. The pencils are red. The chair _____ .

   a) is black

   b) are black

   c) is red

   d) red

10. " _____ on the table?"

   "Yes, they are."

   a) Are the books

   b) Is the book

   c) Are the book

   d) Is the books

Lesson 2

A. Simple present tense with verbs other than *be*
   Statements: He works.
   Questions with *do, does*: Does he work?
   Short answers: Yes, he does. No, he doesn't.

B. Single-word adverbs of frequency: *always, usually, often,* etc.
   Position in statements and questions

Vocabulary List

adverb	every	never	speak
afternoon	has	night	study
always	have	often	supper
arrive	home	orange	tea
begin	juice	practice	teach
breakfast	leave	pronounce	toast
coffee	lesson	pronunciation	understand
come	letter	restaurant	usually
cornflakes	light	sad	very
day	like	sandwich	week
drink	live	seldom	well
eat	lunch	sing	white
egg	milk	sometimes	word
ever	morning	soup	work

Exercise 1 (A.1, pp. 11–12)
Write the forms of the verbs in simple present tense. Use *I, you, he, she, we,* and *they*. Follow the examples.

work

1. __I work__
2. __you work__
3. __he works__
4. __she works__
5. __we work__
6. __they work__

speak

7. _____
8. _____
9. _____
10. _____
11. _____
12. _____

have	*practice*
13. _____	19. _____
14. _____	20. _____
15. _____	21. _____
16. _____	22. _____
17. _____	23. _____
18. _____	24. _____

study	*do*
25. _____	31. _____
26. _____	32. _____
27. _____	33. _____
28. _____	34. _____
29. _____	35. _____
30. _____	36. _____

Exercise 2   (A.1, pp. 11–12)
Underline the correct form of the verb.

> We (<u>study,</u> studies) in the library.
> He (eat, <u>eats</u>) his lunch at noon.

1. He (begin, begins) class at 8:00 A.M.
2. They (drink, drinks) orange juice for breakfast.
3. You (have, has) two books and three pencils.

4. She (pronounce, pronounces) English well.
5. I (work, works) in writing class.
6. The bus (arrive, arrives) at 10 A.M.
7. The student (come, comes) late every morning.
8. Mary (eat, eats) soup for lunch.
9. Mary and Mark (leave, leaves) in the morning.
10. You and I (sing, sings) well.
11. The book (is, are) on the table.
12. The boys (go, goes) to school in the morning.
13. You and I (am, are) friends.
14. Mr. Lee (speak, speaks) Chinese.
15. The teacher (arrive, arrives) late every day.
16. The students (study, studies) English.
17. He (have, has) four books for grammar class.
18. Mike (like, likes) cornflakes.
19. I (teach, teaches) French.
20. I (have, has) my book at home.

Exercise 3 (A.1, pp. 11–12)
Write the correct form of the verb on the line.

(practice) He __**practices**__ in the morning.

(read) They __**read**__ in the classroom.

1. (arrive) I _____ late every day.

2. (begin) The students _____ their homework after supper.

3. (come) Mary and Bill _____ to class at 10 A.M.

4. (drink) Mark _____ milk for lunch.

5. (eat) You _____ eggs and toast for breakfast.

6. (have) Bill ———————— three books for grammar class.

7. (leave) He ———————— school at 3:30 P.M.

8. (pronounce) We ———————— words in pronunciation class.

9. (sing) The girls ———————— very well.

10. (work) The doctor ———————— every day.

11. (be) She ———————— a teacher.

12. (like) Joe and Matt ———————— soup.

13. (have) We ———————— juice for breakfast.

14. (be) Breakfast ———————— in the morning.

15. (speak) The teacher ———————— English, French, and Spanish.

16. (live) Mr. Hart ———————— in Germany.

17. (practice) They ———————— tennis in the park.

18. (eat) Mike ———————— soup for lunch.

19. (be) The students ———————— in class every morning.

20. (study) Pat ———————— English and French.

Exercise 4 (A.2–3, pp. 12–14)

Write the question forms of the verbs in simple present tense. Use *I, you, he, she, we,* and *they*.
Follow the examples.

work

1. __do I work__

2. __do you work__

3. __does he work__

4. __does she work__

5. __do we work__

6. __do they work__

speak

7. _____

8. _____

9. _____

10. _____

11. _____

12. _____

have

13. _____

14. _____

15. _____

16. _____

17. _____

18. _____

practice

19. _____

20. _____

21. _____

22. _____

23. _____

24. _____

study

25. _____

26. _____

27. _____

28. _____

29. _____

30. _____

do

31. _____

32. _____

33. _____

34. _____

35. _____

36. _____

Lesson 2

Exercise 5 (A.2–3, pp. 12–14)
Make a question form.

I work   _____ **do I work** _____

she works   _____ **does she work** _____

1. they drink   _____

2. I have   _____

3. we work   _____

4. they teach   _____

5. you sing   _____

6. he drinks   _____

7. you leave   _____

8. we study   _____

9. she speaks   _____

10. Bill eats   _____

11. he works   _____

12. she studies   _____

13. you like   _____

14. you have   _____

15. he goes   _____

16. they like   _____

17. he has   _____

18. we go   _____

19. you live   _____

20. John has   _____

Exercise 6 (A.2–3, pp. 12–14)
Change the statement into a question.

We study English. __Do we study English?__

1. They sing well. _____

2. She comes late every day. _____

3. They have ten books. _____

4. Paul has a new watch. _____

5. Mary arrives at 9:00 A.M. _____

Exercise 7 (A.1–3, pp. 11–14)
Write the correct form of the verb on the line.

(write) You __write__ long letters.

__Do__ you __write__ long letters?

1. (eat)   He _____ lunch here.

   _____ he _____ lunch here?

2. (have) He _____ ten pencils.

   _____ he _____ ten pencils?

3. (drink) She _____ juice.

   _____ she _____ juice?

4. (study) Bob _____ mathematics.

   _____ Bob _____ mathematics?

5. (speak) Mark _____ Spanish and French.

   _____ Mark _____ Spanish and French?

Exercise 8   (A.4, pp. 14–15)
Write a short affirmative answer.

Does Mary like coffee?

_____ Yes, she does. _____

Do they like coffee?

_____ Yes, they do. _____

1. Do they eat lunch at noon?

   _____

2. Does the library have books?

   _____

3. Do Bob and Carol study in the afternoon?

   _____

4. Does the girl come to class on time?

   _____

5. Does Mr. Allen teach reading class?

   _____

6. Do you have a cat?

   _____

7. Does Sue like tea?

   _____

8. Does the boy have a book?

   _____

9. Do they like the class?

   _____

10. Do I pronounce well?

   _____

Exercise 9 (A.5, pp. 15–16)
Write a negative short answer.

Does Mary like coffee?

_____ No, she doesn't. _____

Do they like coffee?

_____ No, they don't. _____

1. Does grammar class begin at 7:00 A.M.?

   _____

2. Do the students eat breakfast at night?

   _____

3. Do Ann and Dan play tennis?

   _____

4. Does the book have the answers?

   _____

5. Does Bill have two pencils?

   _____

6. Does Ann have class every morning?

   _____

7. Do you speak French?

   _____

8. Do I pronounce well?

   _____

9. Do you and Sue speak French?

   _____

10. Does the cat like oranges?

   _____

Lesson 2

Exercise 10   (A.4–5, pp. 14–16)
Write a short answer.

Does Mary have a book?

Yes, __she does__ .

1. Do you have a book?

   Yes, _____ .

2. Does he have a bicycle?

   No, _____ .

3. Do they eat lunch at noon?

   Yes, _____ .

4. Does she have a car?

   Yes, _____ .

5. Do you and I speak French well?

   Yes, _____ .

6. Do they like milk?

   No, _____ .

7. Does Mary eat apples?

   Yes, _____ .

8. Do John and Mark like apples?

   Yes, _____ .

9. Does he like juice?

   No, _____ .

10. Does Ann work here?

    No, _____ .

Exercise 11: Review of Question Forms   (pp. 1–5, 12–14)
Write *do, does, am, is,* or *are* on the line.

__Do__ you speak English?

1. _____ the boys good students?

2. _____ they study every night?

3. _____ today Monday?

4. _____ I a good student?

5. _____ he have a car?

6. _____ the car a new car?

7. _____ Mark have a new watch?

8. _____ Mark like his watch?

9. _____ you hungry now?

10. _____ John in class?

__Are__ you a doctor?

11. _____ they speak English?

12. _____ I wrong?

13. _____ Paul and Sue at home?

14. _____ they walk home?

15. _____ they tired?

16. _____ the class very difficult?

17. _____ Mr. Green a good teacher?

18. _____ the teacher pronounce well?

19. _____ your father a doctor?

20. _____ you like apples?

Exercise 12: Review of Question Forms (pp. 1–5, 12–14)
Write *do, does, am, is,* or *are* on the line.

__Do__ you speak English?

1. _____ you live with your family?

2. _____ you from France?

3. _____ you speak French?

4. _____ she a good student?

5. _____ she study with you?

6. _____ they work here?

7. _____ Joe have a new car?

8. _____ the new car blue or green?

9. _____ the teacher have two books?

10. _____ Mr. South a good teacher?

__Are__ you a doctor?

11. _____ they tall?

12. _____ she play tennis in the afternoon?

13. _____ Mark like coffee?

14. _____ the coffee good?

15. _____ we have a test today?

16. _____ the grammar tests difficult?

17. _____ I right?

18. _____ you understand?

19. _____ you very tired?

20. _____ Mary and Sue like apples?

Exercise 13: Review of Short Answers (pp. 6–8, 14–16)
Write a short answer.

Do the boys have a book?

Yes, __they do__ .

1. Are they here?

Yes, _____ .

2. Is John hungry?

No, _____ .

3. Do they speak English?

Yes, _____ .

4. Are the boys here?

No, _____ .

Is Paul here?

No, __he isn't__ .

5. Does John have a book?

Yes, _____ .

6. Is the book green?

Yes, _____ .

7. Do you like the book?

No, _____ .

8. Are you and John hungry?

Yes, _____ .

23

9. Does Mary have a car?

Yes, _____ .

10. Is the car blue?

No, _____ .

11. Do the boys study?

Yes, _____ .

12. Do you understand the lesson?

No, _____ .

13. Is English easy?

Yes, _____ .

14. Are pencils heavy?

No, _____ .

15. Do you need a pencil?

Yes, _____ .

16. Are you hungry?

Yes, _____ .

17. Are you a student?

Yes, _____ .

18. Are you students?

Yes, _____ .

19. Do you have a pen?

Yes, _____ .

20. Do you have a nickel?

Yes, _____ .

21. Do Joe and Mark like bread?

Yes, _____ .

22. Are they in class now?

No, _____ .

23. Am I a teacher?

Yes, _____ .

24. Are you a student?

Yes, _____ .

25. Do you study every night?

Yes, _____ .

Exercise 14: Review of Short Answers   (pp. 6–8, 14–16)
Write a short answer.

Do the boys have a book?

Yes, __they do__ .

1. Is your name John?

No, _____ .

2. Are you John?

No, _____ .

Are you sick now?

No, __I'm not__ .

3. Is today Monday?

No, _____ .

4. Do you like fish?

Yes, _____ .

5. Do you speak English?

Yes, _____ .

6. Are the girls here?

Yes, _____ .

7. Am I tall?

No, _____ .

8. Are you tall?

Yes, _____ .

9. Does the man have a pencil?

Yes, _____ .

10. Does Mr. Miller write long letters?

No, _____ .

11. Is the pencil green?

No, _____ .

12. Are the pencils heavy?

No, _____ .

13. Does the teacher have a pencil?

Yes, _____ .

14. Is vocabulary class difficult?

No, _____ .

15. Do we have a green grammar book?

Yes, _____ .

16. Is the book blue?

No, _____ .

17. Do you like the book?

Yes, _____ .

18. Is the watch new?

Yes, _____ .

19. Do you like the watch?

Yes, _____ .

20. Are John and I good students?

Yes, _____ .

21. Are you and I good students?

Yes, _____ .

22. Is the test difficult?

No, _____ .

23. Does John like bread?

No, _____ .

24. Is the pencil yellow?

Yes, _____ .

25. Do John, Mary, and Paul have a bicycle?

Yes, _____ .

Exercise 15 (B.1, p. 17)
Write the correct adverb of frequency.

1. _____always_____ = all of the time

2. _____ = most of the time

3. _____ = much of the time

4. _____ = some of the time

5. _____ = almost never

6. _____ = not at any time

Exercise 16 (B.1, p. 17)
Write the correct frequency word and verb form on the lines.

He <u>writes</u> letters <u>all of the time.</u>

He __always__ __writes__ letters.

1. John <u>has</u> eggs for breakfast <u>much of the time.</u>

   John _____ _____ eggs for breakfast.

2. I do <u>not</u> <u>eat</u> soup <u>at any time.</u>

   I _____ _____ soup.

3. They <u>almost never</u> <u>study</u> grammar.

   They _____ _____ grammar.

4. We <u>drink</u> orange juice for breakfast <u>some of the time.</u>

   We _____ _____ orange juice for breakfast.

5. Mark <u>drinks</u> milk for breakfast <u>much of the time.</u>

   Mark _____ _____ milk for breakfast.

Exercise 17 (B.1, p. 17)
Write a new sentence by substituting a word like *always* for the group of words that expresses the same idea.

Pam eats lunch in a restaurant most of the time.

Pam usually eats lunch in a restaurant.

1. I study grammar at night some of the time.

_____

2. He studies vocabulary most of the time.

_____

3. We practice pronunciation all of the time.

_____

4. They almost never write letters to their parents.

_____

5. You have coffee for breakfast all of the time.

_____

6. Jack comes to class late much of the time.

_____

7. Mary does not sing at any time.

_____

8. We almost never speak Spanish in class.

_____

9. They study at night much of the time.

_____

10. I do not eat toast at any time.

_____

Exercise 18   (B.2, p. 18)
Write the correct verb form and frequency word on the lines.

Mary <u>is</u> tired <u>some of the time</u>.

Mary ____**is**____ ____**sometimes**____ tired.

1. I <u>am</u> hungry <u>all of the time</u>.

   I _____ _____ hungry.

2. They <u>are</u> <u>not</u> sad <u>at any time</u>.

   They _____ _____ sad.

3. Joseph <u>is</u> late <u>most of the time</u>.

   Joseph _____ _____ late.

4. The lessons <u>are</u> easy <u>much of the time</u>.

   The lessons _____ _____ easy.

5. We <u>are</u> <u>almost never</u> sleepy.

   We _____ _____ sleepy.

Exercise 19   (B.2, pp. 18–19)
Write a new sentence. Use a word like *always* for the group of words that expresses the same idea.

Mary is tired some of the time. ___**Mary is sometimes tired.**___

1. The class is at 8 A.M. all of the time. _____

2. The letters are almost never long. _____

3. He is hungry most of the time. _____

4. We are almost never at home in the morning. _____

5. Bill is not absent at any time. _____

6. They're almost never in class. _____

7. I'm well all of the time. _____

8. Mary's happy much of the time. _____

9. The teacher is busy in the afternoon some of the time. _____

10. She is not sick at any time. _____

Exercise 20   (B.1–2, pp. 17–19)
Underline the correct form.

Mary (<u>usually comes</u>, comes usually) to class.

1. Mark (never is, is never) sad.
2. They (always eat, eat always) in the kitchen.
3. We (never study, study never) in the morning.
4. He (sometimes is, is sometimes) late for class.
5. Maria (seldom drinks, drinks seldom) coffee.
6. You (always arrive, arrive always) late for lunch.
7. My teacher (always is, is always) correct.
8. We (seldom speak, speak seldom) Spanish in class.
9. You and I (never go, go never) to the bookstore.
10. They (seldom are, are seldom) hungry at night.
11. He (usually is, is usually) wrong.
12. The teacher (always has, has always) his book.
13. Breakfast (always is, is always) at 8 A.M.
14. Don (often is, is often) absent from class.
15. She (never studies, studies never).

Exercise 21   (B.3, p. 19)
Change the statement into a question.

He is usually busy. _____ **Is he usually busy ?** _____

They always eat bread at lunch. **Do they always eat bread at lunch ?**

1. The man is often in class. _____

2. They usually work in the afternoon. _____

3. He often studies grammar. _____

4. You're often in the library. _____

5. Pencils are always yellow. _____

6. We always write our homework. _____

7. They're usually on time. _____

8. They usually drink milk. _____

9. She always eats a sandwich for lunch. _____

10. She is sometimes late. _____

Exercise 22   (B.4, p. 20)
Write a question using *ever*.

You read a book. _**Do you ever read a book ?**_____

He is tired at night. _**Is he ever tired at night ?**_____

1. They are at home in the morning. _____

2. They eat hamburgers for dinner. _____

3. You sing in class. _____

4. I am wrong. _____

5. We have toast for breakfast. _____

Exercise 23   (B.4, p. 20)
Write a short answer to the question.

Do you ever eat hamburgers for lunch? (yes / much of the time)

___**Yes, often.**_____

1. Are you ever late for class? (no / not at any time)

_____

2. Do you ever write letters? (yes / most of the time)

_____

3. Do you ever eat dinner in a restaurant? (yes / all of the time)

_____

4. Are you ever sad? (yes / some of the time)

_____

5. Do you ever drink juice for breakfast? (yes / much of the time)

_____

30

Exercise 24: Review Test
A. Write a question and give a short answer.

1. You eat toast.

   _____

   Yes, _____ .

2. They're sick.

   _____

   No, _____ .

3. He always arrives late.

   _____

   Yes, _____ .

4. I'm usually right.

   _____

   No, _____ .

B. Write a new sentence using a word like *always*.

1. We eat lunch in the kitchen all of the time.

   _____

2. They are in class most of the time.

   _____

3. I write letters some of the time.

   _____

4. You do not understand the lesson at any time.

   _____

5. He is almost never late.

   _____

C. Write a question using *ever*. Give an appropriate answer.

1. You are in the library.

   _____

   Yes, _____ . (most of the time)

2. We eat lunch at noon.

   _____

   No, _____ . (not at any time)

D. Underline the correct form.

1. John (is always, always is) on time.
2. Mary (begin, begins) class at 8:00 A.M.
3. (Do, Does) they have ten books?
4. (Is, Are) we late?

5. They (eat usually, usually eat) after class.
6. I (write, writes) letters every morning.
7. I (always do, do always) my homework.

Exercise 25: Review Test
Choose the correct answer. Put a circle around the letter of the answer.

1. Mary almost never comes to class on time. She _____ always late.
   a) is
   b) arrive
   c) are
   d) arrives

2. "Do the boys have books?"
   "No, _____ ."
   a) they aren't
   b) he isn't
   c) they don't
   d) he doesn't

3. "Does he ever eat hamburgers for lunch?"
   "No, _____ ."
   a) always
   b) often
   c) usually
   d) never

4. Mr. Miller almost never has coffee in the morning. He _____ coffee in the morning.
   a) seldom has
   b) has seldom
   c) has often
   d) often has

5. "Do you have two books for class?"
   "Yes, _____ ."
   a) I'm
   b) I am
   c) I do
   d) I does

6. He does not come to class.
   He _____ to class.
   a) ever comes
   b) comes ever
   c) never comes
   d) comes never

7. " _____ heavy?"
   "Yes, the grammar book is very heavy."
   a) Do it
   b) Does it
   c) Are it
   d) Is it

8. "Do they have class in the morning?"
   "No, _____ ."
   a) ever
   b) not have
   c) they no have
   d) they do not

9. " _____ to class?"
   "Yes, I always do."
   a) Always do you go
   b) Do always you go
   c) Do you always go
   d) Do you go always

10. We read in the morning, and they _____ in the morning.
    a) reads
    b) read
    c) are
    d) does

Lesson 3

A. Adverbials of place and time

B. Past tense of *be* in statements, questions, and short answers:
   He was here. Was he here? Yes, he was.

C. Past tense of regular verbs
   Regular past tense ending: He worked.
   Questions and short answers with *did*: Did he work? Yes, he did.

Vocabulary List

attend	hot	noon	talk
building	hot dog	o'clock	town
difficult	kitchen	past	visit
dinner	last	place	wait
fish	learn	present	walk
glass	library	repeat	want
go	listen (to)	sleep	watch
hamburger	minute	store	

Exercise 1 (A, pp. 21–22)

Write *place, time,* or *frequency* to tell the type of adverbial.

at 9:00 A.M.	time
in class	place
never	frequency

1. in the library _____

2. here _____

3. at 7:00 A.M. _____

4. in New York _____

5. in ten minutes _____

6. usually _____

7. in the morning _____

8. now _____

9. always _____

10. at the store _____

33

Exercise 2   (A, pp. 21–22)
Put *C* by the correct sentences and *X* by the wrong sentences.

__C__   They study in the library every day.

__X__   They study every day in the library.

_____ 1. We eat lunch in the cafeteria at noon.

_____ 2. Mary studies at night in the library.

_____ 3. She reads books in the morning in class.

_____ 4. I don't sing in the bathroom at night.

_____ 5. She drinks tea in the kitchen in the afternoon.

Exercise 3   (A, pp. 21–22)
Write a new sentence from the parts.

(in the morning / We eat / in the kitchen)

We eat in the kitchen in the morning.

(every day / at home / The man has supper)

The man has supper at home every day.

1. (We eat lunch / at noon / in a restaurant)

   _____

2. (at 10 A.M. / They have class / at the university)

   _____

3. (there / before class / I have coffee)

   _____

4. (in the library / He studies / every night)

   _____

5. (She practices pronunciation / in the laboratory / every day)

   _____

6. (to class / every day / They go)

_____

7. (You drink milk / at the table / in the morning)

_____

8. (at night / in the library / You write letters)

_____

9. (every day / in class / She studies)

_____

10. (to class / He comes / every day)

_____

Exercise 4   (A, pp. 21–22)
Write a new sentence from the parts.

(English / We / study / in class / every day)

_We study English in class every day._____

1. (teach / in my school / They / every day / Spanish)

_____

2. (usually / the lessons / Mary / in class / understands)

_____

3. (every day / goes / at 7:00 A.M. / He / to the office)

_____

4. (at 8:30 / breakfast / eat / They / in the morning)

_____

5. (I / have / coffee / in the morning / in the kitchen)

_____

6. (is / in class / always / The girl / in the morning)

_____

7. (my homework / do / seldom / in my room / I)

_____

8. (every day / He / to class / at noon / comes)

_____

9. (in Atlanta / on Main Street / in a big house / lives / He)

_____

10. (baseball / usually / at 4:00 P.M. / plays / John)

_____

Exercise 5 (B.1, p. 23; p. 3)
Write the forms of *be* in *present* and *past*. Follow the examples.

am, is, are

1. I ____am____ a student.

2. You _____ in class.

3. He _____ here now.

4. She _____ sick now.

5. It _____ ten o'clock.

6. We _____ students.

7. They _____ at home now.

was, were

8. I ___was___ a student in 1970.

9. You _____ in class yesterday.

10. He _____ here last night.

11. She _____ sick last week.

12. It _____ cold yesterday.

13. We _____ students two years ago.

14. They _____ at home last night.

Exercise 6   (B.1–2, pp. 23–24)
Underline the correct form.

He (<u>was</u>, were) here yesterday.
(<u>Was</u>, Were) he here yesterday?

1. Mrs. Smith (was, were) right yesterday.
2. They (was, were) late yesterday.
3. We (was, were) in class an hour ago.

4. (Was, Were) you at home last night?
5. (Was, Were) it a green book?

Exercise 7   (B.1–2, pp. 23–24)
Write the correct form of *to be*.

He ___**was**___ late yesterday.

1. Jack _____ sick last week.

2. _____ they in England last month?

3. I _____ tired yesterday.

4. He _____ a good student last course.

5. _____ she in class yesterday?

6. The class _____ difficult yesterday.

7. The students _____ on time yesterday.

8. _____ Matt absent last week?

9. She _____ a student in 1980.

10. We _____ very hungry an hour ago.

Lesson 3

Exercise 8 (B.2–3, pp. 24–26)
Change each statement into a question. Give an affirmative short answer and a negative short answer.

The chair was black.

Was the chair black ?

Yes, it was .

No, it wasn't .

1. You were hungry.

_____

_____

_____

2. The boys were cold.

_____

_____

_____

3. I was wrong.

_____

_____

_____

4. They were late for class.

_____

_____

_____

5. Mary was in the kitchen.

_____

_____

_____

38

Exercise 9 (C.1, p. 26; p. 11)
Write the forms of *work* in *present* and *past* tense. Follow the examples.

verb

1. I _____work_____ every day.
2. You _____ at night.
3. He _____ all of the time.
4. She _____ every day.
5. It _____ most of the time.
6. We _____ every afternoon.
7. They _____ in class every day.

verb + *ed*

8. I _____worked_____ yesterday.
9. You _____ last night.
10. He _____ an hour ago.
11. She _____ yesterday.
12. It _____ last week.
13. We _____ last summer.
14. They _____ in class yesterday.

Exercise 10 (C.1, p. 26)
Write the past tense form.

I want _____I wanted_____

1. he studies _____
2. she listens _____
3. they attend _____
4. I am _____
5. you present _____
6. he learns _____
7. you talk _____
8. she is _____
9. you arrive _____
10. he waits _____
11. I repeat _____
12. I work _____
13. he works _____

14. they study ——————————————

15. you like ——————————————

Exercise 11 (C.2–3, pp. 27–29)
Change each statement into a question. Give an affirmative short answer and a negative short answer.

John studied French.

_Did John study French?_____

_Yes, he did._____

_No, he didn't._____

1. We practiced writing.

————————————————————————————————————

———————————————————

———————————————————

2. I studied the right lesson.

————————————————————————————————————

———————————————————

———————————————————

3. He asked the question.

————————————————————————————————————

———————————————————

———————————————————

4. Mary and John liked the book.

————————————————————————————————————

———————————————————

———————————————————

5. He waited for Pat.

_____

_____

_____

6. They wanted to go home.

_____

_____

_____

7. She repeated the words.

_____

_____

_____

8. The student arrived late.

_____

_____

_____

9. Mr. Miller worked there for two years.

_____

_____

_____

10. The cat liked the milk.

_____

_____

_____

Exercise 12: Verb Discrimination: Present/Past, Be / *Regular Verbs*
Circle the correct verb forms. Read the sentences carefully.

John and Mary (study, studies, (studied)) vocabulary yesterday.

1. They always (eat, have, are) their books.
2. She (is, was, has) tired yesterday.
3. We (are, were, do) not want a glass of milk now.
4. (Do, Does, Did) John come to class yesterday?
5. (Was, Were, Are) they thirsty an hour ago?
6. You (wants, worked, wait) last year.
7. John and Mary did not (practice, practices, practiced) tennis.
8. The boys (are, was, were) here last night.
9. The boys and girls (work, works, worked) every day last month.
10. I (am, did, was) not late for class last week.
11. The student (do, does, did) not have his book now.
12. It (is, was, did) not hot yesterday.
13. You and Mary never (listened, speaks, asks) to the teacher.
14. She (is, was, does) not speak English.
15. (Do, Did, Does) you do the homework last night?

Exercise 13: Short Answer Practice
Change the question to past tense. Write a short answer.

Did
~~Do~~ the boys have a book?

Yes, **they did** .

Was
~~Is~~ Paul here?

Yes, **he was** .

1. Are they here?

   Yes, _____ .

2. Is John hungry?

   No, _____ .

3. Do they speak English?

   Yes, _____ .

4. Are the boys here?

   No, _____ .

5. Does John have a book?

   Yes, _____ .

6. Is the book green?

   Yes, _____ .

7. Do you like the book?

   No, _____ .

8. Are you and John hungry?

   Yes, _____ .

9. Does Mary have a car?

Yes, _____ .

10. Is the car blue?

No, _____ .

11. Do the boys study?

Yes, _____ .

12. Do you understand the lesson?

No, _____ .

13. Is the test easy?

Yes, _____ .

14. Are the tests easy?

No, _____ .

15. Do you need a pencil?

· Yes, _____ .

16. Are you hungry?

Yes, _____ .

17. Are you a student?

Yes, _____ .

18. Are you students?

Yes, _____ .

19. Do you have a pen?

No, _____ .

20. Do you have a nickel?

Yes, _____ .

21. Do John and Mary like the sandwich?

Yes, _____ .

22. Are they in class?

No, _____ .

23. Am I a good teacher?

Yes, _____ .

24. Are you a good student?

Yes, _____ .

25. Do you study at night?

Yes, _____ .

Exercise 14: Short Answer Practice
Change the question to past tense. Write a short answer.

Did
~~Do~~ the boys have a book?

Yes, _they did_____ .

Were
~~Are~~ you sick?

No, _I wasn't_____ .

1. Is your father the president?

No, _____ .

2. Are you the president?

No, _____ .

3. Is the man hungry?

No, _____ .

4. Do you like the movie?

Yes, _____ .

43

5. Do you speak English?

   Yes, ——————————— .

6. Are the girls here?

   Yes, ——————————— .

7. Am I right?

   No, ——————————— .

8. Are you right?

   Yes, ——————————— .

9. Does the man have a pencil?

   Yes, ——————————— .

10. Does Mr. Miller write long letters?

    No, ——————————— .

11. Is the pencil green?

    No, ——————————— .

12. Are the books heavy?

    No, ——————————— .

13. Does the teacher have a pencil?

    Yes, ——————————— .

14. Is vocabulary class difficult?

    No, ——————————— .

15. Do we have a green grammar book?

    Yes, ——————————— .

16. Is the book blue?

    No, ——————————— .

17. Do you like the book?

    Yes, ——————————— .

18. Is the watch new?

    Yes, ——————————— .

19. Do you like the watch?

    Yes, ——————————— .

20. Are John and I good students?

    Yes, ——————————— .

21. Are you and I good students?

    Yes, ——————————— .

22. Is the test difficult?

    No, ——————————— .

23. Does John like bread?

    No, ——————————— .

24. Is the test easy?

    Yes, ——————————— .

25. Do Paul, Mary, and John have a car?

    No, ——————————— .

Exercise 15: Review Test
A. Write a new sentence from the parts.

1. (in class / We study / every day / English)

   _____

2. (every day / to the bank / at 7:00 A.M. / He goes)

   _____

3. (in the library / I was / last night / at 8:00)

   _____

B. Write the past tense.

1. I watch   _____

2. you study   _____

3. he works   _____

4. they practice _____

5. she is   _____

6. we are   _____

C. Make a question. Give an affirmative short answer and a negative short answer.

1. The man listened to the radio.

   _____ ?

   _____ .

   _____ .

2. He played tennis yesterday.

   _____ ?

   _____ .

   _____ .

45

3. You practiced the verbs yesterday.

_____ ?

_____ .

_____ .

4. Mary and Matt arrived at noon.

_____ ?

_____ .

_____ .

D. Underline the correct word.

1. I (am, is, was, were) here yesterday.
2. Bob and I (walk, walks, walked) to school last month.
3. The teacher (pronounce, pronounces, pronounced) the words yesterday.
4. (Do, Does, Did) he ask the question yesterday?
5. (Am, Is, Was, Were) he here now?
6. Did you (listen, listens, listened) to the radio last night?
7. (Was, Were, Does, Did) Mary call you yesterday?
8. (Does, Is) the book blue?
9. (Are, Do) they study every night?
10. (Do, Does, Is, Are) they speak English well?

Exercise 16: Review Test
Choose the correct answer. Put a circle around the letter of the answer.

1. We study grammar ____ at 10 A.M.
   a) every day
   b) every week
   c) in the library
   d) always
2. "Did John work with you?"
   "Yes, _____ ."
   a) he did
   b) he is
   c) he was
   d) he does

3. " _____ read the book last night?"
   "Yes, I did."
   a) Do you
   b) Did you
   c) Do I
   d) Did I
4. We like to write. We write _____ .
   a) every day letters in our room
   b) letters every day in our room
   c) in our room every day letters
   d) letters in our room every day

5. He _____ coffee at 7:00 A.M.
    a) have usually
    b) has usually
    c) usually have
    d) usually has
6. He _____ in class last year.
    a) never practiced
    b) practiced never
    c) never practices
    d) practices never
7. The boy _____ busy.
    a) didn't
    b) weren't
    c) don't
    d) wasn't

8. "Did she _____ yesterday?"
   "No, she didn't."
    a) studied
    b) studies
    c) study
    d) studyed
9. "_____ you watch television?"
   "No, never."
    a) Are
    b) Do
    c) Were
    d) Does
10. "Were you busy last night?"
    "Yes, I ____ the radio for four hours."
    a) listen
    b) listen to
    c) listened to
    d) listened

Lesson 4

A. Wh-questions: *who, what, where, when*

B. Present progressive: He is writing.

C. Using adjectives and nouns to modify nouns: small class, grammar class.

Vocabulary List

actual	dozen	know	rarely
ago	entire	lamp	simple
apple	exist	large	spoon
assist	expensive	mean	squirrel
beer	flower	need	telephone
bottle	funny	penny	tiny
card	garden	pocket	tomato
cover	hard	prefer	tooth
cream	hear	quarter	wine
desk	huge	quiet	wrist
dime	intelligent		

Exercise 1 (A.1, pp. 30–31)

Write a yes/no question and a wh-question using *what*. Give a short answer for the questions.

Paul reads *books*.

(yes/no) _____ Does Paul read books? _____

_____ Yes, he does. _____

(wh-) _____ What does Paul read? _____

_____ Books. _____

1. John studies *history*.

(yes/no) _____

_____

(wh-) _____

_____

48

2. We like *hamburgers*.

(yes/no) _____

_____

(wh-) _____

_____

3. You write *letters*.

(yes/no) _____

_____

(wh-) _____

_____

4. They eat *soup* for lunch.

(yes/no) _____

_____

(wh-) _____

_____

5. We liked *grammar class*.

(yes/no) _____

_____

(wh-) _____

_____

6. Mark writes *letters* every day.

(yes/no) _____

_____

(wh-) _____

_____

7. Paul studied *French*.

(yes/no) _____

_____

(wh-) _____

_____

8. She pronounced *the word*.

(yes/no) _____

_____

(wh-) _____

_____

9. The student learned *the lesson*.

(yes/no) _____

_____

(wh-) _____

_____

10. The teacher presented *the vocabulary*.

(yes/no) _____

_____

(wh-) _____

_____

Exercise 2 (A.1, pp. 31–32)
Make a question asking what the word in italics means. Give an answer.

Mark and John are very *smart*.

_____**What does smart mean?**_____

_____**It means intelligent.**_____

1. The clock is very *large*.

   _____

   _____

2. The baby is very *tiny*.

   _____

   _____

3. They *rarely* go to church.

   _____

   _____

4. We eat lunch at *noon*.

   _____

   _____

5. The vocabulary test was very *hard*.

   _____

   _____

6. The new student is very *unhappy*.

   _____

   _____

7. We go to class every *week*.

   _____

   _____

8. Do you have a *dozen* pencils?

_____

_____

9. The reading class was *excellent*.

_____

_____

10. Jane is a very *smart* girl.

_____

_____

Exercise 3   (A.1, p. 32)
Write a yes/no question and a wh-question using *when*. Give a short answer for the questions.

Paul arrives *in the morning*.

(yes/no) _Does Paul arrive in the morning?_____

_Yes, he does._____

(wh-) _When does Paul arrive?_____

_In the morning._____

1. Mary studies *at night*.

(yes/no) _____

_____

(wh-) _____

_____

2. We eat *at noon*.

(yes/no) _____

_____

(wh-) _____

_____

3. John arrived *yesterday*.

(yes/no) _____

_____

(wh-) _____

_____

4. They practiced *on Monday*.

(yes/no) _____

_____

(wh-) _____

_____

5. She has class *in the afternoon*.

(yes/no) _____

_____

(wh-) _____

_____

Exercise 4 (A.1, p. 32)
Write a question using *when*. Give a short answer.

Paul arrives in the morning.

When does Paul arrive?

In the morning.

1. Mary studied every day.

_____

_____

2. She worked yesterday.

_____

_____

3. You eat breakfast at 10 o'clock.

_____

_____

4. He arrives in the afternoon.

_____

_____

5. John has class at 2 P.M.

_____

_____

Exercise 5   (A.1, p. 32)

Write a yes/no question and a wh-question using *where*. Give a short answer for the questions.

He works *at the bank*.

(yes/no) ___Does he work at the bank?_____

___Yes, he does._____

(wh-) ___Where does he work?_____

___At the bank._____

1. You learned French *in France*.

(yes/no) _____

_____

(wh-) _____

_____

2. She studies *at home*.

(yes/no) _____

_____

(wh-) _____

_____

3. They play tennis *in the park*.

(yes/no) _____

_____

(wh-) _____

_____

4. Sam studied *in the library*.

(yes/no) _____

_____

(wh-) _____

_____

5. Ruth lives *in Texas*.

(yes/no) _____

_____

(wh-) _____

_____

Exercise 6   (A.1, p. 32)
Write a question using *where*. Give a short answer.

They eat lunch at home.

___Where do they eat lunch ?_____

___At home ._____

1. We study in the library.

_____

_____

2. Mary has class in room four.

_____

_____

Lesson 4

3. John and Sam lived in New York.

_____

_____

4. You practiced English in the laboratory.

_____

_____

5. You eat lunch in the kitchen.

_____

_____

Exercise 7 (A.1, p. 32)
Make a question using *who*. Give a short answer.

Mary knows John.

Who knows John ?

Mary does.

1. *Mary* visited Mr. Miller.

_____

_____

2. *He* asked Mark.

_____

_____

3. *Joe* helped Alan with the homework.

_____

_____

4. *The girl* telephoned Paul.

_____

_____

5. *Ann* plays tennis with John.

_____

_____

6. *You* know Jack well.

_____

_____

7. *Bill* understands Mary.

_____

_____

8. *We* waited for Greg.

_____

_____

9. *She* listened to the doctor.

_____

_____

10. *Rick and Sue* work with Pat.

_____

_____

Exercise 8   (Lesson 9.C, p. 94)
Make a question using *whom*. Give a short answer.

Mary knows *John*.

_Whom does Mary know ?_____

_John._____

1. Mary visited *Mr. Miller*.

_____

_____

2. He asked *Mark*.

_____

_____

3. Joe helped *Alan* with the homework.

_____

_____

4. The girl telephoned *Paul*.

_____

_____

5. Ann plays tennis with *John*.

_____

_____

6. You know *Jack* well.

_____

_____

7. Bill understands *Mary*.

_____

_____

8. We waited for *Greg*.

_____

_____

9. She listened to *the doctor*.

_____

_____

10. Rick and Sue work with *Pat*.

_____

_____

Exercise 9 (A.1, p. 32; p. 94)
Make a question with *who* and *whom*.

Mr. Miller called Paul.

(who)   Who called Paul ?

(whom)   Whom did Mr. Miller call ?

1. Jane visited Martha yesterday.

   (who)   _____

   (whom)   _____

2. Anne studies with Matt.

   (who)   _____

   (whom)   _____

3. Anne and Bob study with Matt in the evening.

   (who)   _____

   (whom)   _____

4. John and Martha play tennis with Anne and Matt every day.

   (who)   _____

   (whom)   _____

5. The teacher waited for all the students.

   (who)   _____

   (whom)   _____

Exercise 10 (A.1, p. 32; p. 94)
Write *who* or *whom* on the line.

___Who___ has my book?

1. _____ does Mary like?

2. _____ knows John?

3. _____ knows the answer?

4. _____ understands the lesson?

5. _____ did you ask?

6. _____ do you see?

7. _____ has my pen?

8. _____ needs a pencil?

9. _____ did the homework?

10. _____ does he play tennis with?

Exercise 11 (A.1, pp. 30–32; p. 94)
Make a question by substituting *who*, *whom*, *what*, *when*, and *where* for the italicized words.

Mary called John. ___Who called John?_____

They speak *English*. ___What do they speak?_____

1. She arrives *at 8 o'clock*. _____

2. Mary learned French *in France*. _____

3. She asked *John*. _____

4. *Rick* wants a new car. _____

5. Jane has *a new watch*. _____

Exercise 12   (A.1, pp. 30–32; p. 94)
Make questions according to the italicized words.

Mary called *John* *last night.*
   a   b   c

a) __Who called John last night ?__

b) __Whom did Mary call last night?__

c) __When did Mary call John?__

1. *Susan* studied *English* *in England*.
    a   b   c

a) _____

b) _____

c) _____

2. *Joe* practices *tennis* *in the park*.
    a   b   c

a) _____

b) _____

c) _____

3. *Mike* usually studies *history* with *Peter*.
    a   b   c

a) _____

b) _____

c) _____

Exercise 13   (A.1, pp. 30–32; p. 94)
Underline the correct question word.

(<u>Who</u>, When) has my book?

1. (Who, Whom) studied German?
2. (Who, Whom) did you ask?
3. (Who, Whom) did they see?
4. (Who, Whom) sees Mary?
5. (Who, Where) did you go?

6. (When, Who) did you go?
7. (Who, Whom) called you?
8. (Where, What) do you live?
9. (When, Who) do you study?
10. (Whom, When) do you have class?

Lesson 4

Exercise 14   (A.2, p. 33)
Make a wh-question. Substitute a wh-word for the italicized word or words.

John is *at home*.   **Where is John?**

Joe and Sue are in the kitchen.   **Who is in the kitchen?**

1. He's usually hungry *in the afternoon*. _____

2. She is *at home* now. _____

3. Mark is tired *at night*. _____

4. *John and Mary* are in New York. _____

5. The book is *on the table*. _____

6. *The book* is on the table. _____

7. *They* were late to class yesterday. _____

8. He is absent *every Friday*. _____

9. *He* is a teacher. _____

10. He is *a teacher*. _____

Exercise 15   (A.2, p. 33)
Make questions according to the italicized words.

John is *at home*.
  a   b

a) _____ **Who is at home?** _____

b) _____ **Where is John?** _____

1. *Mary* is *in class* *now*.
   a   b   c

a) _____

b) _____

c) _____

2. *The school* is *in Florida*.
   a   b

a) _____

b) _____

3. *Mrs. Jones* is always hungry *at noon*.
       _a   _b

   a) _____

   b) _____

4. *Peter* is *the president*.
       _a   _b

   a) _____

   b) _____

Exercise 16   (A.3, pp. 34–35)
Make a wh-question with *what*. Substitute *do* for the verb in the original sentence.

Mary *eats lunch* at noon.   <u>What does Mary do at noon?</u>

1. They *read books* in the library. _____

2. Joe *eats his lunch* at noon. _____

3. She *learned the vocabulary* last night. _____

4. Bob *writes letters* at night. _____

5. She *watches television* after dinner. _____

6. Paul and Peter *learned French* in France. _____

7. They *talked to the teacher* at noon. _____

8. You *have breakfast* at 9 o'clock. _____

9. We *go to class* every morning. _____

10. They *watch television* at night. _____

Exercise 17   (A.4, pp. 35–36)
Make a wh-question by substituting *who*, *whom*, *what*, *when*, or *where* for the italicized words.

She is from *Spain*.   <u>Where is she from?</u>

He played tennis with *Mary*.   <u>Whom did he play tennis with?</u>

1. John waited for *Mary*. _____

2. The students listened to *the teacher*. _____

3. He gives presents to *his family*. _____

4. She arrives *at 10:00* A.M. _____

5. He looked for *the book*. _____

6. They are from *the United States*. _____

7. You always watch *television* in the afternoon. _____

8. The students write letters to *their parents*. _____

9. *Mark* has class at 9 A.M. _____

10. You listen to *the radio* every evening. _____

Exercise 18   (B.1, p. 36; p. 11)
Read the sentence and write the correct verb form. Follow the examples.

verb

1. I __work__ every day.

2. You _____ every night.

3. He _____ every day.

4. She _____ every night.

5. We _____ every morning.

6. They _____ every afternoon.

be + **verb** + *ing*

7. I __am working__ now.

8. You _____ right now.

9. He _____ today.

10. She _____ this week.

11. We _____ this course.

12. They _____ now.

Exercise 19   (B.1, pp. 36–37)
Write the verbs in the present progressive tense.

(read) Mary ___is reading___ now.

1. (study) She _____ English now.

2. (teach) Mr. Miller _____ class today.

3. (write) I _____ a letter now.

4. (watch) We _____ television now.

5. (eat) They _____ hamburgers now.

6. (use) I _____ your book now.

7. (walk) John _____ home now.

8. (look) Mary _____ at the football game now.

9. (do) You _____ the work now.

10. (look) John _____ at the newspaper now.

Exercise 20   (B.1–2, pp. 36–38)
Write the expression in the present progressive tense. Put an *X* by the verbs that *cannot* be changed.

I eat ___I am eating___

you go ___you are going___

I know ___X___

1. you read	_____	8. we need	_____
2. he is	_____	9. we write	_____
3. I study	_____	10. we hear	_____
4. I see	_____	11. they prefer	_____
5. he likes	_____	12. we believe	_____
6. you work	_____	13. I drink	_____
7. they want	_____	14. he has	_____

15. she plays _____
16. she eats _____
17. I write _____

18. we walk _____
19. they study _____
20. they know _____

Exercise 21   (B.1–2, pp. 36–38)
Read the sentence and write the verb in the correct tense.

(read) He ___*is reading*___ a book now.

(read) He ___*reads*___ every day.

1. (eat) They _____ lunch now.

2. (like) Mary _____ the new dress.

3. (have) We _____ a new house now.

4. (be) I _____ very sick today.

5. (see) I _____ you now.

6. (write) She _____ a letter now.

7. (watch) They _____ television now.

8. (go) He _____ to class now.

9. (have) He _____ my pencil right now.

10. (listen) I _____ to the radio now.

Exercise 22   (B.3, p. 39)
Write a yes/no question and then give a short answer.

He is reading a book. (no)

___*Is he reading a book?*___
___*No, he isn't.*___

1. They are speaking Japanese. (yes)

_____

_____

2. Martha is writing a letter. (no)

_____

_____

3. The teacher is teaching lesson 6. (no)

_____

_____

4. The students are studying. (yes)

_____

_____

5. Patti is eating lunch. (yes)

_____

_____

Exercise 23   (B.4, pp. 39–40)
Make a wh-question by substituting *who, whom, what, when,* or *where* for the italicized words.

Paul is studying *grammar*.
 ᵃ   ᵇ

a) _____ Who is studying grammar? _____

b) _____ What is Paul studying? _____

1. *Mary* is talking to *Paul*.
   ᵃ   ᵇ

   a) _____

   b) _____

2. *They* like *coffee and tea*.
   ᵃ   ᵇ

   a) _____

   b) _____

3. *My sisters* are studying *English in Canada*.
      ᵃ   ᵇ   ᶜ

   a) _____

   b) _____

   c) _____

4. *She* is drinking *tea in the kitchen*.
    ᵃ   ᵇ   ᶜ

   a) _____

   b) _____

   c) _____

Exercise 24: Wh-Word Discrimination
Read the conversations. Write the correct question word on the line. Write *who*, *whom*, *what*, *when*, or *where*.

Mary: **When** do you eat lunch?

John: At noon.

1. Sue: _____ is my pencil?

   John: On the table.

2. Paul: _____ gave the book to you?

   Mary: Mr. Miller did.

3. John: _____ did you drink some water?

   Paul: After grammar class.

4. Bill: _____ did you see in the afternoon?

   Carl: John and Sam.

5. Paul: _____ is he doing?

   Mary: He's writing a letter.

6. Mary: _____ does "dozen" mean?

   Paul: That's easy. It means twelve.

7. John: _____ do you live?

   Bill: In Mexico.

8. John: _____ is your name?

   Sam: Sam.

9. Mark: _____ did Bill visit?

   John: Paul.

10. Mark: _____ visited Paul?

    John: Bill did.

11. Bill: _____ do you have class?

    Sam: In the morning.

12. John: _____ are you listening to?

    Bob: My new radio.

13. Bob: _____ did you buy?

    Ann: Two dresses and a skirt.

14. Bill: _____ did you go last night?

    John: To the library.

15. Sue: _____ did you write a letter to?

    Paul: John and Bill.

16. John: _____ are you eating now?

    Mary: An apple.

17. Paul: _____ is in the kitchen?

    Mark: My mother.

18. Bill: _____ are those boys?

    Tim: They're John and Joe.

19. John: _____ are those boys?

    Mary: In the store.

20. John: _____ does Mary finish class?

    Paul: At 3 o'clock.

21. Joe: _____ did they eat for lunch?

    Ann: A hamburger and a salad.

22. Bill: _____ has fifty cents?

    Mary: I do.

23. Bill: _____ has fifty cents?

    Mary: Paul does.

24. John: _____ does the girl play tennis?

    Jane: In the afternoon.

25. Mary: _____ are they doing now?

    John: They're studying for the test.

Exercise 25: Verb Discrimination—Present, Past, Present Progressive
Underline the correct verb form. Read the sentence carefully.

The boys (work, <u>worked</u>, are working) in class yesterday.

1. The man (walks, walked, is walking) with his dog now.
2. John and Mary (have, did have, are having) the books now.
3. Bill (opens, opened, is opening) the door five minutes ago.
4. It (rains, rained, raining) last night.
5. We do not (play, played, playing) tennis at night.
6. Susan always (repeat, repeats, is repeating) the words every day.
7. The students (need, needed, are needing) three books right now.
8. You and I (study, studied, are studying) vocabulary and writing this semester.
9. They (go, goes, are going) to the library now.
10. Mr. Smith (work, is work, is working) in a big office this year.
11. My cat (like, likes, is liking) fish for breakfast.
12. The girl (isn't, doesn't, didn't) talking to John.
13. The book (is, are, is being) on the table now.
14. He (play, plays, is playing) tennis right now.
15. They (don't, weren't, aren't) eating lunch now.

Exercise 26 (C, pp. 41–42)
Combine the two sentences to make one good sentence.

It's a book. It's green.

_____It's a green book._____

It's a tree. It has apples.

_____It's an apple tree._____

1. It's a clock. It's on the wall.

_____

2. They're pencils. They're red.

_____

3. It's a dog. It's big.

_____

4. I'm a student. I'm intelligent.

_____

5. It's a watch. It's gold.

_____

6. They're books. They're for grammar.

_____

7. It's a tree. It has apples.

_____

8. She is a teacher. She teaches French.

_____

9. He is a man. He is good.

_____

10. It's a factory. It makes cars.

_____

Lesson 4

Exercise 27 (C, pp. 41–42)
Answer the question.

What's a telephone book?

_____It's a book._____

1. What's a baby bottle?

   _____

2. What's an apple tree?

   _____

3. What's a flower garden?

   _____

4. What's a garden flower?

   _____

5. What is a bus station?

   _____

6. What is a pocket watch?

   _____

7. What is a watch pocket?

   _____

8. What's a car magazine?

   _____

Exercise 28: Review Test
A. Make wh-questions by substituting *who, whom, what, when,* or *where* for the italicized words.

1. *Paul arrived late every day.*
      a   b   c

   a) _____

   b) _____

   c) _____

2. *The book* was *on the table*.
   _a   _b

   a) _____

   b) _____

3. *The teacher* is explaining *the lesson* to *the class*.
   _a   _b   _c

   a) _____

   b) _____

   c) _____

4. Dozen means *twelve*.
   _a

   a) _____

5. *They* are *playing* *tennis* *now*.
   _a   _b   _c

   a) _____

   b) _____

   c) _____

B. Write a yes/no question and give a short answer.

1. The man is waiting for the bus. (yes)

   _____

   _____

2. They are eating lunch now. (no)

   _____

   _____

C. Write the correct form of the verb.

1. (read) He _____ a book now.

2. (read) He _____ every night.

3. (prefer) I _____ this pen.

4. (see) She _____ the bus now.

5. (need) I _____ ten cents now.

73

Lesson 4

D. Combine the sentences to make one good sentence.

1. It's a watch. It's small.

   _____

2. They're books. They're good.

   _____

3. It's a tree. It has apples.

   _____

4. It's a car. It's expensive.

   _____

5. It's a factory. It makes cars.

   _____

Exercise 29: Review Test
Choose the correct answer. Put a circle around the letter of the answer.

1. Mary has a book. It's for grammar class. It's _____ .
   a) a book grammar
   b) a grammar book
   c) a book class
   d) a grammar class

2. " _____ French?"
   "In France."
   a) When did study Paul
   b) When did Paul study
   c) Where did study Paul
   d) Where did Paul study

3. " _____ John every day?"
   "Mary and Bill do."
   a) Who see
   b) Who sees
   c) Whom see
   d) Whom sees

4. "When _____ ?"

"At ten o'clock."

   a) arrived he

   b) he arrived

   c) did arrive he

   d) did he arrive

5. "I don't understand 'smart'. What _____ ?"

"It means 'intelligent'."

   a) means 'smart'

   b) does 'smart' mean

   c) says 'smart'

   d) wants to say 'smart'

6. "What _____ at noon?"

"I studied grammar."

   a) do you did

   b) did you do

   c) do you do

   d) did you did

7. We like television. We are _____ a television program now.

   a) seeing

   b) listening

   c) watching

   d) going

8. " _____ write letters to?"

"John."

   a) Whom you

   b) Whom do you

   c) Who you

   d) Who do you

9. "Is the girl eating soup?"

"Yes, _____ ."

   a) she's

   b) she is

   c) she's eating

   d) the soup

10. " _____ Matt writing letters right now?"

"No, he isn't."

   a) Does

   b) Is

   c) Was

   d) Do

Lesson 5

A. *Be + going to* to indicate future time: He is going to sing.

B. Negative statements: He isn't here. He didn't come.

C. Negative statements with single-word adverbs of frequency: He isn't always here. He doesn't always study.

D. *Some* and *any*

Vocabulary List

bread	history	picture	song
dentist	ink	pie	stamp
engineer	magazine	potato	umbrella
fruit	museum	run	vacation
get up	newspaper	smoke	wear

Exercise 1   (A.1, p. 43; p. 11; p. 26)
Write the forms of *work* in *present*, *past*, and *future* (*going to*). Follow the examples.

verb

1. I __work__ all of the time.

2. You _____ every day.

3. He _____ most of the time.

4. She _____ every morning.

5. It _____ most of the time.

6. We _____ some of the time.

7. They _____ every day.

verb + *ed*

8. I __worked__ yesterday.

9. You _____ last night.

10. He _____ a year ago.

11. She _____ last Monday.

12. It _____ yesterday.

13. We _____ in 1974.

14. They _____ last summer.

be + *going to* + verb

15. I ___ **am going to work** ___ next week.

16. You _____ tomorrow.

17. He _____ in five minutes.

18. She _____ next year.

19. It _____ tomorrow.

20. We _____ next Monday.

21. They _____ next summer.

Exercise 2 (A.1, pp. 43–44)

Read the time expression and then write the correct form of the verb. Follow the example.

every day	*tomorrow*
1. I study	**I am going to study.**
2. she reads	_____
3. they do	_____
4. he eats	_____

now	*tomorrow*
5. he is eating	_____
6. we are going	_____
7. I am studying	_____

yesterday	*tomorrow*
8. she studied	_____
9. he worked	_____
10. they visited	_____

Exercise 3 (A.1, pp. 43–44)
Read the sentences. Use *be + going to* in the second sentence to express future time.

John reads a book every week.

John ___is going to read___ a book next week.

1. I worked hard yesterday.

   I _____ hard tomorrow.

2. Mary goes to school every day.

   She _____ to school tomorrow.

3. We eat sandwiches in the cafeteria.

   We _____ sandwiches tomorrow.

4. They study in the library all of the time.

   They _____ in the library tomorrow.

5. The boy is writing a letter to his father now.

   He _____ a letter to his father tomorrow.

6. You and I go to class every morning.

   We _____ to class tomorrow morning.

7. They are reading a newspaper now.

   They _____ a newspaper tomorrow.

8. We play tennis every afternoon.

   We _____ tennis tomorrow afternoon.

9. You are buying a watch now.

   You _____ a watch next year.

10. Her family visited France last summer.

   They _____ France next summer.

Exercise 4 (A.1, p. 44)
Read the question and then answer *no* to the question. Write a statement using the word *tomorrow*.

Did John write the letter yesterday?

No, he's going to write the letter tomorrow.

1. Did you eat the cake last night?

_____

2. Did we study all of the lessons yesterday?

_____

3. Did Jane speak with Paul yesterday?

_____

4. Did John and Sue go to New York yesterday?

_____

5. Did Mark do the homework last night?

_____

Exercise 5 (A.2, pp. 45–46)
Write a yes/no question and a short answer. Then write a wh-question by substituting *who*, *whom*, *when*, *where*, or *what* for the italicized words. Give a short answer.

Ruth is going to read *a book*. (yes)

(yes/no) _Is Ruth going to read a book?_
Yes, she is.
(wh-) _What is Ruth going to read?_
A book.

1. The students are going to study *history*. (yes)

(yes/no) _____

_____

(wh-) _____

_____

79

2. *Rick* is going to write a letter tomorrow. (no)

(yes/no) _____

_____

(wh-) _____

_____

3. *Judy and Jane* are going to play tennis tomorrow. (no)

(yes/no) _____

_____

(wh-) _____

_____

4. We are going to *study math* tomorrow afternoon. (yes)

(yes/no) _____

_____

(wh-) _____

_____

5. Mrs. Sanders is going to call *Joe*. (yes)

(yes/no) _____

_____

(wh-) _____

_____

6. Bob and Bill are going to go *to Florida*. (no)

(yes/no) _____

_____

(wh-) _____

_____

7. The party is going to begin *at seven o'clock*. (yes)

(yes/no) _____

_____

(wh-) _____

_____

Exercise 6 (B.1–2, pp. 47–49)
Write the contractions.

you are ____you're____

it is ____it's____

1. I am not _____
2. they do not _____
3. it was not _____
4. he is not _____
5. we do not _____
6. I did not _____
7. you are not _____
8. I do not _____
9. I was not _____
10. you did not _____
11. it does not _____
12. he did not _____
13. you were not _____
14. she is not _____

15. they were not _____
16. you do not _____
17. she did not _____
18. we are not _____
19. he was not _____
20. it did not _____
21. he does not _____
22. we did not _____
23. they are not _____
24. they did not _____
25. we were not _____
26. she does not _____
27. she was not _____

Lesson 5

Exercise 7 (B.1–2, pp. 47–49)
Make a negative statement.

John speaks English. *John doesn't speak English.*

John is here now. *John isn't here now.*

1. He works hard. _____

2. They're studying. _____

3. He studied French. _____

4. I'm hungry now. _____

5. They're writing letters. _____

6. You have all your books. _____

7. She has all her books. _____

8. He was sick. _____

9. He speaks French. _____

10. They arrived late. _____

11. I'm going to write two letters. _____

12. You liked the movie. _____

13. She plays tennis. _____

14. They were hungry. _____

15. Mr. Smith teaches German. _____

16. They do the work on time. _____

17. He does the work on time. _____

18. They did the work on time. _____

19. He did the work on time. _____

20. He is going to do the work on time. _____

Exercise 8 (B.1–2, pp. 47–49)
Make a negative statement.

John speaks English. _John doesn't speak English._

John is here now. _John isn't here now._

1. He played tennis. _____

2. He is playing tennis. _____

3. She is going to call Paul. _____

4. He likes toast with butter. _____

5. He liked the book. _____

6. I am tired. _____

7. He has a new car. _____

8. I do my work all of the time. _____

9. I did my work last week. _____

10. I am doing my work. _____

11. I am going to do my work tomorrow. _____

12. They have my keys. _____

13. We were very tired. _____

14. Mike knows all the answers. _____

15. Mike studies at night. _____

16. The student from Mexico was absent yesterday. _____

17. She studied last night. _____

18. She's going to study tomorrow. _____

19. Pat writes well. _____

20. They were late to class today. _____

Exercise 9 (C, pp. 49–51)
Make a negative statement. Practice contractions.

Mary is often late. _____ Mary isn't often late. _____

1. He is always sick. _____

2. He usually studies. _____

3. I'm often late. _____

4. I always arrive on time. _____

5. The students usually read well. _____

6. She always does her work. _____

7. Mark always arrives late. _____

8. Mark always arrived late. _____

9. They are usually early. _____

10. He always did his work on time. _____

Exercise 10 (C, pp. 49–51)
Put a circle around the *negative* adverbs of frequency.

1. often   3. usually   5. sometimes   7. never
2. (seldom)   4. rarely   6. always

Exercise 11 (C, pp. 49–51)
Write a new sentence that includes the frequency word. Follow the example.

She doesn't arrive on time.

1. usually _____ She doesn't usually arrive on time. _____

2. seldom _____

3. always _____

4. rarely _____

5. never _____

6. often _____

Exercise 12 (C, p. 49–51)

Write a negative statement. If the sentence is negative already, write the word *negative* on the line.

He is usually on time. __He isn't usually on time.__

He is never late. __negative__

1. They usually study at night. _____

2. They are always at home. _____

3. She is seldom in class. _____

4. They always do the work. _____

5. Pamela never writes long letters. _____

Exercise 13 (D, pp. 51–53)

Underline the correct answer. Sometimes two answers are possible.

We need (<u>some</u>, any) books.

Do you have (<u>some</u>, <u>any</u>) pencils?

1. I don't have (some, any) money.
2. They're going to eat (some, any) potatoes.
3. John has (some, any) stamps.
4. John doesn't have (some, any) stamps.
5. They would like (some, any) magazines.
6. We don't need (some, any) money.
7. Did he buy (some, any) paper?
8. She isn't going to buy (some, any) fruit.
9. He didn't buy (some, any) pencils.
10. Are you going to write (some, any) letters tomorrow?

Exercise 14   (D, pp. 51–53)
Write *some* or *any* on the line. If two answers are possible, write *some/any*.

I want _____**some**_____ books.

Do you need _**some/any**_____ money?

1. He has _____ magazines.

2. They don't want _____ stamps.

3. Do you need _____ paper and pencils?

4. Are you going to buy _____ tables?

5. The children are playing _____ games.

6. Did he eat _____ fruit last night?

7. Is she going to make _____ sandwiches for the boys?

8. We didn't watch _____ movies yesterday.

9. They're going to buy _____ tea.

10. He is watching _____ birds.

Exercise 15   (D, pp. 51–53)
Read the question and then write four possible answers.

Do you want some bread?

Yes, ___**I do**_____ .

No, ___**I don't**____ .

Yes, __**I want some**_____ .

No, __**I don't want any**__ .

1. Does Paul have any pencils?

Yes, _____ .

No, _____ .

Yes, _____ .

No, _____ .

2. Are John and Mike going to buy any stamps?

Yes, _____ .

No, _____ .

Yes, _____ .

No, _____ .

3. Do you have some sugar?

Yes, _____ .

No, _____ .

Yes, _____ .

No, _____ .

4. Did you want some water?

Yes, _____ .

No, _____ .

Yes, _____ .

No, _____ .

Exercise 16: Verb Discrimination—Present, Past, Present Progressive, Future
Underline the correct form of the verb.

The boys (are going to work, are working, worked, work) here tomorrow.

1. The boy (is going to play, is playing, played, plays) tennis last week.
2. Mark and Joe (are going to study, are studying, studied, study) vocabulary next week.
3. We (are going to be, are being, were, are) on the plane in one hour from now.
4. Susan (is going to attend, is attending, attends, attend) class every day.
5. They (are going to need, are needing, needed, need) a camera right now.
6. John, Mike, and Susan (are going to listen, are listening, listened, listen) to the radio now.
7. I (am going to assist, am assisting, assisted, assist) the doctor yesterday.
8. It (is going to rain, is raining, rained, rains) right now.
9. You and John (are going to do, are doing, did, do) the homework last night.
10. They usually (are going to visit, are visiting, visits, visit) Mrs. Jones on Monday.

Exercise 17: Verb Discrimination—Present, Past, Present Progressive, Future
Write the correct form of the verb on the line.

play

They **are playing** tennis now.

We **played** tennis yesterday.

He **is going to play** tennis tomorrow.

She **plays** tennis every day.

study

1. She _____ grammar now.

2. They _____ vocabulary last night.

3. He always _____ spelling.

4. I _____ grammar tomorrow.

87

Lesson 5

do

5. You —————————— the homework last night.

6. I —————————— the exercises every day.

7. We —————————— lesson 5 right now.

8. She —————————— the questions tomorrow.

need

9. We —————————— some help last week.

10. We —————————— a car next week.

11. I always —————————— more money.

12. I —————————— money right now.

be

13. I —————————— a businessman.

14. I —————————— in Venezuela last year.

15. I —————————— in France next month.

16. I —————————— in the United States now.

work (use *you* in the questions)

17. —————————— every day?

18. —————————— in a nice office now?

19. —————————— in France last year?

20. —————————— there next month?

rain (use *it* in the questions)

21. —————————— tomorrow?

22. —————————— yesterday?

23. —————————— every day in August?

24. —————————— right now?

88

Exercise 18: Review Test
A. Make a yes/no question and wh-questions by substituting *who, whom, what, when,* or *where* for the italicized words.

George is going to study Spanish next year.
    a   *b*   *c*

1. yes/no: _____

2. *a)* _____

3. *b)* _____

4. *c)* _____

B. Write a negative statement.

1. Paul is here. _____

2. He usually studies hard. _____

3. She was absent. _____

4. We played for one hour. _____

5. She smokes most of the time. _____

C. Write the contractions.

1. I am not   _____

2. I was not   _____

3. they are not   _____

4. it is not   _____

5. you were not   _____

D. Write *some, any,* or *some/any*.

1. John wants _____ good books.

2. He doesn't want _____ bad books.

3. Did Mary buy _____ meat for dinner?

4. Is she going to write _____ letters?

5. No, she's not going to write _____ letters.

Lesson 5

Exercise 19: Review Test
Choose the correct answer. Put a circle around the letter of the answer.

1. "Do you have some bread?"
   "No, I do not _____ ."
   a) have some
   b) have any
   c) some bread
   d) any bread

2. Mary comes to class almost every day.
   She _____ absent.
   a) is seldom
   b) seldom is
   c) isn't seldom
   d) doesn't seldom

3. "Is Paul writing a letter now?"
   "No, he _____ a letter now."
   a) doesn't writing
   b) doesn't write
   c) isn't writing
   d) isn't write

4. "Are they going to eat dinner in ten minutes?"
   "No, they _____ ."
   a) don't
   b) no are
   c) aren't
   d) aren't going

5. Mary _____ at night.
   a) always doesn't study
   b) doesn't always study
   c) always doesn't studies
   d) doesn't always studies

6. We _____ play tennis next week.
   a) don't going to
   b) aren't going to
   c) don't going
   d) aren't going

7. "What _____ read next week?"
   "A book."
   a) is going Mary to
   b) is Mary going to
   c) does Mary
   d) Mary does

8. "Are you going to play baseball tomorrow?"
   "Yes, _____ ."
   a) I'm
   b) I am
   c) I'm going
   d) I am going

9. "Does Mrs. Miller usually drink tea?"
   "No, she _____ drink tea."
   a) doesn't seldom
   b) seldom doesn't
   c) doesn't usually
   d) usually doesn't

10. I do not smoke. My brother does not _____ smoke.
   a) never
   b) rarely
   c) seldom
   d) often

90

Lesson 6

A. The articles: *the, a, an*

B. Count and noncount nouns: *a pencil; some ink*

C. Quantity expressions: *much, many, a few,* etc.

D. Demonstratives: *this, that, these, those*

E. Possessives: *my, your, his,* etc.

Vocabulary List

algebra	cover	important	quantity
apartment	cup	information	ready
architecture	dictionary	interesting	slice
art	discussion	invite	soap
bar (of soap)	drug store	knife	sugar
banana	envelope	loaf	ticket
bit	exciting	meeting	tie
broken	fresh	mistake	time
butter	furniture	oxygen	toothbrush
buy	gasoline	philosophy	toothpaste
chalk	grow	piece	tube
cheese	hat	pound	use
city	help	professor	yellow
comfortable	house		

Exercise 1   (A, pp. 54–55)

Write a short answer to the question.

I have a book and a shirt. What do I read?

_____The book._____

1. Mary has an apple and a skirt. What does she eat?

   _____

2. We bought a chair and a radio. What did we listen to?

   _____

3. Jim has a pencil sharpener and a car. What does he drive?

   _____

4. I bought a comb and a spoon yesterday. What did I eat with?

   _____

5. They have a new car and a new house. What do they live in?

   _____

6. I have a glass of water and some bread. What do I drink?

   _____

7. We have a television, a telephone, and a radio. What do we watch?

   _____

8. Mary has a dress and some shoes. What does she wear on her feet?

   _____

9. My mother bought an apple, a book, and a newspaper. What did she eat?

   _____

10. They are going to buy some coffee and some cups. What are they going to drink?

   _____

Exercise 2 (A, pp. 54–57)
Write *a, an,* or *the*. Draw a line if no article is possible.

   _—_ Mr. Jones lives in **the** United States.

1. _____ Mr. Smith is _____ teacher.

2. _____ John is studying _____ architecture.

3. _____ University of California is on _____ College Street in _____ Los Angeles.

4. I bought _____ comb and _____ pen yesterday. _____ comb is black, and _____ pen is green.

5. Do you prefer _____ American history or _____ history of _____ France?

6. _____ Mrs. Miller bought _____ newpaper and _____ watch. She was reading _____ newspaper last night.

7. _____ Spanish is _____ popular language.

8. _____ John likes _____ coffee.

9. I prefer _____ music of _____ Mexico, but she likes _____ French music.

10. _____ Doctor Allen is from _____ Netherlands. He has _____ new office here.

11. _____ Mrs. Allen is _____ good nurse.

12. I live in _____ Bogotá. It is _____ capital of _____ Colombia.

13. We visited _____ Atlantic Ocean, but we didn't visit _____ Mississippi River.

14. _____ Harvard University is in _____ United States.

15. Last summer we visited _____ Switzerland, _____ Egypt, _____ South Africa, and _____ Soviet Union.

16. Ann: "Do you like _____ oranges?"

    Sam: "Yes, but I prefer _____ apples."

17. _____ Hawaiian Islands are in _____ Pacific Ocean.

18. Peter is from _____ Dominican Republic.

19. He studied _____ English, _____ algebra, and _____ architecture of _____ Greece this semester.

20. _____ Argentina is in _____ South America.

21. _____ Orinoco River is in _____ Venezuela.

22. _____ United States is in _____ North America.

23. _____ people in Switzerland speak _____ French, _____ German, and _____ Italian.

24. I eat _____ salad for _____ lunch every day.

25. Sue: "How was lunch?"

    Pat: " _____ salad was excellent."

Exercise 3 (A, pp. 55–57)
Write *the* where it is necessary. If *the* is not possible, draw a line.

He is studying ——— art.

I attend **the** University of Florida.

1. I like ——— coffee for ——— breakfast.

2. ——— United States is a large country.

3. Did you ever see ——— Amazon River?

4. He speaks ——— Japanese and ——— Chinese.

5. Who visited ——— Soviet Union?

6. She studied ——— American history.

7. Did you study ——— history last semester?

8. Did you study ——— history of ——— Greece last semester?

9. ——— Professor Jones teaches ——— mathematics.

10. Matt doesn't like ——— tea.

Exercise 4 (A, pp. 55–57)
Write *the* where it is necessary. If *the* is not possible, draw a line.

He is studying ——— art.

I attend **the** University of Florida.

1. I like ——— hamburgers.

2. Do you like ——— tea?

3. Did you ever visit ——— Argentina?

4. We study ——— English in school.

5. ——— Greek architecture is interesting.

6. Joe is studying ——— music.

7. He likes ——— music of Mozart.

8. I'm going to see ——— Canada.

9. ——— Dr. Borman is a busy man.

10. ——— Netherlands is in ——— Europe.

Exercise 5 (B, pp. 57–59)

Write *C* by the count nouns and *NC* by the noncount nouns.

___C___ book

__NC__ water

1. _____ banana

2. _____ chair

3. _____ air

4. _____ apple

5. _____ ink

6. _____ soup

7. _____ stamp

8. _____ butter

9. _____ milk

10. _____ radio

11. _____ pencil

12. _____ money

13. _____ dollar

14. _____ salt

15. _____ student

Exercise 6 (B, pp. 57–59)

Write *a*, *an*, or *some*.

_____a_____ book

__some__ books

__some__ water

1. _____ soup

2. _____ pen

3. _____ pens

4. _____ paper

5. _____ apple

6. _____ tomato

7. _____ sugar

8. _____ house

9. _____ food

10. _____ cups

11. _____ information

12. _____ help

13. _____ homework

14. _____ bank

15. _____ banks

16. _____ plate

17. _____ university

18. _____ milk

19. _____ hot dog
20. _____ telephone
21. _____ salt
22. _____ sand
23. _____ air
24. _____ pencil

25. _____ dollar
26. _____ car
27. _____ cars
28. _____ apples
29. _____ apple
30. _____ work

Exercise 7   (B, pp. 57–59; p. 56)
Write *a, an, the,* or *some* on the line. If no article is possible, draw a line.

Would you like ___**an**___ apple?

Would you like ___**the**___ apple on the table?

Would you like ___**some**___ apples?

Do you like ___—___ apples?

1. Would you like _____ water?

2. Would you like _____ tea?

3. Would you like _____ book?

4. Would you like _____ books?

5. Would you like _____ books on the table?

6. Do you like _____ books?

7. Would you like _____ orange?

8. Would you like _____ orange juice?

9. Would you like _____ paper now?

10. Would you like _____ slice of bread?

11. Would you like _____ bread?

12. Would you like _____ red shirt?

13. Would you like _____ red shirt on the bed?

14. Do you like _____ coffee?

96

15. Would you like _____ coffee now?

16. Would you like _____ elephant?

17. Would you like _____ elephant in the zoo?

18. Would you like _____ application?

19. Would you like _____ university application?

20. Would you like _____ ink?

21. Do you like _____ meat?

22. Do you like _____ meat in your sandwich?

23. Would you like _____ meat now?

24. Do you need _____ apples?

25. Do you like _____ apples?

Exercise 8 (B, pp. 58–59)
Combine the two sentences.

I want some water. I want two cups.

___I want two cups of water._____

1. I need some bread. I need three pieces.

   _____

2. She wants some orange juice. She wants two glasses.

   _____

3. He wants some cake. He wants two slices.

   _____

4. They are going to buy some sugar. They are going to buy five pounds.

   _____

5. You need some toothpaste. You need three tubes.

   _____

6. I need some paper. I need two sheets.

_____

7. Mr. Smith wants some coffee. He wants a cup.

_____

Exercise 9   (C, pp. 60–62)
Write *a few* or *a little*.

___a few___ books
___a little___ coffee

1. _____ cents

2. _____ cars

3. _____ ink

4. _____ books

5. _____ pencils

6. _____ milk

7. _____ friends

8. _____ work

9. _____ flour

10. _____ money

11. _____ time

12. _____ tea

13. _____ furniture

14. _____ sugar

15. _____ students

16. _____ bread

17. _____ paper

18. _____ tables

19. _____ homework

20. _____ meat

Exercise 10   (C, pp. 60–62)
Write *many* or *much*.

___many___ books
___much___ coffee

1. _____ tea

2. _____ homework

3. _____ pencils

4. _____ ink

5. _____ paper

6. _____ students

7. _____ teachers   14. _____ keys

8. _____ cars   15. _____ classes

9. _____ fruit   16. _____ money

10. _____ bread   17. _____ milk

11. _____ countries   18. _____ furniture

12. _____ time   19. _____ water

13. _____ tests   20. _____ questions

Exercise 11   (C, pp. 60–62)

Write the correct quantity word on the line.

    (large) I want __a lot of__ apples.

    (small) I want __a few__ apples.

Quantity

1. (small) I want _____ sugar.

2. (large) He wants _____ apples.

3. (small) I wanted _____ water.

4. (small) I need _____ chairs.

5. (large) I wanted _____ bananas.

6. (large) She wanted _____ money.

7. (small) They want _____ ink.

8. (small) He wants _____ stamps.

9. (large) I want _____ books.

10. (large) He wants _____ paper.

Lesson 6

Exercise 12 (C, pp. 60–62)
Complete the sentences with the correct quantity words.

I didn't see *a large number of* students.

I didn't see ____many____ students.

I didn't see __a lot of__ students.

1. We didn't drink *a large quantity of* beer.

   We didn't drink _____ beer.

   We didn't drink _____ beer.

2. I don't have *a large number of* ties.

   I don't have _____ ties.

   I don't have _____ ties.

3. You don't have *a large number of* pencils.

   You don't have _____ pencils.

   You don't have _____ pencils.

4. He doesn't have *a large quantity of* money.

   He doesn't have _____ money.

   He doesn't have _____ money.

5. She does not have *a large quantity of* fruit.

   She does not have _____ fruit.

   She does not have _____ fruit.

Exercise 13 (C, pp. 60–62)
Complete the sentences with the correct quantity words.

Does Mary have *a small number of* books?

Does Mary have ___**a few**___ books?

1. Do you have *a large quantity of* coffee?

   Do you have _____ coffee?

   Do you have _____ coffee?

2. Do you have *a small quantity of* tea?

   Do you have _____ tea?

3. Does Mike have *a large number of* friends?

   Does Mike have _____ friends?

   Does Mike have _____ friends?

4. Do we need *a large number of* coins to make the call?

   Do we need _____ coins to make the call?

   Do we need _____ coins to make the call?

5. Do you want *a small number of* books?

   Do you want _____ books?

Exercise 14 (C, pp. 60–62)
Underline the correct quantity word.

He wants (many, <u>a little</u>) sugar.

1. I don't have (much, many) books.
2. You need (a few, a little) money.
3. Does she need (a lot of, a few) sugar?
4. We have (a lot of, much) books.
5. She has (a few, much) pencils.
6. They want (a little, a lot of) pens.
7. Bob didn't buy (much, a few) milk.
8. We need (a lot of, a few) coffee.
9. They would like (many, a little) sugar in the coffee.
10. Would you like (a few, much) butter?

Lesson 6

Exercise 15   (C, p. 62)
Make a question with *how much* or *how many*. Give a short answer with *a little* or *a few*.

(water) ___How much water do you want ?___
___A little .___

1. (ink) _____

_____

2. (bottles of ink) _____

_____

3. (apples) _____

_____

4. (orange juice) _____

_____

5. (coffee) _____

_____

6. (books) _____

_____

7. (money) _____

_____

8. (homework) _____

_____

9. (stamps) _____

_____

10. (furniture) _____

_____

Exercise 16 (C, pp. 62–63)
Write the negative quantity expression.

1. many _____

2. much _____

3. all _____

4. any _____ (_____)

Exercise 17 (C, pp. 62–63)
Answer the questions with negative quantity expressions.

Are many of the students here now? (no)

__No, not many of the students are here now.__

1. Was much of the class interesting? (no)

_____

2. Are many of the students excellent? (no)

_____

3. Are any of the teachers bad? (no)

_____

4. Are all of the girls going to New York? (no)

_____

5. Are any of the stories very good? (no)

_____

6. Is much of the food delicious? (no)

_____

7. Were many of the tests in the class good? (no)

_____

Lesson 6

Exercise 18 (D, pp. 63–64)
Write the demonstrative adjective on the line.

(here) __This__ book is green.

(there) __That__ book is blue.

1. (here) _____ flower is red.

2. (there) _____ apples are from Washington.

3. (here) _____ apples are delicious.

4. (there) _____ man is my father.

5. (here) _____ child is my sister.

6. (here) _____ children are my sisters.

7. (here) Is _____ book a grammar book?

8. (there) _____ pants are blue jeans.

9. (there) I know _____ man.

10. (here) Do _____ pencils write well?

11. (there) Are _____ shirts blue or green?

12. (there) _____ students are from Mexico.

13. (there) _____ cars are expensive.

14. (here) _____ man is a teacher.

15. (there) _____ car is very small.

Exercise 19 (E, pp. 64–65)
Write the correct possessive form.

John has __his__ book.

She has __her__ book.

1. Jane has _____ books.   4. I have _____ car.

2. Mike has _____ books.   5. You have _____ car.

3. Jane and Mike have _____ books.   6. You and I have _____ cars.

7. The students have _____ money. 9. Your sister has _____ notebooks.

8. My father has _____ keys. 10. Her cat has _____ food.

Exercise 20 (E, pp. 64–65)
Write the correct possessive form.

I washed __**my**__ face.

He has __**his**__ books.

1. John washed _____ face and hands.

2. Mary has _____ money.

3. My son has _____ car.

4. The boy is eating _____ dinner.

5. You and I have _____ books.

6. Do they want _____ coats now?

7. She is washing _____ face.

8. Mrs. Miller is combing _____ hair.

9. You need _____ friends.

10. We want _____ pencils and pens.

11. Do I need _____ coat today?

12. You and Mary have _____ books and pencils.

13. John and I are doing _____ homework now.

14. Mary and Jill are going to eat _____ dinner at six o'clock.

15. I don't have _____ book with me.

Lesson 6

Exercise 21: Review Test
A. Write the correct article (*a, an, the, some*). Draw a line if none is necessary.

1. _____ Mr. Jones studies _____ English in _____ United States.

2. I bought _____ pencil and _____ newspaper. I use _____ pencil

to write letters and I read _____ newspaper.

3. _____ Netherlands and _____ Germany are in _____ Europe.

4. Mary is going to study _____ Greek philosophy and _____ philosophy

of _____ Rome.

5. Would you like _____ oranges?

6. Would you like _____ orange?

7. Would you like _____ orange on the table?

8. Do you like _____ oranges?

B. Combine the two sentences.

1. I need some paper. I need two sheets.

   _____

2. I want some bread. I want two slices.

   _____

C. Write the correct quantity expression on the line.

Quantity

1. (small) I want _____ sugar.

2. (large) Do you need _____ books?

3. (large) I don't want _____ new pens.

4. (small) I want _____ good students.

D. Write *this, that, these,* or *those* on the line.

1. (here) We like _____ tables.

2. (there) We want _____ chairs.

3. (here) They prefer _____ pencil.

4. (there) I need _____ grammar book.

E. Write the correct possessive adjective.

1. I washed _____ face.

2. You like _____ books.

3. Did they eat _____ dinner?

4. She likes _____ little dog.

5. The man is drinking _____ beer.

Exercise 22: Review Test
Choose the correct answer. Put a circle around the letter of the answer.

1. "Where did you go last summer?"
   "I visited _____ ."
   a) the New York
   b) the Argentina
   c) Canada
   d) United States

2. The books there are red. _____ books are red.
   a) This
   b) These
   c) That
   d) Those

3. "Are any of the students sick?"
   "No, _____ are sick now."
   a) no any
   b) not many
   c) none
   d) not much

4. I don't need a large quantity of sugar. I only need _____ sugar.

    a) a few

    b) a little

    c) much

    d) a lot of

5. I bought a comb yesterday. _____ is very good.

    a) A comb

    b) The comb

    c) Some combs

    d) Many combs

6. "What are you studying?"

   "I'm studying _____ ."

    a) the art

    b) the Greek art

    c) the art of Greece

    d) art of Greece

7. I'm very thirsty! I would like _____ .

    a) a juice of orange

    b) a orange juice

    c) a glass of orange juice

    d) an orange juice

8. "Do Mr. and Mrs. Jones have a car?"

   "Yes, _____ car is new."

    a) its

    b) his

    c) their

    d) our

9. I need to buy some toothpaste. I need _____ toothpaste.

    a) two

    b) two tubes of

    c) a few

    d) many

10. John likes coffee very much. He drinks a large quantity. He drinks _____ coffee.

    a) many

    b) much

    c) a lot of

    d) some

Lesson 7

A. Requests: Please read the book. (*would you; let's*)

B. Irregular nouns: *man, men; people*

C. The noun substitute *one*

D. The use of *other* and *another*

E. The object forms of pronouns: *me, him, them,* etc.

Vocabulary List

automobile	fast	movie	policeman
beside	follow	name	rapidly
blackboard	foot	near	salt
check	forget	news	sheep
child	gentleman	notebook	shelf
clothes	glad	paint	shirt
concert	lend	parent	translate
conversation	luggage	park	wash
elephant	man	pattern	waste
eraser	miss	please	wife
factory	mouse	police	women

Exercise 1 (A, pp. 66–67)
Write a request with *please*.

(open your book) ___Please open your book._____

1. (write your name) _____

2. (go to the bank) _____

3. (give me a sheet of paper) _____

4. (lend me a dollar) _____

Exercise 2   (A, pp. 66–67)
Write a request with *would you please*.

(sit down) ___Would you please sit down.___

1. (read page 95) _____

2. (close the window) _____

3. (pass me the salt) _____

4. (come in) _____

Exercise 3   (A, pp. 66–67)
Write a negative request.

(speak rapidly) ___Don't speak rapidly.___

1. (sleep late) _____

2. (forget your ticket) _____

3. (eat my lunch) _____

4. (call me tonight) _____

5. (arrive late) _____

Exercise 4   (A, pp. 66–67)
Write a request with *let's*.

(play tennis) ___Let's play tennis.___

1. (leave soon) _____

2. (sing some songs) _____

3. (go to a movie) _____

4. (do our homework) _____

5. (eat lunch now) _____

Exercise 5 (B, pp. 68–69)
Write the form that is missing. Draw a line if there is no other form of the word.

<u>child</u>   children

businessman   <u>businessmen</u>

Singular	*Plural*
1. _____	shelves
2. _____	loaves
3. knife	_____
4. wife	_____
5. _____	children
6. woman	_____
7. _____	businessmen
8. _____	clothes
9. man	_____
10. foot	_____
11. _____	police
12. _____	sheep
13. fish	_____
14. _____	people
15. tooth	_____
16. _____	policemen
17. mouse	_____
18. gentleman	_____

Lesson 7

Exercise 6 (B, pp. 68–69)
Underline the correct answer.

The women (is, <u>are</u>) talking in the kitchen.
The (<u>man</u>, men) is here now.

1. The news (is, are) good.
2. I see the two (childs, children).
3. We need some (knifes, knives).
4. The mice (is, are) very bad in this house.
5. His clothes (is, are) very nice.
6. These sheep (is, are) fat.
7. Every person has two (foot, feet).
8. My (tooth, teeth) are white.
9. They bought two (loafs, loaves) of bread.
10. This fish (is, are) very small.
11. The businessmen always (arrive, arrives) at nine o'clock.
12. The (man, men) in the car work at the bank.
13. (This, These) shirts are not expensive.
14. The knives on the table (is, are) sharp.
15. The people in my class (has, have) new books.

Exercise 7 (C, pp. 69–70)
Write *it, one,* or *some.*

I see the book. I see ___it___ .

1. I need a pen. Please give me _____ .

2. They want the answer now. They want _____ now.

3. He needs some water. He needs _____ .

4. Did you write a letter today? No, I'm going to write _____ tomorrow.

5. Did you buy any apples? Yes, I bought _____ .

6. I want a red pen. I want _____ .

7. I need a good book. I need _____ .

8. Does she want any ink? Yes, she wants _____ .

9. The chair is not old. _____ is new.

10. Do you have a car? No, I don't have _____ .

Exercise 8 (D.1, pp. 71–72)
Write *another one* or *the other one*.

I have a pen here on the table. I have __another one__ in my car.

1. Mary is writing a letter now. She is going to write _____ tomorrow.

2. Mary needs to write two letters. She's going to write one now. She's going to write _____ _____ tomorrow.

3. I'm going to buy two shirts. I'm going to buy one today. I'm going to buy _____ _____ tomorrow.

4. John's reading a book now. He wants to read _____ next week.

5. I have three cats. Two of my cats are black. _____ is white.

6. I have many books. I like books very much. I'm going to buy _____ _____ tomorrow.

7. Mary has four books. Two are grammar books, and one is a reading book. _____ _____ is a writing book.

8. I am reading a book now. Tomorrow I'm going to read _____.

9. She has two sisters. One is short, and _____ is tall.

10. I have two pens here. This one doesn't write well. I'm going to use _____ _____.

Exercise 9 (D.1, pp. 71–73)
Write *another one, the other one, others,* or *the others*.

I bought a shirt today. I'm going to buy __another one__ tomorrow.

1. I have a pen here on the table. I have _____ in my car. The pen on the table is old, and _____ is new.

2. Mary bought three apples. She ate two of the apples. Now she is going to eat _____ _____.

3. We have two pages of homework. I did one page last night, and I'm going to do _____

_____ in a few minutes.

4. Many students speak English. A few _____ speak French.

5. Five people came to class. One has his book, but _____ don't have their books.

6. Susan has two classes. She's attending one now. She's going to go to _____

_____ after lunch.

7. A few students arrive late every day. A few _____ arrive on time.

8. Many students do not eat breakfast. Many _____ do not eat lunch.

9. I have two pens. I don't like this pen. I prefer _____.

10. John has two brothers. One is in France, and _____ is in Spain.

11. Four men work here at night. Four _____ work here in the day.

12. One student is writing a letter. _____ is studying math.

13. I have five dollars. I'm going to give four dollars to Jane, and I'm going to give _____

_____ to Mark.

14. She doesn't like her new car. She's going to buy _____.

15. He has a pencil on his desk in class. He has some _____ at home.

Exercise 10   (D.1, pp. 71–73)
Write *another one, the other one, others,* or *the others*.

I bought a shirt today. I'm going to buy **another one** tomorrow.

1. A few students study in the morning. Many _____ study at night.

2. One student is standing near the door. _____ is sitting at his desk.

3. She's singing some songs now. She's going to sing some _____ tonight.

4. I'm going to write three letters. I'm writing two letters now, and I'm going to write

_____ tomorrow.

5. I have a lot of good books. These books are excellent, but _____ are much more interesting.

Exercise 11   (E, pp. 74–75; p. 3; p. 64)
Write the pronoun and adjective forms.

subject pronoun	object pronoun	possessive adjective
1. I	8. __me__	15. __my__
2. _____	9. _____	16. your
3. _____	10. him	17. _____
4. she	11. _____	18. _____
5. it	12. _____	19. _____
6. _____	13. _____	20. our
7. they	14. _____	21. _____

Exercise 12   (pp. 64–65, 74–75)
Write the correct form of the pronoun or adjective.

John explained the question. __He__ explained __it__ .

1. Ann is going to call Sally. _____ is going to call _____ .

2. John studies with Paul and Joe. _____ studies with _____ .

3. Mark studies with Sue and Jane. _____ studies with _____ .

4. Mary is eating two sandwiches for lunch. _____ is eating _____ for lunch.

5. Mr. and Mrs. Smith live near the school. _____ live near _____ .

6. John and I see Mary and you every day. _____ see _____ every day.

7. John is leaving. Does _____ have _____ luggage with _____ ?

8. The girls are going to buy some books. Do _____ have _____ money with _____ ?

9. We are going to class now. Do _____ have _____ books with _____ ?

10. Matt and I watched the movie. _____ watched _____ .

Exercise 13: Pronoun Discrimination: Subject Pronoun, Object Pronoun, Possessive Adjective
Underline the correct form.

John has (<u>his</u>, him) books.
John and I hear (they, <u>them</u>) now.

1. (We, Us) eat lunch at noon.
2. The boys write (their, them) homework at night.
3. She eats (her, his) lunch at noon.
4. (I, Me) am going to study (it, its) tonight.
5. Mary sees (he, him) every day.
6. I have a class with (she, her) in the afternoon.
7. We are going to give (it, its) to (he, him) tomorrow.
8. (I, Me, My) book is on the table.
9. John and (them, I) are always late.
10. We are calling (they, them) now.
11. (She, Her) sees John, but he doesn't see (she, her).
12. My friend has (he, his, him) car with (he, his, him).
13. Does John study with Mary and Matt?
    Yes, (he, his, him) studies with (they, them, their).
14. They asked (I, me, my) some questions.
15. Did you practice the vocabulary?
    Yes, (I, me, my) practiced (it, him, her) last night.
16. I have some apples.
    I'm going to eat (they, them, their) for lunch.
17. What is your name?
    (I, It, You) is John.
18. Please call (me, she, we) at noon.
19. (We, Them, His) dog is eating now.
20. What is the answer?
    (He, She, It) is letter B.

Exercise 14: Review Test
A. The words in this exercise are requests. Write the words in the correct order.

1. (the / pass / please / sugar) _____

2. (you / pass / please / would / sugar / the) _____

3. (party / have / let's / a) _____

4. (don't / please / loudly / speak) _____

B. Write the plural.

1. man _____   4. mouse _____

2. knife _____   5. sheep _____

3. child _____   6. foot _____

C. Underline the correct form.

1. My clothes (is, are) on the bed.
2. The news (is, are) good.
3. The people (is, are) hungry now.

D. Write *it, one, some, another one, the other one, other,* or *others*.

1. Bill needs a coat. Please lend him _____ .

2. I have a pen here on the table. I have _____ in my car.

3. Three dogs are black. Three _____ are brown.

4. "Do you need any bread?" "Yes, I need _____ ."

5. Where is the newspaper? I want to read _____ now.

6. Some students study hard. Many _____ students do not study.

E. Write the correct pronoun or adjective form.

1. Mary knows John and Bill. _____ knows _____ .

2. The new car is blue. _____ is blue.

3. I see the new cars. I see _____ .

4. John asked Mary the question. _____ asked _____ the question.

5. The dog sees you. The dog sees _____ .

6. You are going to class now. Do _____ have _____ books with _____ ?

Exercise 15: Review Test
Choose the correct answer. Put a circle around the letter of the answer.

1. "What are we going to do now?"
   " _____ ."
   a) Going to the store.
   b) Let's go to the store.
   c) Don't go to the store.
   d) Would you please.

2. I have two _____ .
   a) foot
   b) mice
   c) child
   d) knife

3. "Did you buy a pencil yesterday?"
   "No, but I'm going to buy ___ tomorrow."
   a) some
   b) one
   c) other
   d) it

4. I need my watch.
   Who has _____ ?
   a) some
   b) it
   c) other
   d) one

5. John's reading a newspaper now.
   He's going to read ___ tomorrow.
   a) another one
   b) other one
   c) other
   d) it

6. I have four cats. Three are black.
   _____ is white.
   a) Four
   b) It
   c) The other
   d) Another

7. "Do John and Mary have _____ ?"
   "Yes, they do."
   a) their luggage with they
   b) their luggage with them
   c) his luggage with them
   d) her luggage with they

8. One of the students is reading a book.
   "What are _____ doing?"
   "They're reading also."
   a) the other one
   b) the others ones
   c) the others
   d) the ones

9. Four men work here in the morning.
   Four _____ work here at night.
   a) ones
   b) others
   c) others ones
   d) the others

10. Be quiet! Please _____ loudly!
    a) no speak
    b) do speak
    c) don't speak
    d) speak not

Lesson 8

A. Verb and indirect object: Give her a book. Give a book to her.

B. Past tense forms of irregular verbs: *eat, ate; give, gave*

Vocabulary List

address	direction	meet	show
announce	dish	plan	sit
ask	do	plate	speech
bank	explain	pleasant	spend
become	favor	postcard	sportcoat
break	feel	prescribe	stand
cake	find	price	story
cash	fine	problem	suggest
cat	food	progress	take
charge	get	prove	tear
choose	give	put	tell
cloth	introduce	report	think
cost	journey	save	train
custom	make	say	under
cut	mathematics	see	wake up
dark	medicine	sell	wish
describe	mention	send	

Exercise 1   (A.1, pp. 76–77)
Write a sentence with *to*.

Joe gives Mark the books. __Joe gives the books to Mark.__

1. Susan writes Sam a letter. _____

2. I always read my brother the newspaper. _____

3. We show the class our gift. _____

4. She teaches the students new words. _____

5. Please tell Mary the good news. _____

6. I'm going to sell Bob my bicycle. _____

7. I usually lend Paul my car. _____

8. Did she bring the teacher an apple? _____

9. Would you please take your father the food. _____

10. He passed me the salt. _____

119

Exercise 2 (A.1, pp. 76–77)
Write a sentence without *to*.

John gives the books to Mark. ___*John gives Mark the books.*___

1. I teach the lesson to Bill. _____

2. You showed the map to Mr. Smith. _____

3. He brings the newspaper to my family._____

4. Please lend the money to John. _____

5. Did you write a long letter to your sister? _____

6. I sold my car to Bill. _____

7. Pass the glass to your father. _____

8. She is going to read the letter to me. _____

9. Take the money to Mrs. Jones. _____

10. I never tell lies to my father. _____

Exercise 3 (A.1, pp. 76–77)
Circle the letter of the correct sentences.

(*a*) Joe gives the books to Mary.
(*b*) Joe gives Mary the books.

1. *a*) He is writing a letter to Susan.
   b) He is writing Susan a letter.
2. *a*) Pass the salt to me.
   b) Pass me the salt.
3. *a*) He showed his new car to me.
   b) He showed me his new car.
4. *a*) I am going to sell my car to Mike.
   b) I am going to sell Mike my car.
5. *a*) Are you taking the money to Mr. Miller?
   b) Are you taking Mr. Miller the money?

Exercise 4 (A.2, pp. 77–78)
Write a new sentence with the words in parentheses.

He wished a good trip. (Mary)

He wished Mary a good trip.

1. He's going to ask a question. (the teacher)

2. They charged twenty dollars. (Mr. Smith)

3. She saved ten cents. (Joe)

4. We asked the time of day. (the man)

5. Santa Claus wished Merry Christmas. (the child)

6. The bicycle cost fifty dollars. (me)

7. The store charged ten dollars for a new shirt. (them)

Exercise 5 (A.2, pp. 77–78)
Circle the letter of the correct sentences.

a) The man asked the question to us.
b) The man asked us the question.

1. *a*) My mother wished a good day to us.
   b) My mother wished us a good day.
2. *a*) That shirt cost ten dollars to me.
   b) That shirt cost me ten dollars.
3. *a*) The restaurant charged three dollars to us.
   b) The restaurant charged us three dollars.

4. *a*) The ladies saved fifty cents to us.

   b) The ladies saved us fifty cents.

5. *a*) The students asked several questions to the teacher.

   b) The students asked the teacher several questions.

Exercise 6 (A.3, pp. 78–79)

Write a new sentence with the words in parentheses.

The teacher announced the test. (the class)

<u>The teacher announced the test to the class.</u>

1. She explained the vocabulary. (the students)

_____

2. Mary reported the news. (the women)

_____

3. We suggested that restaurant. (them)

_____

4. I introduced Susan. (Mike)

_____

5. I described my trip. (my family)

_____

6. Bill mentioned the idea. (the men)

_____

7. I spoke English. (Mr. Jones)

_____

8. He proved his age. (the girl)

_____

9. The teacher repeated the answers. (the class)

_____

10. I always say "hello." (Jane)

_____

122

Exercise 7   (A.3, pp. 78–79)
Circle the letter of the correct sentences.

a) He announced the schedule to the students.
b) He announced the students the schedule.

1. *a)* Mrs. Smith explained the lesson to the class.
   b) Mrs. Smith explained the class the lesson.
2. *a)* Mike introduced John to Bill.
   b) Mike introduced Bill John.
3. *a)* They described the picture to us.
   b) They described us the picture.
4. *a)* My father mentioned the trip to the children.
   b) My father mentioned the children the trip.
5. *a)* He repeated the words to me.
   b) He repeated me the words.

Exercise 8   (A.1–3, pp. 76–80)
Write *a, b,* or *ab* on the line to show the possible answers.

He mentioned _____ **a** _____ .
a) the idea to us
b) us the idea

1. John gave _____ .
   a) the books to Joe
   b) Joe the books
2. Mike asked _____ .
   a) some questions to the students
   b) the students some questions
3. He explained _____ .
   a) the lesson to me
   b) me the lesson
4. She sent _____ .
   a) the letter to Paul
   b) Paul the letter
5. The teacher showed _____ .
   a) the test to the boys
   b) the boys the test
6. The shirt cost _____ .
   a) ten dollars to me
   b) me ten dollars

7. I wrote _____ .
   a) the note to him
   b) him the note
8. We told _____ .
   a) the news to them
   b) them the news
9. Gary repeated _____ .
   a) the sentence to us
   b) us the sentence
10. They described _____ .
    a) their trip to us
    b) us their trip
11. She brought _____ .
    a) their lunch to them
    b) them their lunch
12. That store charged _____ .
    a) ten dollars to us
    b) us ten dollars

13. We took _____ .
    a) the money to them
    b) them the money

14. Mary introduced _____ .
    a) John to me
    b) me John

15. We usually spoke _____ .
    a) English to him
    b) him English

16. Mr. Jones wished _____ .
    a) a Merry Christmas to us
    b) us a Merry Christmas

17. I mentioned _____ .
    a) the idea to him
    b) him the idea

18. She lent _____ .
    a) the money to her friend
    b) her friend the money

19. He passed _____ .
    a) the salt to Jane
    b) Jane the salt

20. Sam and Sue taught _____ .
    a) the verbs to me
    b) me the verbs

21. We reported _____ .
    a) the news to my father
    b) my father the news

22. The lady is reading _____ .
    a) the story to the children
    b) the children the story

23. The students sent _____ .
    a) a present to the teacher
    b) the teacher a present

24. My friend saved _____ .
    a) some money to me
    b) me some money

25. Those people suggested _____ .
    a) that restaurant to us
    b) us that restaurant

Exercise 9 (A.4, pp. 80–82)
Write a sentence with *for*.

He is going to buy Mary a book.

___He is going to buy a book for Mary.___

1. I'm going to get John some water.

   _____

2. She found Mr. Miller the newspaper.

   _____

3. She made the girl a cake.

   _____

4. The teacher got the student a test.

   _____

5. My brother did me a favor.

   _____

Exercise 10   (A.4, pp. 80–82)
Write a sentence without *for*.

He is going to buy a book for Mary.   <u>He is going to buy Mary a book.</u>

1. I made some tea for the students. _____

2. Mr. Smith bought a dress for his wife. _____

3. He found a pencil for me. _____

4. He did a favor for me. _____

5. They got a ticket for me. _____

Exercise 11   (A.4, pp. 80–82)
Circle the letter of the correct sentences.

(a) I'm going to buy a book for Mary.
(b) I'm going to buy Mary a book.

1. *a*) I did a favor for Bill.
   b) I did Bill a favor.
2. *a*) He got a chair for the lady.
   b) He got the lady a chair.
3. *a*) She made dinner for us.
   b) She made us dinner.

4. *a*) They found the keys for me.
   b) They found me the keys.
5. a) I bought a present for him.
   b) I bought him a present.

Exercise 12   (A.4, pp. 80–82)
Write a new sentence with the words in parentheses.

He opened the door. (Mary)

_____ <u>He opened the door for Mary.</u> _____

1. The doctor prescribed the medicine. (me)

_____

2. She cashed the check. (Mike)

_____

3. The teacher pronounced the word. (the students)

_____

125

4. He closed the window. (the girl)

_____

5. Martha did the homework. (Bill)

_____

6. The teacher answered the question. (the boy)

_____

7. The teacher changed the test grade. (the student)

_____

Exercise 13   (A.4, pp. 80–82)
Circle the letter of the correct sentences.

    a) Please open the door for Mary.
    b) Please open Mary the door.

1. *a*) They did the dishes for us.
    b) They did us the dishes.
2. *a*) The doctor prescribed the medicine for me.
    b) The doctor prescribed me the medicine.
3. *a*) He answered the questions for us.
    b) He answered us the questions.
4. *a*) Would you please close the window for me.
    b) Would you please close me the window.
5. *a*) The class pronounced the words for the teacher.
    b) The class pronounced the teacher the words.
6. *a*) The lady cashed the check for him.
    b) The lady cashed him the check.
7. *a*) He changed his plans for us.
    b) He changed us his plans.
8. *a*) Would you please open the door for the woman.
    b) Would you please open the woman the door.

Exercise 14   (A.4, pp. 80–82)
Write *a*, *b*, or *ab* to show the possible answers.

He brought __a b__ .
a) the car for me
b) me the car

1. He pronounced _____ .
   a) the word for me
   b) me the word
2. The doctor prescribed _____ .
   a) the medicine for me
   b) me the medicine
3. We made _____ .
   a) the reservation for them
   b) them the reservation
4. I opened _____ .
   a) the door for him
   b) him the door
5. I am going to find _____ .
   a) the map for you
   b) you the map
6. Please do _____ .
   a) a favor for me
   b) me a favor
7. They changed _____ .
   a) their plans for me
   b) me their plans

8. Mary did _____ .
   a) the dishes for me
   b) me the dishes
9. We got _____ .
   a) some tickets for the students
   b) the students some tickets
10. I found _____ .
    a) a chair for Mrs. Smith
    b) Mrs. Smith a chair
11. Would you please close _____ .
    a) the window for us
    b) us the window
12. The man cashed _____ .
    a) the check for me
    b) me the check
13. She's going to buy _____ .
    a) a shirt for you
    b) you a shirt

Exercise 15   (A.1–4, pp. 76–82)
Write *to me, for me,* or *me* on the line.

He gave the book __to me__ .

He gave __me__ the book.

1. He repeated the words _____ .

2. She opened the door _____ .

3. He bought _____ the shirt.

4. He bought the shirt _____ .

5. They spoke _____ .

6. Please tell _____ the answer.

7. Pass the salt _____ .

8. He is going to read the story _____ .

9. He asked _____ the question.

10. They explained the answer _____ .

11. The doctor prescribed the medicine _____ .

12. She sent _____ the letter.

13. She sent the letter _____ .

14. Please close the door _____ .

15. He described his trip _____ .

16. He wished _____ a happy birthday.

17. He got _____ a nice present.

18. He gave _____ a new shirt.

19. They found a chair _____ .

20. He is getting _____ a chair.

21. He is getting a chair _____ .

22. She made a cake _____ .

23. He wrote a letter _____ .

24. Please pronounce the new vocabulary words _____ .

25. He answered the questions _____ .

Exercise 16: Verb Pattern Discrimination Using Grammatical Context Clues (A.1–4, pp. 76–82)
Write the correct verb on the line.

John ____**gave**____ the book to me. (gave, bought, opened)

1. The teacher _____ the question to me. (asked, answered, explained)

2. He _____ a cake for me. (gave, made, described)

3. I am going to _____ my new car to them. (save, show, change)

4. My sister always _____ long letters to me. (finds, sends, answers)

5. Please _____ me the salt. (open, pass, repeat)

6. Mary _____ the words for me. (explained, repeated, pronounced)

7. Did John _____ the books to them? (find, take, close)

8. Mrs. Smith _____ ten dollars to John. (sent, saved, charged)

9. Did the doctor _____ the medicine to you? (buy, bring, prescribe)

10. My parents did not _____ me a new bicycle. (get, change, suggest)

11. I often _____ money to Paul. (lend, change, charge)

12. They _____ it for us. (found, wished, explained)

13. John usually _____ me "hello." (says, tells, speaks)

14. She _____ me a happy birthday. (said, wished, described)

15. He _____ the idea to my class. (made, asked, mentioned)

16. We are going to _____ her a watch. (open, give, submit)

Lesson 8

Exercise 17 (B.1, pp. 82–84)
Write the past tense of the verbs.

come _came_

buy _bought_

1. drink _____

2. give _____

3. become _____

4. read _____

5. begin _____

6. get _____

7. see _____

8. wear _____

9. take _____

10. sit _____

11. wake _____

12. break _____

13. eat _____

14. know _____

15. speak _____

16. forget _____

17. meet _____

18. tear _____

19. come _____

20. write _____

21. choose _____

Exercise 18 (B.1, pp. 82–84)
Write the correct form of the verb on the line.

(meet) I _____met_____ him yesterday.

1. (give) She _____ me a check a few minutes ago.

2. (come) Did you _____ late?

3. (take) I _____ my medicine an hour ago.

4. (forget) He didn't _____ the answer.

5. (break) Did you _____ the window?

6. (be) I _____ in France last summer.

7. (begin) His class _____ ten minutes ago.

8. (give) He didn't _____ me the money yesterday.

9. (eat) My family _____ steak last night.

10. (get) Martha _____ sick yesterday.

Exercise 19 (B.1, pp. 82–84)
Answer these questions with complete answers.

Did John eat an apple? (yes)

<u> Yes, he ate an apple .   </u>

Did you come late? (no)

<u>No, I didn't come late .   </u>

1. Did Mark choose a car? (yes)

   _____

2. Did they break the glass? (no)

   _____

3. Did she begin the work? (no)

   _____

4. Did you see the movie? (yes)

   _____

5. Did you forget my book? (no)

   _____

Exercise 20 (B.2–3, pp. 84–88)
Write the past tense of the verbs.

go   <u> went   </u>

eat   <u> ate   </u>

1. leave	_____	7. feel	_____
2. do	_____	8. spend	_____
3. understand	_____	9. make	_____
4. send	_____	10. put	_____
5. have	_____	11. sleep	_____
6. stand	_____	12. cost	_____

13. lend _____   18. teach _____

14. mean _____   19. tell _____

15. cut _____   20. buy _____

16. hear _____   21. think _____

17. bring _____   22. say _____

Exercise 21   (B.2–3, pp. 84–88)
Write the correct form of the verb on the line.

(bring) He __**brought**__ the book yesterday.

1. (have) He _____ a cold last week.

2. (buy)   She _____ a new house in 1979.

3. (hear) Did you _____ the news?

4. (send) She _____ me a letter last month.

5. (cut)   I _____ my finger last night.

6. (make) He _____ a sandwich for me a few minutes ago.

7. (tell) She didn't _____ me the answer.

8. (say)   She _____ ''hello'' to me in the last class.

9. (feel) He _____ sick yesterday.

10. (sleep) I didn't _____ well last night.

Exercise 22   (B.2–3, pp. 84–88)
Write a complete answer to the question. Use the italicized words as the answer.

Did he send *a box* or a cake?

__He sent a box .__

1. Did they eat cake or *steak*?

_____

2. Did I tell you *yes* or no?

_____

3. Did Robert make coffee or *tea*?

_____

4. Did you sleep *six hours* or seven hours?

_____

5. Did she bring *one book* or two books?

_____

Exercise 23   (B.1–3, pp. 82–88)
Write the past tense of the verbs.

eat   __ate__

1. break _____

2. bring _____

3. eat _____

4. do _____

5. wake _____

6. cut _____

7. attend _____

8. feel _____

9. drink _____

10. send _____

11. speak _____

12. sleep _____

13. want _____

14. know _____

15. mean _____

16. wear _____

17. are _____

18. buy _____

19. study _____

20. choose _____

21. go _____

22. put _____

23. make _____

24. get _____

25. begin _____

26. have _____

Lesson 8

27. give _____   39. take _____

28. think _____   40. teach _____

29. sit _____   41. tell _____

30. spend _____   42. cost _____

31. say _____   43. understand _____

32. read _____   44. become _____

33. is _____   45. write _____

34. see _____   46. forget _____

35. meet _____   47. hear _____

36. leave _____   48. come _____

37. work _____   49. lend _____

38. tear _____   50. stand _____

Exercise 24: Review Test
A. Write a new sentence with the words in parentheses. If there are two possible sentences, write both of them.

1. She cashed a check. (me)

_____

_____

2. I did a favor. (the boys)

_____

_____

3. He announced the schedule. (us)

_____

_____

4. Mr. Jones bought a present. (Bill)

_____

_____

5. The shirt cost six dollars. (him)

_____

_____

B. Write *to me*, *for me*, or *me*.

1. Mary sent the letter _____ .

2. Mary sent _____ the letter.

3. She made a sandwich _____ .

4. He gave _____ a sheet of paper.

5. Please cash the check _____ .

6. They introduced Mike _____ .

7. Please pronounce the words _____ .

8. They wrote _____ a long letter.

9. She's reading the answers _____ .

10. He prescribed the medicine _____ .

C. Write the past tense of the verbs.

1. bring _____

2. tell _____

3. buy _____

4. read _____

5. spend _____

6. sleep _____

7. mean _____

8. find _____

9. give _____

10. see _____

11. choose _____

12. hear _____

13. cut _____

14. teach _____

15. drink _____

Exercise 25: Review Test
Choose the correct answer. Put a circle around the letter of the answer.

1. "Did he begin his homework last night?"
   "Yes, he _____ it."
   a) begin
   b) begins
   c) began
   d) beginned

2. "Did you hear the news?"
   "Yes, I did. That man announced _____ ."
   a) it us
   b) us it
   c) it to us
   d) it for us

3. "Did she give Bob the book?"
   "Yes, she _____ ."
   a) give Bob the book
   b) gave the book to Bob
   c) give Bob to the book
   d) gave the book Bob

4. "How much did the shirt cost?"
   "It _____ me ten dollars."
   a) costed
   b) costed to
   c) cost
   d) cost to

5. "Did she have her key?"
   "No, she didn't. Peter opened _____ ."
   a) her the door
   b) her for the door
   c) the door her
   d) the door for her

6. "Are you going to write her a letter today?"
   "No, I'm not. I _____ yesterday."
   a) writed her a letter
   b) writed a letter to her
   c) wrote a letter for her
   d) wrote a letter to her

7. The ladies _____ that little dog in the street.
   a) finds
   b) found
   c) finded
   d) founded

8. I need some help. Please _____ me a favor.
   a) do
   b) did
   c) do for
   d) did for

9. I was sick last night.
   The doctor prescribed _____ .
   a) me some medicine
   b) some medicine me
   c) some medicine to me
   d) some medicine for me

10. She always _____ every day.
    a) says him "hello"
    b) says "hello" to him
    c) tell to him "hello"
    d) tell "hello" to him

Lesson 9

A. Adverbs of manner: *correctly, well*, etc.

B. Noun phrase + modifier: the chair near the door

C. Wh-questions: Whom does Mary see? Who sees Mary?

Vocabulary List

advise	corner	mile	silent
beautiful	correct	nice	sincere
blond	downtown	peace	slow
bookstore	ear	prompt	swim
briefcase	everywhere	punctual	thin
careful	friendly	quick	wise
clear	hair	shoe store	zoo
clown	loud	short	

Exercise 1   (A.1, pp. 89–90)
Write the adverb form for these adjectives.

correct __correctly__

quick __quickly__

1. quiet _____

2. wise _____

3. clear _____

4. fast _____

5. sad _____

6. easy _____

7. silent _____

8. sincere _____

9. bad _____

10. hard _____

11. loud _____

12. slow _____

13. careful _____

14. good _____

15. beautiful _____

16. prompt _____

17. real _____

18. poor _____

19. rapid _____

20. sudden _____

Lesson 9

Exercise 2 (A.1, pp. 89–90)
Change the adjective in the first sentence to an adverb in the second sentence.

He is a quiet worker. He works ____*quietly*____ .

1. His answer was correct. He answered the question _____ .

2. She is a careful driver. She drives _____ .

3. Mark is a fast reader. He reads _____ .

4. They are good singers. They sing _____ .

5. This is a beautiful painting. Martha paints _____ .

6. I am a hard worker. I work _____ .

7. The doctor is very careful. He works _____ all of the time.

8. Matt is a sincere person. He talks with his friends _____ .

9. John is a quick runner. He runs _____ .

10. She is a good adviser. She advises _____ .

Exercise 3 (A.1, pp. 89–90)
Read the first sentence and then complete the second sentence with an adjective and a noun.

He runs quickly. He is ____*a quick runner*____ .

1. He writes excellently. He is _____ .

2. She eats slowly. She is _____ .

3. They read fast. They are _____ .

4. I drive carefully. I am _____ .

5. They sing well. They are _____ .

6. He works hard. He is _____ .

7. Jack speaks clearly. Jack is _____ .

8. He swims rapidly. He is _____ .

9. Mr. Miller advises well. Mr. Miller is _____ .

10. They work very well. They are _____ .

138

Exercise 4   (A.1, pp. 89–90)
Underline the correct word.

He is a (<u>good</u>, well) teacher. He teaches (good, <u>well</u>).

1. She answered (correct, correctly).
2. The test was (easy, easily).
3. He always drives (careful, carefully).
4. The children are very (quiet, quietly) tonight.
5. His typewriter runs (silent, silently).
6. We heard a (loud, loudly) noise last night.
7. The new man did the work (rapid, rapidly).
8. Be (careful, carefully) with that knife.
9. His (clear, clearly) explanation is going to help us.
10. He gave me a (sincere, sincerely) answer to my question.
11. He is a (sad, sadly) person most of the time.
12. He said the answer (quick, quickly).
13. The (wise, wisely) man is going to become the president in the future.
14. His car is very (slow, slowly).
15. She wrote me some (beautiful, beautifully) letters.

Exercise 5   (A.2, pp. 90–91)
Write a new sentence from the parts.

(opened / carefully / the / He / door) He opened the door carefully.

1. (correctly / The / students / words / the / yesterday / pronounced)

2. (rapidly / cooks / always / She / dinner)

3. (called / store / He / immediately / the)

4. (drives / She / night / always / at / carefully)

5. (to / He / sincerely / spoke / me / night / last)

139

Lesson 9

6. (home / I / at / never / fast / eat)

_____

7. (read / going / is / to / the / He / lesson / carefully)

_____

8. (bank / He / a / the / careful / at / worker / is)

_____

9. (good / arrive / punctually / The / always / students)

_____

10. (a / spoke / Steven / year / English / ago / well)

_____

Excerise 6   (B, pp. 92–93)
Combine the two sentences.

The girl is playing tennis. She is tall.

___The tall girl is playing tennis.___

The man is a doctor. He has a large book.

___The man with the large book is a doctor.___

1. The lady is reading. She is quiet.

_____

2. The student is from Colombia. He has a blue shirt.

_____

3. The store sells shoes. It's on Green Street.

_____

4. The boy speaks English and French. He's from Canada.

_____

5. The question is difficult. It's about verbs.

_____

140

6. That story is very good. It is short.

_____

7. The chair is old. It is near the door.

_____

8. The lady is a nurse. She has blond hair.

_____

9. Those students are intelligent. They're from Canada.

_____

10. The book is about tennis. It's very good.

_____

Exercise 7   (C, pp. 94–97)
Write questions with the question words.

Bill called Mary yesterday.

(who) ___Who called Mary yesterday?_____

(when) ___When did Bill call Mary?_____

1. They talked to Mary last night.

   (who) _____

   (when) _____

   (whom) _____

2. She visited Jack in Miami last month.

   (who) _____

   (whom) _____

   (where) _____

3. That blue shirt cost him ten dollars.

   (how much) _____

   (which) _____

4. Mike ate two hamburgers at noon.

(when) _____

(how many) _____

(what) _____

5. Tim walked six miles this morning.

(who) _____

(how far) _____

6. Mr. Smith was a teacher in New York in 1977.

(who) _____

(what) _____

(when) _____

7. They gave a present to him.

(what) _____

(whom) _____

Exercise 8   (C, pp. 94–97)
Write questions by substituting wh-words for the italicized words.

They live *in New York*.
  a   b

a) _____ Who lives in New York? _____

b) _____ Where do they live? _____

1. *We* saw *Bill* *yesterday*.
   a   b   c

a) _____

b) _____

c) _____

2. *That book* cost *ten dollars*.
   a   b

a) _____

b) _____

142

3. *He* bought *two* pens for *Jill*.
　　_a　　　_b　　　　_c

    a) _____

    b) _____

    c) _____

4. George *studied Portuguese in Brazil*.
　　　　　　　　_a　　　　　　_b

    a) _____

    b) _____

5. The girls spent *twenty dollars at the store*.
　　　　　　　　　　_a　　　　　_b

    a) _____

    b) _____

Exercise 9: Review Test
A. Write the adverb forms.

1. fast _____   3. easy _____   5. sincere _____

2. wise _____   4. hard _____   6. good _____

B. Write the adverb form.

1. He is a good runner. He runs _____ .

2. They are careful drivers. They drive _____ .

C. Write the adjective form.

1. Tim reads carefully. He is a _____ reader.

2. He reads slowly. He is a _____ reader.

D. Write a new sentence from the parts.

1. (carefully / questions / Please / the / read)

_____

2. (slowly / always / in / They / read / class)

_____

E. Combine the two sentences.

1. That store is expensive. It's on State Street.

_____

2. That student studies a lot. He's from Brazil.

_____

F. Make questions from the sentences.

1. *John* bought *two* shirts for *his father yesterday*.
   a   *b*   *c*   *d*

   a) _____

   b) _____

   c) _____

   d) _____

2. Bill spent five dollars in the store.

   a) Who _____

   b) Where _____

   c) How much _____

Exercise 10: Review Test
Choose the correct answer. Put a circle around the letter of the answer.

1. " _____ yesterday?"
   "John."
   a) Who visited Mary
   b) Who did visit
   c) Whom did Mary visited
   d) Whom did visited Mary

2. "Is Jane a good announcer?"
   "Yes, she talks _____ ."
   a) loudly and clearly
   b) fast and clear
   c) rapid and fast
   d) clear and rapidly

3. The chair is old. It's near the door.
   The chair _____ .
   a) old is near the door
   b) near the door is old
   c) old and near the door
   d) is near the old door

4. "Is John a good worker?"
   "Yes, he works _____ ."
   a) good
   b) well
   c) goodly
   d) workly

5. "Which man is John?"
   " _____ is John."
   a) The man newspaper
   b) The man old
   c) The man with a sweater
   d) John in the class

6. They ate _____ last night.
   a) dinner rapid
   b) rapid dinner
   c) dinner rapidly
   d) rapidly dinner

7. The students are good workers. They're
   from France. _____ are good workers.
   a) The France students
   b) The students France
   c) The from France students
   d) The students from France

8. " _____ ?"
   "Mike does."
   a) Who works careful?
   b) Who works carefully?
   c) Whom works careful?
   d) Whom works carefully?

9. He is an excellent _____ .
   a) sing
   b) sings
   c) singer
   d) singing

10. " _____ ate the bread?"
    "Mike and Pete did."
    a) Who
    b) Whom
    c) Which
    d) How many

Review Test 1 (Lessons 1–9)

Choose the best answer and put a circle around the letter of the correct answer.

1. "Mary is never on time."
   "She always _____ late for class."
   a) arrive
   b) arrives
   c) is
   d) are

2. I did a favor _____ yesterday.
   a) for he
   b) for him
   c) to he
   d) to him

3. Mrs. Smith _____ him the book yesterday.
   a) gives
   b) spoke
   c) mentioned
   d) lent

4. "Did you buy a few pencils yesterday?"
   "No, I'm going to buy _____ tomorrow."
   a) any
   b) some
   c) it
   d) another

5. They _____ sandwiches last night.
   a) no make any
   b) did not made
   c) never makes
   d) did not make

6. "Whom _____ now?"
   "She sees Bill."
   a) sees Mary
   b) sees Bill
   c) does Mary see
   d) does Bill see

7. We have our books.
   They have _____ books.
   a) they're
   b) there
   c) them
   d) their

8. I need some bread. I'm going to buy _____ .
   a) one bread
   b) two breads
   c) one loaf of bread
   d) two loafs of bread

9. "What _____ at noon every day?"
   "I eat lunch."
   a) did you do
   b) do you did
   c) do you do
   d) did you did

10. They don't have a small quantity of
    money. They have _____ money.
    a) a lot of
    b) a little
    c) many
    d) a few

11. His books are there on the table.
    _____ are his books.
    a) That
    b) This
    c) Those
    d) These

12. "Did you eat your lunch
    _____ yesterday?"
    "Yes, I did."
    a) usually
    b) rapidly
    c) fastly
    d) often

13. "Mary has the correct answer."
    "Yes, she _____ right."
    a) has
    b) have
    c) does
    d) is

146

14. "Mrs. Smith was absent yesterday."
"Did Mrs. Jones _____ in her place?"
 a) teach
 b) taucht
 c) taught
 d) teached

15. They are trees. They have apples.
They are _____ .
 a) apples tree
 b) apple trees
 c) apples trees
 d) trees of apples

16. "Do you need some fruit?"
"Yes, I need _____ ."
 a) a few
 b) many
 c) some
 d) any

17. I like apples. I really like _____
apples from Washington.
 a) some
 b) the
 c) a little
 d) much

18. "May I use the pen on the table?"
"No, do not use _____ ."
 a) it
 b) one
 c) another
 d) the other

19. Paul showed the books to me.
He showed _____ .
 a) the books me
 b) them to me
 c) they to me
 d) they me

20. The large shoe store is very good. It's on
State Street. The _____ is very good.
 a) shoe store large on State Street
 b) large shoe store on State Street
 c) on State Street is large shoe store
 d) large shoe store is on State Street

21. "Is Paul usually busy at 3:00 P.M.?"
"Yes, _____ ."
 a) he does
 b) he is
 c) he's ever
 d) ever

22. " _____ is writing a letter to John?"
"One of the students is."
 a) When
 b) Where
 c) Whom
 d) Who

23. "I do not understand this lesson."
"I am going _____ ."
 a) explain it to you
 b) explain you it
 c) to explain it to you
 d) to explain you it

24. "Where are they?"
"I don't know. Those _____ are
never on time."
 a) childs
 b) wifes
 c) men
 d) womans

25. Mr. Allen is writing a letter now.
He's going to write _____ tomorrow.
 a) the other one
 b) other
 c) other one
 d) another one

26. Mr. Jones is a good teacher.
He teaches _____ .
 a) good
 b) goodly
 c) well
 d) usually

27. "John and Mike are leaving."
"Do they have their luggage with _____ ?"
 a) they
 b) them
 c) they're
 d) their

28. "Are you _____ the soccer game now?"
"Yes, I am."
a) listening
b) watching
c) hearing
d) seeing

29. I do not smoke. My brother does not _____ smoke.
a) never
b) seldom
c) usually
d) rarely

30. "Is any of the chalk yellow?"
"No, _____ is yellow. All of it is white."
a) not many
b) not much
c) no all
d) none

31. John was very dirty. He washed _____ face and hands.
a) him
b) his
c) the
d) him the

32. Joe, Greg, and I _____ hungry now.
a) have
b) are
c) are having
d) are being

33. We have coffee _____ at seven.
a) often
b) always
c) in the kitchen
d) in the morning

34. He is going _____ tonight.
a) read
b) reads
c) to read
d) reading

35. "Was George very happy?"
"No, he wasn't. He _____ a car."
a) never have
b) wasn't having
c) didn't have
d) didn't had

36. "Did you buy a shirt and a tie last night?"
"Yes, I did. I _____ shirt today."
a) weared a
b) weared the
c) wore a
d) wore the

37. It's cold in this room. Would you please _____ the window.
a) close
b) closing
c) to close
d) to closing

38. We gave the books to _____ .
a) she
b) his
c) them
d) whom

39. I bought a very good book. It _____ .
a) cost five dollars to me
b) costed five dollars to me
c) cost me five dollars
d) costed me five dollars

40. "_____ did they visit yesterday?"
"Some friends."
a) Who
b) Whom
c) When
d) Where

41. "_____ grammar books do you need?"
"We need a lot of them."
a) Which
b) How many
c) How much
d) What number

42. " _____ did he drive yesterday?"
"He drove two hundred miles."
   a) How
   b) How far
   c) How a lot
   d) How a lot of

43. "Did you go to other countries last year?"
"Yes, I went to _____ ."
   a) the Japan and United States
   b) Japan and the United States
   c) Japan and United States
   d) the Japan and the United States

44. The teacher pronounced the words
_____ students in class yesterday.
   a) to this
   b) for this
   c) to the
   d) for the

45. I have a pencil here on the table.
I have _____ in my car.
   a) another
   b) other one
   c) anothers
   d) others ones

46. "Do you need _____ ?"
"Yes, just a little, please."
   a) some bananas
   b) any bananas
   c) some sugar
   d) many sugar

47. She did _____ .
   a) the work for Bill
   b) for Bill the work
   c) the work to Bill
   d) to Bill the work

48. "Did the men bring some food?"
"No, they didn't _____ ."
   a) bring some
   b) bring any
   c) brought some
   d) brought any

49. Mary is not a good speaker.
She speaks very _____ .
   a) loudly and fast
   b) fast and rapid
   c) bad and rapidly
   d) rapid and carefully

50. "Are they your friends?"
"Yes, they are. They often _____
before class."
   a) say me 'hello'
   b) say to me 'hello'
   c) tell to me 'hello'
   d) tell me 'hello'

Review Test 2 (Lessons 1–9)

Choose the best answer and put a circle around the letter of the correct answer.

1. They _____ to the store a few minutes ago.
   a) arrive
   b) begin
   c) buy
   d) went

2. "Did you call John?"
   "Yes, I _____ last night."
   a) called he
   b) called him
   c) he called
   d) him called

3. Please give the letter _____ .
   a) to her
   b) at her
   c) for her
   d) her

4. "Does Pat know the answer?"
   "Yes, he _____ ."
   a) is
   b) was
   c) does
   d) knows

5. "Do you ever go to church?"
   "Yes, _____ ."
   a) ever
   b) often
   c) seldom
   d) never

6. " _____ is he doing?"
   "He's making a sandwich."
   a) When
   b) What
   c) How many
   d) How much

7. " _____ the news good?"
   "I don't know."
   a) Does
   b) Did
   c) Are
   d) Was

8. We don't have many books. We only have _____ .
   a) a few
   b) a little
   c) any
   d) much

9. "Which tree is tall?"
   "The _____ is very tall."
   a) apples tree
   b) apple tree
   c) apples of tree
   d) tree of apples

10. "What is he doing now?"
    "He's _____ a story."
    a) write
    b) wrote
    c) writes
    d) writing

11. "Did you understand the word?"
    "Yes, he _____ it to me."
    a) asked
    b) answered
    c) explained
    d) pronounced

12. "Are you hungry now?"
    "No, I _____ ."
    a) don't
    b) amn't
    c) do not
    d) am not

13. "Does she have the correct answer?"

"Yes, her answer _____ right."

a) has

b) does

c) is

d) had

14. "Does she arrive late?"

"Yes, she _____ arrives late."

a) ever

b) often

c) never

d) seldom

15. "When is your party?"

"It _____ next Friday."

a) goes to be

b) goes to being

c) is going to be

d) is being to go

16. " _____ did he walk?"

"He walked seven miles."

a) What

b) When

c) How far

d) How near

17. He isn't _____ .

a) a tired

b) a doctor

c) good driver

d) fast writer

18. "Would you like some coffee?"

"Yes, just _____ , please."

a) some

b) much

c) a few

d) a little

19. She doesn't _____ .

a) read rapid

b) write well

c) a rapid reader

d) a good writer

20. Joe usually _____ me "hello."

a) announces

b) speaks

c) tells

d) says

21. " _____ did the watch cost?"

"It cost thirty dollars."

a) Whom

b) When

c) How much

d) Would you

22. My sister _____ it for me.

a) gave

b) found

c) wished

d) explained

23. Those children ____ not like vegetables.

a) is

b) are

c) do

d) does

24. "Where is your homework?"

"I _____ it."

a) don't

b) didn't

c) don't do

d) didn't do

25. "Are you busy?"

"Yes, I wrote one letter and now I'm writing _____ ."

a) the others ones

b) the others one

c) another one

d) other one

26. "Please describe your new car."

"It's a _____ ."

a) small

b) green

c) small car

d) car green

27. " _____ are you going to call?"
"John and Paul."
a) Which
b) Whom
c) Where
d) How

28. "Do you want any water?"
"Yes, I'm thirsty. Please give me ____ ."
a) much
b) some
c) none
d) any

29. "Is he a good student?"
"Yes, sometimes. He _____ study."
a) always doesn't
b) doesn't always
c) always isn't
d) isn't always

30. Please give me a _____ .
a) juice
b) bread
c) toothbrush
d) toothpaste

31. Four men work here at night.
Four _____ work here in the day.
a) others
b) anothers
c) the others
d) others ones

32. The boy _____ is from England.
a) near them
b) near they
c) is near them
d) is near they

33. "Is she a good student?"
"Yes, she always answers ____ in class."
a) good
b) rapidly
c) careful
d) correct

34. He is studying the _____ .
a) art
b) English
c) math
d) lesson

35. "Did you get those clothes for your birthday?"
"Yes, my brother gave _____ ."
a) it to me
b) me to it
c) them to me
d) me to them

36. "Where did you go?"
"We went to the _____ ."
a) South America
b) Philippines
c) Northern University
d) Japan

37. "Are ____ books on that table for you?"
"Yes, they are."
a) this
b) that
c) those
d) these

38. I have an apple and a knife.
I'm going to eat _____ .
a) a apple
b) an apple
c) the apple
d) some apples

39. "Did you go to the party?"
"Yes, I _____ there."
a) go
b) do
c) was
d) did

40. The people in my country ____ German.
a) speak
b) speaks
c) speaking
d) is speaking

41. "Who _____ at the party?"
"All of your friends were there."
a) do
b) was
c) did
d) were

42. "John is late."
"That's strange. He _____ on time."
a) ever comes
b) comes ever
c) usually is
d) is usually

43. "Does Dan have a car?"
"Yes, he _____ ."
a) has
b) had
c) did
d) does

44. "Do you need your coat?"
"Yes, I _____ cold now."
a) have
b) has
c) am
d) was

45. "Where is Martha?"
"She _____ lunch at this time."
a) always eats
b) eats always
c) always is
d) is always

46. "Did Mike do the homework?"
"Yes, he _____ all of the lesson."
a) do
b) does
c) read
d) reads

47. "Are any of the questions difficult?"
" _____ are difficult.
Some of them are very easy."
a) No
b) Any
c) Not many
d) Not much

48. "It's hot in here."
"Would you please _____ that window."
a) open
b) opened
c) opening
d) to opening

49. She studies _____ .
a) at home English
b) history never
c) carefully grammar
d) in class every day

50. "Would you like an apple?"
"Yes, I'd like _____ ."
a) it
b) an
c) one
d) few

Lesson 11

A. Modal auxiliaries: *will, can*, etc.

B. Statements connected with *and . . . too, and . . . either*, and *but*

Vocabulary List

able	grow	ought	should
about	hall	pass	sidewalk
but	have to	permission	sign
can	immediately	permit	someone
conclude	matches	possible	therefore
conclusion	may	probable	too
could	might	recently	will
either	must		

Exercise 1 (A.1, pp. 109–11)

Complete this exercise by writing the modal and the verb. Use *I, you, he, she, we*, and *they*.
Follow the examples.

will + go

1. I will go
2. you will go
3. he will go
4. she will go
5. we will go
6. they will go

can + play

7. _____
8. _____
9. _____
10. _____
11. _____
12. _____

should + study

13. _____
14. _____
15. _____
16. _____
17. _____
18. _____

must + be

19. _____
20. _____
21. _____
22. _____
23. _____
24. _____

154

might + have   *may + use*

25. ───────────────────── 31. ─────────────────

26. ───────────────────── 32. ─────────────────

27. ───────────────────── 33. ─────────────────

28. ───────────────────── 34. ─────────────────

29. ───────────────────── 35. ─────────────────

30. ───────────────────── 36. ─────────────────

Exercise 2   (A.1, pp. 109–11)
Underline the correct modal.

She is going to call John tomorrow.
She (might, <u>will</u>) call John tomorrow.

1. Mr. Miller has to get a new car soon.
   Mr. Miller (should, must) get a new car soon.
2. It is possible that the students will need some pencils.
   The students (will, might) need some pencils.
3. Mark ought to sleep more at night.
   Mark (should, can) sleep more at night.
4. He is able to speak four languages.
   He (can, could) speak four languages.
5. They are going to eat lunch in a nice restaurant.
   They (must, will) eat lunch in a nice restaurant.
6. It is very probable that Mr. Prince is calling his wife.
   Mr. Prince (must, might) be calling his wife.
7. We have permission to spend the money.
   We (might, may) spend the money.
8. I was able to watch television every day last month.
   I (could, should) watch television every day last month.
9. Mr. Johnson ought to buy a present for his wife.
   Mr. Johnson (may, should) buy a present for his wife.
10. It is possible that it will rain next week.
    It (will, might) rain next week.

Exercise 3 (A.1, pp. 109–11)
Write the correct modal on the line.

John ought to study vocabulary tonight.

John ___**should**___ study vocabulary tonight.

1. Paul is able to play tennis very well.

   Paul _____ play tennis very well.

2. They are going to arrive tomorrow morning.

   They _____ arrive tomorrow morning.

3. John and I have to do our homework every day.

   John and I _____ do our homework every day.

4. It is possible that Mr. Brown will be late.

   Mr. Brown _____ be late.

5. I conclude that you are sick.

   You _____ be sick.

6. Do I have permission to smoke here?

   _____ I smoke here?

7. I conclude that his sister is about twenty-five years old.

   His sister _____ be about twenty-five years old.

8. You have an obligation to call your mother.

   You _____ call your mother.

9. It is possible that Mary will send us a long letter.

   Mary _____ send us a long letter.

10. It is going to snow tonight and tomorrow.

    It _____ snow tonight and tomorrow.

11. Everyone has to know how to read and write.

    Everyone _____ know how to read and write.

12. My little sister is able to cook well.

    My little sister _____ cook well.

13. Last year I was able to swim very well.

    Last year I _____ swim very well.

14. I conclude that he has a lot of money.

    He _____ have a lot of money.

15. I conclude that it is raining.

    It _____ be raining.

Exercise 4   (A.1, pp. 109–11)
Write the correct modal and verb form on the line.

John ought to study grammar.

John __**should study**_____ grammar.

1. Tom and Joe are able to drive very well.

   Tom and Joe _____ very well.

2. He has to get up very early every morning.

   He _____ up very early every morning.

3. Miss Smith is able to type very fast.

   Miss Smith _____ very fast.

4. The boys were able to play baseball all of the time.

   The boys _____ baseball all of the time.

5. She has permission to use the telephone.

   She _____ the telephone.

6. It is possible that Bill will receive a letter today.

   Bill _____ a letter today.

7. The plane is going to arrive late.

   The plane _____ late.

8. I conclude that you are very intelligent.

   You ————————— very intelligent.

9. They have to take a test in the morning.

   They ————————— a test in the morning.

10. It is very probable that he has two cars.

    He ————————— two cars.

11. All of the students are able to speak and write English.

    All of the students ————————— English.

12. She is able to run one mile in six minutes.

    She ————————— one mile in six minutes.

13. Each student ought to have a good dictionary.

    Each student ————————— a good dictionary.

14. They're able to sing very well.

    They ————————— very well.

15. She's going to leave soon.

    She ————————— soon.

Exercise 5   (A.1, pp. 112–13)
Write the negative form of the modal or verb. Use contractions when possible.

   (can) They _____**can't**_____ go to class now.

   (have to) Jack **doesn't have to** do his work now.

1. (be able to) We ————————— speak Chinese.

2. (will) Mr. Smith ————————— call you later.

3. (could) They ————————— eat all of the food.

4. (can) The students ————————— understand the new lesson.

5. (might) Tom ————————— have the correct answers.

6. (must) You ————————— go outside now.

7. (be going to) He _____ read any more long books.

8. (may) You _____ use my car now.

9. (be able to) We _____ pay for all of our books.

10. (will) The girls _____ go to see a movie.

11. (have to) You _____ arrive early.

12. (have to) He _____ do the work right now.

13. (can) I _____ go out tonight.

14. (should) We _____ make many phone calls.

15. (should) You _____ eat a lot of candy.

Exercise 6   (A.3, pp. 113–15)
Make a yes/no question from the statement. Then give a short answer.

Jack can play tennis. (yes)

_Can Jack play tennis ?_____

_Yes, he can.____

1. Paul will arrive in a few minutes. (yes)

   _____

   _____

2. Mark should study grammar now. (yes)

   _____

   _____

3. They might be at home now. (no)

   _____

   _____

4. He could get up late every day. (no)

   _____

   _____

5. I may smoke in this room. (no)

_____

_____

6. Your mother can cook very well. (yes)

_____

_____

7. Every student must do his homework. (yes)

_____

_____

8. We may help you. (yes)

_____

_____

9. You can speak Spanish. (no)

_____

_____

10. You should go to bed early. (yes)

_____

_____

Exercise 7 (A.3, pp. 113–15)
Write questions with the question words.

She can speak French.

(who) __Who can speak French?__

(what) __What can she speak?__

1. They could play tennis every day.

   (who) _____

   (what) _____

   (when) _____

2. We must study vocabulary tonight.

   (what) _____

   (when) _____

3. She should be here around nine o'clock.

   (who) _____

   (where) _____

   (when) _____

4. Henry will see Mary tonight.

   (who) _____

   (whom) _____

   (when) _____

5. That man might have five chairs for sale.

   (which) _____

   (how many) _____

Lesson 11

Exercise 8 (A.3, pp. 113–15)
Write questions by substituting wh-words for the italicized words.

John can speak *English* very well.
_a   _b

a)   Who can speak English very well ?

b)   What can John speak very well ?

1. *He* should listen to *the radio* more often.
   _a   _b

   a) _____

   b) _____

2. *The girls* might arrive *tonight*.
   _a   _b

   a) _____

   b) _____

3. Mr. and Mrs. Jones must be *here tomorrow morning*.
                              _a   _b

   a) _____

   b) _____

4. *Children* shouldn't play with *matches*.
   _a   _b

   a) _____

   b) _____

5. *You* will talk to *the doctor* at *the hospital*.
   _a   _b   _c

   a) _____

   b) _____

   c) _____

Exercise 9: Review of question forms, verbs/modals
Write questions with the question words.

He studies history.

(what) ___ **What does he study ?** ___

1. Martha speaks English.

   (who) ___

   (what) ___

2. They arrived at noon.

   (who) ___

   (when) ___

3. She saw Joe at school.

   (whom) ___

   (where) ___

4. They can play tennis very well.

   (who) ___

   (what) ___

5. Bob has a new car.

   (who) ___

   (what) ___

Exercise 10: Review of Question Forms, Verbs/Modals
Write questions with the question words.

He studies history.

(what) ___ **What does he study.** ___

1. Paul had a history test yesterday.

   (who) ___

   (which) ___

2. They will drive four hundred miles tonight.

(who) _____

(how many) _____

3. Everyone should send a card to the sick boy.

(what) _____

(whom) _____

4. This new shirt cost him twenty dollars.

(what) _____

(how much) _____

5. The students will take a history test tomorrow.

(who) _____

(what) _____

Exercise 11 (B.1, pp. 116–17)
Read the two sentences and then complete the third sentence.

John can speak English. Mark can speak English.

John can speak English, *and Mark can too* .

1. Paul is a good student. Suzy is a good student.

Paul is a good student, _____ .

2. We will go to France in June. They will go to France in June.

We will go to France in June, _____ .

3. I like hamburgers very much. She likes hamburgers very much.

I like hamburgers very much, _____ .

4. Paul reads two books every month. Mr. Todd reads two books every month.

Paul reads two books every month, _____ .

5. They are going to buy a new car. She is going to buy a new car.

They are going to buy a new car, _____ .

6. We wrote a letter to our parents. They wrote a letter to their parents.

   We wrote a letter to our parents, _____ .

7. She might have a dime. He might have a dime.

   She might have a dime, _____ .

8. I have to learn English. Mike has to learn English.

   I have to learn English, _____ .

9. You should be happy now. He should be happy now.

   You should be happy now, _____ .

10. They were hungry. I was hungry.

    They were hungry, _____ .

Exercise 12   (B.2, pp. 117–18)
Read the two sentences and then complete the third sentence.

   John can't speak English. Mark can't speak English.

   John can't speak English, **and Mark can't either** .

1. Paul won't go with us to Mexico. John won't go with us to Mexico.

   Paul won't go with us to Mexico, _____ .

2. The grammar book isn't new. The reading book isn't new.

   The grammar book isn't new, _____ .

3. She didn't understand the lesson. I didn't understand the lesson.

   She didn't understand the lesson, _____ .

4. We couldn't arrive on time. Peter couldn't arrive on time.

   We couldn't arrive on time, _____ .

5. Alice might not be hungry. Jane might not be hungry.

   Alice might not be hungry, _____ .

6. You weren't here last night. He wasn't here last night.

   You weren't here last night, _____ .

7. They don't have a car. We don't have a car.

   They don't have a car, ————————————— .

8. She didn't need any help. He didn't need any help.

   She didn't need any help, ————————————— .

9. Mr. Smith isn't going to Italy. Mr. Jones isn't going to Italy.

   Mr. Smith isn't going to Italy, ————————————— .

10. They aren't hungry now. I'm not hungry now.

    They aren't hungry now, ————————————— .

Exercise 13 (B.3, pp. 119–20)
Read the two sentences, and then complete the third sentence.

   Paul is a good student. Joe isn't a good student.

   Paul is a good student, _**but Joe isn't**_ .

1. I don't work on Saturday. My sister works on Saturday.

   I don't work on Saturday, ————————————— .

2. They are from Europe. She isn't from Europe.

   They are from Europe, ————————————— .

3. Paul won't call you. Jane will call you.

   Paul won't call you, ————————————— .

4. Mr. Doe has two daughters. Mr. Art doesn't have two daughters.

   Mr. Doe has two daughters, ————————————— .

5. You can't eat a lot of candy. Your brother can eat a lot of candy.

   You can't eat a lot of candy, ————————————— .

6. That lady wasn't hungry at lunch. Her husband was hungry at lunch.

   That lady wasn't hungry at lunch, ————————————— .

7. We couldn't understand the teacher. She could understand the teacher.

   We couldn't understand the teacher, ————————————— .

8. My brother didn't know my telephone number. My sister knew my telephone number.

   My brother didn't know my telephone number, —————————— —————————— .

9. They'll arrive tomorrow night. Their friends won't arrive tomorrow night.

   They'll arrive tomorrow night, —————————————————— .

10. She always studies. I never study.

    She always studies, ———————————————— .

Exercise 14   (B.1–3, pp. 116–20)
Read the two sentences and then complete the third sentence. Use *and . . . too, and . . . either*, or *but*.

   John can skate well. Mary can skate well.

   John can skate well, _and Mary can too_ .

   I have a car. She doesn't have a car.

   I have a car, **but she doesn't** .

   He doesn't read fast. I don't read fast.

   He doesn't read fast, **and I don't either** .

1. We like fish. They don't like fish.

   We like fish, ———————————————— .

2. They should have a dictionary. We should have a dictionary.

   They should have a dictionary, —————————————————— .

3. I couldn't go with them. He couldn't go with them.

   I couldn't go with them, ————————————————— .

4. Peter saw that movie. She saw that movie.

   Peter saw that movie, ———————————————— .

5. We weren't hungry. John and Mary weren't hungry.

   We weren't hungry, ———————————————— .

Lesson 11

6. She won't go to class today. Her brother will go to class today.

   She won't go to class today, ———————————————————— .

7. I'm writing a letter to my aunt. My sister is writing a letter to my aunt.

   I'm writing a letter to my aunt, ———————————————————— .

8. He is a good student. I am not a good student.

   He is a good student, ———————————————————— .

9. He speaks French well. She speaks French well.

   He speaks French well, ———————————————————— .

10. They have some new books. She has some new books.

    They have some new books, ———————————————————— .

Exercise 15   (B.1–3, pp. 116–20)
Read the sentence and then complete it by adding the missing words.

   I want a new book, and she ___does too___ .

   They weren't sick, but we ___were___ .

   She doesn't understand, and I ___don't either___ .

1. You might win, but she ———————————————————— .

2. We don't need any pencils, and they ———————————————————— .

3. Paul speaks French well, and Mary and John ———————————————————— .

4. I'm hungry, and my brother ———————————————————— .

5. We won't go, but he ———————————————————— .

6. They were very happy, but the little girl ———————————————————— .

7. Sally wore a new dress, but Mary ———————————————————— .

8. Tim couldn't run fast, and Tom ———————————————————— .

9. He passed the test, but I ———————————————————— .

10. I don't like apples, and she ———————————————————— .

11. We'll go on vacation soon, and they ———————————————————— .

168

12. We'll go on vacation, but they _____ .

13. She couldn't attend class, but I _____ .

14. Mike didn't understand, and his friend _____ .

15. This man doesn't speak French, but that man _____ .

Exercise 16: Review Test
A. Write the correct modal which means the same as the expression.

1. _____ = ought to   6. _____ = be able to

2. _____ = be going to   7. _____ = probable

3. _____ = conclusion   8. _____ = have to

4. _____ = possibility   9. _____ = was able to

5. _____ = permission

B. Write a new sentence using a modal.

1. I was able to play football. _____

2. She is going to do the work. _____

3. It is possible that it will rain. _____

4. I conclude that she has two brothers. _____

C. Read the two sentences and then write a new sentence that means the same thing.

1. John isn't very hungry now. Mary isn't very hungry now.

_____

2. They will come by bus. My brother won't come by bus.

_____

3. They had to study yesterday. We had to study yesterday.

_____

Lesson 11

4. Sally speaks French. Paul speaks French.

_____

5. This man couldn't go with us. That man couldn't go with us.

_____

Exercise 17: Review Test
Choose the correct answer. Put a circle around the letter of the answer.

1. John won't go, but they _____ .
   a) were
   b) will
   c) won't
   d) weren't

2. " _____ must we do now?"
   "You must study very hard."
   a) When
   b) What
   c) Which
   d) Where

3. "What did the doctor tell you?"
   "He said that I _____ smoke again.
   It will kill me."
   a) mayn't
   b) must not
   c) might not
   d) don't have to

4. "Is it possible that she will be late to class?"
   "Yes, she _____ be late."
   a) can
   b) will
   c) must
   d) might

5. " _____ fly fast?"
   "Yes, they can."
   a) Do birds
   b) Does a bird
   c) Can birds
   d) Can a bird

6. Helen is an excellent student, and
   Mary _____ .
   a) too is
   b) is too
   c) either isn't
   d) isn't either

7. Juan is from Mexico. He _____
   speak Spanish.
   a) will
   b) must
   c) won't
   d) mustn't

8. "Everyone ought to have a good dictionary."
   "Yes, everyone _____ have one."
   a) must
   b) must to
   c) should
   d) should to

9. I didn't listen to the news, and she ____ .
   a) listened
   b) did too
   c) either didn't
   d) didn't either

10. Today I must study. Yesterday I _____
    study.
    a) had
    b) had to
    c) musted
    d) must to

Lesson 12

A. Verb + preposition + object: He called on them.
   Verb + particle + object: He called them up.

B. Adverbials of purpose: He went to buy some books.

C. Adverbials of means: He came by plane.
   Adverbials of instrument: He wrote with a pen.

Vocabulary List

ask for	how	nod	talk over
call on	hurry up	pick up	talk to
call up	improve	put away	think of
earn	leave out	put on	throw away
fill out	listen to	put out	turn off
find	look at	run out of	turn on
get along with	look for	shake	wait for
get up	look out for	sit down	wake up
give back	look over	stand up	why
hand in	look up	take off	write down
hand out			

Exercise 1 (A, pp. 121–24)
Include the pronoun in the verb expression.

it

pick _it_ up _____

him

talk _____ to _him_

it

1. ask _____ for _____

2. hand _____ in _____

3. put _____ on _____

4. take _____ off _____

5. listen _____ to _____

you

6. speak _____ to _____

7. wake _____ up _____

8. think _____ of _____

9. wait _____ for _____

10. call _____ on _____

us

11. talk _____ to _____

12. pick _____ up _____

13. wait _____ for _____

14. listen _____ to _____

15. look _____ for _____

them		*me*	
16. look _____ at _____		21. leave _____ out _____	
17. throw _____ away _____		22. think _____ of _____	
18. give _____ back _____		23. call _____ up _____	
19. hand _____ out _____		24. call _____ on _____	
20. look _____ for _____		25. pick _____ up _____	

Exercise 2   (A, pp. 121–24)
Write the verb expression again using a pronoun.

Look at the man. ____Look at him._____

Fill out the form. ____Fill it out._____

I'm writing down the name. I'm ___writing it down_____.

He'll put away the books. He'll ___put them away_____.

1. Look for the answers. _____

2. Think of that name. _____

3. Turn on the lights. _____

4. Look over the lesson. _____

5. Talk to your father. _____

6. Pick up the paper. _____

7. Put on your shoes. _____

8. Ask for Mr. Miller. _____

9. Wait for the bus. _____

10. Put out the fire. _____

11. She didn't listen to the radio. She didn't _____ .

12. I'll throw away the newspaper. I'll _____ .

13. The teacher handed out the tests. The teacher _____ .

14. We handed in our papers. We _____ .

15. I am looking for my pencil. I am _____ .

172

Exercise 3 (A, pp. 121–24)
Answer these questions with complete sentences. Use pronouns.

Did John look at the newspapers?

Yes, __he looked at them_____ .

Did they talk over the problem?

No, __they didn't talk it over_____ .

1. Did Mark look up the new words?

   Yes, _____ .

2. Does the teacher give back the papers?

   Yes, _____ .

3. Did you wake up the baby?

   No, _____ .

4. Will Mike look at the photos?

   No, _____ .

5. Can you think of his telephone number?

   No, _____ .

6. Did Sam turn off the lights?

   Yes, _____ .

7. Did John wait for his sister?

   Yes, _____ .

8. May they take off their coats?

   Yes, _____ .

9. Did Peter talk to his girlfriend?

   No, _____ .

10. Did Mary put up her hand?

    Yes, _____ .

Exercise 4   (B, pp. 125–26)

Questions with *why* often have three possible answers. Make questions with *why* and give three answers.

John came here to get his books.

_____Why did John come here_____ ?

_____In order to get his books_____ .

_____To get his books_____ .

_____For his books_____ .

1. Matt went to the store to buy some fruit.

_____ ?

_____ .

_____ .

_____ .

2. Peter left the room to look for a chair.

_____ ?

_____ .

_____ .

_____ .

3. He had to study a lot to pass the test.

_____ ?

_____ .

_____ .

_____ .

4. Patty will go home to get her homework.

_____ ?

_____ .

_____ .

_____ .

Exercise 5   (B, pp. 125–26)
Write *to* or *for* on the line in order to answer the question *why*.

He came __to__ meet my family.

He went there __for__ some apples.

1. She called me _____ ask for money.

2. We went there _____ eat lunch.

3. I was studying _____ a test.

4. He came _____ help the students.

5. He's coming here _____ dinner.

6. They came _____ get their radio.

7. Please write her _____ the information.

8. He studied _____ pass the test.

9. He came _____ his books.

10. I need a spoon _____ eat my soup.

11. Use the dictionary _____ the difficult words.

12. He studied _____ learn the new words.

13. I got up early _____ do my homework.

14. She went to the store _____ buy some milk.

15. Let's go there _____ see a movie.

16. She's eating salad _____ lunch today.

17. I have two good pencils _____ the test.

18. Did you call your parents _____ some money?

19. He left home _____ go to class.

20. He will go _____ a new tie.

Exercise 6 (C.1, pp. 126–27)
Write *by* or *with* on the line in order to answer the question *how*.

They arrived __by__ bus.

We opened the door __with__ a key.

1. She went to Mexico _____ ship.

2. They got there _____ car.

3. She answered _____ a smile.

4. The student wrote _____ a new pen.

5. We talked _____ telephone.

6. They paid for the present _____ a check.

7. We arrived _____ taxi last night.

8. They sent the news _____ radio.

9. Mr. Smith walks _____ a cane.

10. She speaks English _____ an accent.

11. The letter came _____ air mail.

12. She answered _____ a nod.

13. I ate the soup _____ a spoon.

14. He passed the test _____ an excellent grade.

15. They'll vote _____ machine in this election.

16. He arrived _____ car.

17. I'll open the door _____ my key.

18. We communicated _____ telephone.

19. He sent the letter _____ only one stamp.

20. He usually travels _____ sea.

Exercise 7 (C.1, pp. 126–27)

Write the correct adverb of manner on the line.

How does John speak? (clear)

He speaks __clearly__ .

1. How does Mark read? (slow)

   He reads _____ .

2. How does he play tennis? (good)

   He plays _____ .

3. How does Peter drive? (fast)

   He drives _____ .

4. How do they eat? (rapid)

   They eat _____ .

5. How does Sally sing? (beautiful)

   She sings _____ .

6. How did he study? (hard)

   He studied _____ .

7. How did she cook? (careful)

   She cooked _____ .

8. How did they arrive? (prompt)

   They arrived _____ .

9. How did he answer your question? (sincere)

   He answered it _____ .

10. How does he pronounce? (good)

    He pronounces _____ .

Exercise 8 (C.2, pp. 128–29)

Complete the sentences with the correct preposition and verb form in order to answer the question *how*.

How did John learn German? (practice)

He learned German ___by practicing___ every day.

1. How did they arrive on time? (run)

   They arrived on time _____ very quickly.

2. How did the boy get ten dollars? (work)

   He got the money _____ with his father.

3. How did she pay for her ticket? (write)

   She paid for it _____ a check.

4. How did you learn that song? (listen)

   I learned it _____ to the radio.

5. How does Paul get to school in the morning? (walk)

   He gets there _____ .

6. How did you study for the test? (read)

   I studied for it _____ the lesson many times.

7. How did she wake up early? (use)

   She woke up early _____ her alarm clock.

8. How did they make dinner? (follow)

   They made dinner _____ a recipe.

9. How does Ben make a salad? (mix)

   He makes a salad _____ lettuce and tomatoes together.

10. How do you learn new words? (repeat)

    I learn new words _____ them several times.

Exercise 9   (B–C, pp. 125–29)

Write *how* or *why* to complete the question.

" **Why** did he come here?"
"In order to learn English."

1. " _____ did he study?"
   "With his notes from class."

2. " _____ did he study?"
   "By looking over all the lessons."

3. " _____ did he study?"
   "To pass the test."

4. " _____ did you get to Brazil?"
   "By plane."

5. " _____ did she go there?"
   "For some stamps."

6. " _____ did Mary go there?"
   "By car."

7. " _____ did she take the pictures?"
   "With a camera."

8. " _____ can I learn English fast?"
   "By doing all your homework."

9. " _____ must she sleep now?"
   "To wake up early tomorrow morning."

10. " _____ did they come here?"
    "For some gasoline."

11. " _____ did you pass the test?"
    "By studying hard."

12. " _____ do you eat soup?"
    "With a spoon."

13. " _____ does he pronounce?"
    "Slowly and carefully."

14. " _____ will she go there?"
    "For some books."

15. " _____ can you travel to Europe?"
    "By air or by sea."

Exercise 10   (B–C, pp. 125–29)

Make a question from the statement and then give a short answer.

Paul went to the store to buy a pencil.

_Why did Paul go to the store_____ ?
_To buy a pencil_____ .

1. He answered with a smile.

   _____ ?

   _____ .

2. They called to ask a question.

_____ ?

_____ .

3. We learned French by practicing every day.

_____ ?

_____ .

4. She arrived by bus.

_____ ?

_____ .

5. Kay went to the bank for some money.

_____ ?

_____ .

6. She came to learn English.

_____ ?

_____ .

7. We called to get some information.

_____ ?

_____ .

8. He cut the apple with a knife.

_____ ?

_____ .

9. They are communicating by phone.

_____ ?

_____ .

10. They should go with a group.

_____ ?

_____ .

Exercise 11: Review Test
A. Underline the correct word.

1. Did you turn off the lights?
   Yes, I turned (off them, them off).
2. Did you look at the schedule?
   Yes, I looked (at it, it at).

3. Did the teacher return the books?
   Yes, he gave (back them, them back).
4. Did John write down the answer?
   Yes, he wrote (down it, it down).

B. Make a question with *how* or *why*. Then give a short answer.

1. She went to the store for some bread.

   _____ ?

   _____ .

2. They cooked the meat by frying it.

   _____ ?

   _____ .

3. He wrote a letter to get some information.

   _____ ?

   _____ .

4. She came home by bus.

   _____ ?

   _____ .

5. He prefers to write with a pencil.

   _____ ?

   _____ .

C. Write the correct preposition (*up, to, for, with, by, down*).

1. We went to Europe _____ ship.

2. They opened the door _____ a key.

3. She learned English _____ studying very hard.

4. She learned English _____ get a good job.

5. Mike went to the library _____ some books.

6. She answered _____ a nod.

7. They sent the letter _____ air mail.

8. He looked the word _____ in his dictionary.

9. I wrote the telephone number _____ .

10. She called me _____ last night.

Exercise 12: Review Test
Choose the correct answer. Put a circle around the letter of the answer.

1. "Why did the man call you?"
   " _____ ."
   a) By telephone
   b) With a coin
   c) To ask a question
   d) For know something

2. The teacher _____ the tests.
   a) handed in
   b) handed out
   c) took off
   d) wrote down

3. "How did she send you the money?"
   " _____ ."
   a) By calling
   b) By air mail
   c) For a new car
   d) To buy a new car

4. "Did you study the lesson?"
   "Yes, I _____ ."
   a) looked it at
   b) looked it over
   c) looked up it
   d) looked it for

5. "How did you eat the hot soup?"
   " _____ ."
   a) Fastly
   b) Good
   c) With a spoon
   d) By eating it

6. "Did you complete the form?"
   "Yes, I filled _____ ."
   a) it out
   b) out it
   c) them out
   d) out them

7. "How did you open the door?"
   " _____ ."
   a) By key
   b) By a key
   c) With key
   d) With a key

8. "Will she wait for her brother?"
   "Yes, she'll _____ ."
   a) wait for him
   b) wait him for
   c) wait for her
   d) wait her for

9. "Why did your mother go to the store?"

"She went _____ buy some bread."

a) for

b) by

c) to

d) with

10. "Who turned off the lights last night?"

"I turned _____ last night."

a) it off

b) off it

c) them off

d) off them

Lesson 13

A. Verb + *to* + verb: George wants to go.
   Verb + noun phrase + *to* + verb: George wants John to go.
   George told John to go.

B. *Be* + adjective + *to* + verb: This is easy to learn.

C. *Very, too, enough*

Vocabulary List

agree	feed	lend	reach
angry	fix	nap	safe
carry	force	order	spell
ceiling	help	persuade	sweet
dangerous	hope	plan	try
decide	intend	pleasant	urge
drive	invite	practical	very
enough	learn	promise	whole
expect			

Exercise 1   (A.1, pp. 130–32)

Complete the sentence with the words given. Be sure to use *to* when necessary and make the verb agree with the subject.

(plan go) They ___plan to go___ today.

(want call) Mike ___wants to call___ his friends.

(can speak) She ___can speak___ several languages.

1. (like swim) We _____ a lot in the summer.

2. (might be) She _____ a little late to class.

3. (hope be) James _____ able to take a vacation.

4. (try learn) He is _____ Spanish and German.

5. (will arrive) The airplane _____ in thirty minutes.

6. (intend work) The new man _____ very hard.

7. (might need) She _____ more money for the trip.

8. (plan go) They're _____ to Mexico next month.

184

9. (promise come) She _____ to class on time.

10. (may pick up) The students _____ their books here.

11. (could speak) I _____ Greek well a long time ago.

12. (need write) Susan _____ a letter to her mother.

13. (decide go) Last night we _____ to Miami.

14. (agree pay) He usually _____ for my lunch.

15. (expect arrive) We _____ around eight o'clock.

16. (will try learn) Our class _____ English.

17. (need try learn speak) He _____ English.

18. (should promise help) We _____ him immediately.

19. (must want go) She _____ in my car.

20. (need agree do) Those men _____ the work now.

Exercise 2 (A.2, pp. 132–33)
Read the two sentences, and then complete the third sentence.

John doesn't want to work. He needs to work.

John doesn't want to work, __**but he needs to**_____ .

1. Mr. Miller didn't want to go to Miami. He had to go to Miami.

   Mr. Miller didn't want to go to Miami, _____ .

2. They don't need to eat more. They plan to eat more.

   They don't need to eat more, _____ .

3. I might not go with her. I am hoping to go with her.

   I might not go with her, _____ .

4. They shouldn't be late. They might be late.

   They shouldn't be late, _____ .

5. Susan doesn't want to do the work. She has to do the work.

   Susan doesn't want to do the work, _____ .

6. We might not study tonight. We need to study tonight.

   We might not study tonight, _____ .

7. Our cat doesn't want to eat. It must eat.

   Our cat doesn't want to eat, _____ .

8. Paul called me up. He didn't intend to call me up.

   Paul called me up, _____ .

9. Mr. Smith can't play tennis now. He would like to play tennis now.

   Mr. Smith can't play tennis now, _____ .

10. He can't go now. He should go now.

    He can't go now, _____ .

11. I didn't get a letter. I hoped to get a letter.

    I didn't get a letter, _____ .

12. My mother didn't meet my teacher. She wanted to meet my teacher.

    My mother didn't meet my teacher, _____ .

13. Martha doesn't like to do her work. She has to do her work.

    Martha doesn't like to do her work, _____ .

14. He will arrive late. He shouldn't arrive late.

    He will arrive late, _____ .

15. Carl should try to study more. Carl doesn't want to study more.

    Carl should try to study more, _____ .

Exercise 3   (A.3, pp. 133–34)
Write a new sentence. Make the *first* verb negative.

   He promised to call her.   He didn't promise to call her.

   1. The boys want to eat now. _____

   2. John planned to study for the examination. _____

3. You are trying to learn English rapidly. _____

4. She prefers to drink water. _____

5. I need to eat more at night. _____

Exercise 4   (A.3, pp. 133–34)
Write a new sentence. Make the *second* verb negative.

He promised to call her. __He promised not to call her .__

1. She is trying to talk loudly. _____

2. We prefer to drink that beer. _____

3. I tried to sleep in class. _____

4. Tom and Sue agree to do the work. _____

5. Frank decided to go with me. _____

Exercise 5   (A.4, pp. 134–36)
Complete these sentences with the given words.

(Mary answer) We want __Mary to answer__ the question.

(John write) She wants __John to write__ a letter now.

1. (my brother fix) I would like _____ my car.

2. (Mr. Brown help) They expect _____ with the work.

3. (the students bring) The teacher told _____ their books.

4. (George go) Steve wants _____ to the store now.

5. (I use) My father permitted _____ the car.

6. (we clean) Mother wants _____ our rooms immediately.

7. (Mr. and Mrs. Jones come) I invited _____ to my party.

8. (I write) Judy asked _____ a letter for her.

9. (you look) I would like _____ over my test paper.

10. (the children do) He will tell _____ the dishes after dinner.

Exercise 6 (A.4, pp. 134–36)

Use the words in parentheses to answer these questions with complete sentences.

What did he want Mary to do? (call him)

He wanted Mary to call him.

1. What did the teacher tell Joe to do? (be quiet)

   _____

2. What did Mr. Max ask Mark to do? (mail the letters)

   _____

3. What did she want Paul to do? (go to the store)

   _____

4. What did they invite you to do? (play tennis)

   _____

5. What would George like you to do? (eat lunch with him)

   _____

6. What did Jack tell you to do? (call him up)

   _____

7. What does he expect you to do? (pick him up)

   _____

8. What do they need Bob to do? (carry the box)

   _____

9. What do you want me to do? (go to the bank)

   _____

10. What did Fran ask you to do? (erase the blackboard)

    _____

Exercise 7 (B, pp. 136–38)
Read the two sentences, and then complete the third sentence.

This car is fun. To drive this car is fun.

This car ___**is fun to drive**___ .

This number is easy for me. To remember this number is easy for me.

This number ___**is easy for me to remember**___ .

1. Books can be interesting. To read books can be interesting.

   Books _____ .

2. Dogs are beautiful. To watch dogs is beautiful.

   Dogs _____ .

3. This lesson is easy for me. To understand this lesson is easy for me.

   This lesson _____ .

4. English words are difficult. To pronounce English words is difficult.

   English words _____ .

5. These pants are very comfortable. To wear these pants is comfortable.

   These pants _____ .

6. This medicine is important for you. To take this medicine is important for you.

   This medicine _____ .

7. This song is very pretty. To listen to this song is very pretty.

   This song _____ .

8. This cake was easy. To make this cake was easy.

   This cake _____ .

9. These words are difficult. To spell these words is difficult.

   These words _____ .

10. The book will be easy for us. To read the book will be easy for us.

    The book _____ .

189

11. Cigarettes are bad for you. To smoke cigarettes is bad for you.

    Cigarettes _____ .

12. Hamburgers are not expensive. To eat hamburgers is not expensive.

    Hamburgers _____ .

13. That recipe is hard. To follow that recipe is hard.

    That recipe _____ .

14. This record is nice. To listen to this record is nice.

    This record _____ .

15. That movie is not interesting. To watch that movie is not interesting.

    That movie _____ .

Exercise 8   (C, pp. 139–41)
Complete these sentences with *too* or *enough*.

    Mary is short. She can't reach the ceiling.

    Mary is __too__ short to reach the ceiling.

    I am twenty-three years old. I can drive a car.

    I am old __enough__ to drive a car.

1. Mark is very intelligent. He will pass the test.

    Mark is intelligent _____ to pass the test.

2. John is very angry. He can't speak right now.

    John is _____ angry to speak right now.

3. I'm hungry. I can eat three hamburgers.

    I'm hungry _____ to eat three hamburgers.

4. We are tired. We can't study.

    We are _____ tired to study.

5. She is tall. She can reach the ceiling.

    She is tall _____ to reach the ceiling.

6. The shirt is big. I can't wear it.

   The shirt is _____ big for me to wear.

7. The shirt is small. I can wear it.

   The shirt is small _____ to wear.

8. That car is very expensive. She can't buy it.

   That car is _____ expensive for her to buy.

9. It's very hot. We can go swimming.

   It's hot _____ for us to go swimming.

10. This magazine is hard. I can't understand it.

    This magazine is _____ hard for me to understand.

11. Peter is fat. He can't wear those pants.

    Peter is _____ fat to wear those pants.

12. We were poor. We couldn't buy any books.

    We were _____ poor to buy any books.

13. You have one thousand dollars. You can buy dinner for me.

    You are rich _____ to buy dinner for me.

14. The dog is dangerous. We can't touch it.

    The dog is _____ dangerous to touch.

15. The store is full. We can't enter it.

    The store is _____ full to enter.

16. The food is very salty. We can't eat it.

    The food is _____ salty to eat.

17. Mr. Jones was well. He was able to work yesterday.

    Mr. Jones was well _____ to work yesterday.

18. The weather is cold. We can go skiing.

    The weather is cold _____ for us to go skiing.

19. This book is easy. We can finish it in a few days.

This book is easy _____ for us to finish in a few days.

20. This car is expensive. I can't buy it.

This car is _____ expensive for me to buy.

Exercise 9   (C, pp. 139–40)
Read the two sentences, and then write a new sentence with *too* or *enough*.

John is very tired. He can't play now.

_____ John is too tired to play now. _____

The book is easy. We can read it.

_____ The book is easy enough for us to read. _____

1. James is sick. He can't go on the trip.

_____

2. I'm tall. I can reach the ceiling.

_____

3. Peter is rich. He can buy a new car.

_____

4. It is warm. The children can go swimming.

_____

5. That man is strong. He can pick up this box.

_____

6. The car is cheap. She can buy it.

_____

7. This hat is very large. I can't wear it.

_____

8. You're very happy. You can forget all your problems.

_____

9. We were sick. We couldn't go to class.

_____

10. Those books are heavy. The boys can't carry the books.

_____

11. The window is low. He can reach it.

_____

12. Randy is very hungry. He can eat four sandwiches.

_____

13. James is short. He can't reach the faucet.

_____

14. The food is very hot. We can't eat it.

_____

15. The dog is very dirty. We can't keep it in the house.

_____

Exercise 10: Review Test
A. Write the word *to* where it is necessary.

1. We will _____ learn _____ speak English.

2. John doesn't _____ study, but he should _____ .

3. I want _____ Mary _____ open the window.

4. They promised _____ not _____ arrive early.

5. The doctor ordered _____ me _____ rest.

6. They might _____ arrive late.

7. I didn't _____ get a letter, but I would like _____ .

8. She is going _____ try _____ do the homework.

9. We would like _____ Rosemary _____ be here.

10. We didn't _____ get a letter, but we wanted _____ .

B. Read the two sentences and then write a new sentence that means the same thing.

1. John is young. He can't vote.

   _____

2. Books are interesting. To read books is interesting.

   _____

3. It is cold. We can't go swimming.

   _____

4. The table is heavy. You can't pick it up.

   _____

5. Long words are difficult. To pronounce long words is difficult.

   _____

6. That shirt is expensive. I can't buy it.

   _____

C. Write the correct form of *be* in the present tense (*am, is, are*).

1. Short stories _____ interesting to read.

2. To receive many letters _____ very nice.

3. That shirt _____ too expensive for me to buy.

4. To walk in parks _____ pleasant.

5. To read short stories _____ interesting.

Exercise 11: Review Test
Choose the correct answer. Put a circle around the letter of the answer.

1. "Can you vote?"
   "Yes, I'm _____ to vote."
   a) too old
   b) old too
   c) old enough
   d) enough old

2. They _____ read the lesson.
   a) will try
   b) try will
   c) will try to
   d) will to try

3. "Do you like parks?"
   "Yes, I do. Parks _____ ."
   a) is pleasant to walk
   b) is pleasant to walk in
   c) are pleasant to walk
   d) are pleasant to walk in

4. We would like _____ now.
   a) that she goes
   b) that her goes
   c) her to go
   d) she to go

5. The boys should _____ English.
   a) to learn speak
   b) learn to speak
   c) learn speak
   d) speak learn

6. "The weather is great. Let's go swimming."
   "Yes, it's _____ to go swimming."
   a) too hot for we
   b) too hot for us
   c) hot enough for we
   d) hot enough for us

7. "What do you think of the lessons in the book?"
   "These lessons _____ to understand."
   a) is easy
   b) are easy
   c) is very
   d) are very

8. "Does Joe speak English?"
   "Joe doesn't know English, but he _____ ."
   a) does
   b) does to
   c) wants
   d) wants to

9. "Are you going to buy that hat?"
   "No, I'm not. It's _____ for me."
   a) enough expensive
   b) expensive enough
   c) too expensive
   d) expensive too

10. "Did John go to class today?"
    "No, but he _____ to go tomorrow."
    a) does
    b) will
    c) wants
    d) likes

Lesson 14

A. Some uses of *it* in subject position: It's early. It's easy to understand this lesson.

B. The expletive *there*: There is a book on the table.

C. Possessive *of* and *-'s*: The legs of the table. The dog's legs.

D. Possessive pronouns: *mine, yours*, etc.

E. *Whose*

F. *One* and *ones*

Vocabulary List

assignment	floor	mine	snow
belong	freeze	ours	theirs
block	get	polite	there is
clear up	ground	season	there are
cloudy	hers	seem	unusual
cool off	humid	several	warm up
date	mail	simple	whose
early	marry	ski	yours
far			

Exercise 1   (A.1, pp. 142–44)
Answer the questions in complete sentences.

What time is it? (noon)

_____It's noon._____

What month is it? (June)

_____It's June._____

1. What time is it? (10:45)

   _____

2. What time was it fifteen minutes ago?

   _____

3. What is the date today? (March 6)

   _____

4. What was the date five days ago?

_____

5. How is the weather now? (rain)

_____

6. What day is it today? (Monday)

_____

7. What day will it be tomorrow?

_____

8. Who is at the door? (Mr. Prince)

_____

9. What month is it now? (August)

_____

10. Who was on the phone? (Mary)

_____

Exercise 2   (A.1, pp. 142–44)
Answer these questions in complete sentences.

How far is it from Los Angeles to San Francisco? (400 miles)

It is 400 miles from Los Angeles to San Francisco.

1. How far is it from New Orleans to Washington? (1,100 miles)

_____

2. How far is it from here to the store? (2 miles)

_____

3. How many hours is it from here to Miami? (7 hours)

_____

4. How far is it to the post office? (1 block)

_____

Lesson 14

5. How far is it from New York to Boston? (200 miles)

_____

Exercise 3   (A.3, pp. 146–47)
Write a sentence beginning with *it*.

   To drive a car is fun.   <u>It is fun to drive a car.</u>

1. To understand this lesson is easy. _____

2. To pronounce English sounds is difficult. _____

3. To wear these pants is comfortable. _____

4. To take this medicine is good for you. _____

5. To call long distance is expensive. _____

6. To make that cake was difficult. _____

7. To smoke cigarettes is bad for your health. _____

8. To read the book will be easy for us. _____

9. To play tennis must be fun. _____

10. To eat hamburgers is not expensive. _____

Exercise 4   (A.3, pp. 146–47; p. 136)
Write two other sentences that express the same idea.

   To understand this lesson is easy.

   <u>This lesson is easy to understand.</u>
   <u>It is easy to understand this lesson.</u>

1. To say "thank you" is polite.

_____

_____

2. To drive a motorcycle can be dangerous.

_____

_____

3. To spell these words is difficult.

_____

_____

4. To buy those shoes was very practical.

_____

_____

5. To live in big houses is very expensive.

_____

_____

Exercise 5   (B.1, pp. 148–50)
Write the correct form of *be*.

There __is__ a book on the table now.

There **was** a party last night.

1. There _____ a test tomorrow.

2. There _____ two basketball games last night.

3. There _____ several good students in my class this semester.

4. There _____ no money on the table last night.

5. There _____ some milk in the refrigerator now.

6. There _____ some people studying grammar now.

7. There _____ a good book on the shelf last week.

8. There _____ a meeting in New York next month.

9. There _____ many students absent yesterday.

10. There _____ a few people late to class every day.

Lesson 14

Exercise 6 (B.1, pp. 148–50)
Use the words to make a new sentence that begins with *there*.

(now / on the table / a book)

There is a book on the table now.

(a party / next week / here)

There will be a party here next week.

1. (an apple / in the refrigerator / now)

2. (yesterday / a test / in history class)

3. (now / many students / studying English)

4. (a few books / on the desk / a few minutes ago)

5. (on the table / a lot of bread / now)

Exercise 7 (C, pp. 151–52)
Circle the letter of the usual possessive form.

a) the man's car
b) the car of the man

1. *a)* the boy's watch
   b) the watch of the boy
2. *a)* the cat's tail
   b) the tail of the cat
3. *a)* the machine's work
   b) the work of the machine
4. *a)* Mary's car
   b) the car of Mary
5. *a)* today's homework
   b) the homework of today

a) the table's legs
b) the legs of the table

6. *a)* the girls' purses
   b) the purses of the girls
7. *a)* the book's cover
   b) the cover of the book
8. *a)* yesterday's news
   b) the news of yesterday
9. *a)* the boy's keys
   b) the keys of the boy
10. *a)* the table's top
    b) the top of the table

Exercise 8 (C, pp. 151–52)
Write the possessive expression.

the boy has a book   _the boy's books_

a vacation for a week   _a week's vacation_

1. John has a pencil   _____

2. the child has a toy   _____

3. the table has a top   _____

4. the box has a cover   _____

5. a car belongs to the man   _____

6. the lady owns a ring   _____

7. the ladies have rings   _____

8. the newspaper for today   _____

9. a tie belongs to Mr. Smith   _____

10. the men have cars   _____

11. the girl has a book   _____

12. the girls have books   _____

13. the children have toys   _____

14. the ladies have purses   _____

15. the pencil has a point   _____

16. Ned owns a house   _____

17. the car belongs to Tom   _____

18. the movie has an end   _____

19. the students have test papers   _____

20. the story has a beginning   _____

Lesson 14

Exercise 9 (C, pp. 151–52)
Write the correct possessive form on the line.

(the boy has a book) ___The boy's book___ is on the table.

(the boys have books) ___The boys' books___ are on the table.

1. (John owns a book) _____ was very interesting.

2. (the newspaper for today) _____ had a lot of bad news.

3. (the book has a cover) _____ is very dirty.

4. (a car belongs to Mike) _____ uses a lot of gasoline.

5. (the homework for yesterday) I was doing _____ .

6. (Jack wrote a story) We read _____ .

7. (Sue will have a party) _____ will be next week.

8. (the children have a cat) _____ eats a lot.

9. (the boys have a father) _____ came to speak in our class.

10. (the secretary does work) _____ is very good.

Exercise 10 (D, pp. 152–54)
Write the correct possessive pronoun.

my book = ___mine___

his money = ___his___

1. our car = _____

2. our cars = _____

3. her purse = _____

4. their pens = _____

5. your pencil = _____

6. his arm = _____

7. my books = _____

8. your pens = _____

9. her money = _____

10. its leg = _____

Exercise 11 (D, pp. 152–54)
Complete the sentence with the correct possessive pronoun.

I like my watch, and she likes __hers__ .

I have my book, and you have _yours_ .

1. She will buy her ticket, and I will buy _____ .

2. He called his aunt, and I called _____ .

3. You should have your homework, and he should have _____ .

4. We forgot our money, and she forgot _____ .

5. I did my work, and you did _____ .

6. Paul signed his name, and Ann and Bob signed _____ .

7. I lost all my money, and he lost all _____ .

8. I didn't eat my sandwich, and Bob didn't eat _____ .

9. They finished their report, and Carol and I are finishing _____ .

10. You'll clean your room, and I'll clean _____ .

Exercise 12 (D, pp. 153)
Read the two sentences, and then complete the third sentence with possessive forms.

John's car is new. Mary's car is new.

John's car is new, __and Mary's is too__ .

Her cat eats fish. His cat eats fish.

Her cat eats fish, __and his does too__ .

1. Your class begins at eight. My class begins at eight.

Your class begins at eight, _____ .

2. Their father is a doctor. Our father is a doctor.

Their father is a doctor, _____ .

3. My clothes are new. Her clothes are new.

My clothes are new, _____ .

203

4. Our teacher gave a test today. Their teacher gave a test today.

Our teacher gave a test today, ——————————— .

5. His watch was expensive. Her watch was expensive.

His watch was expensive, ——————————— .

6. Their teacher read the story. His teacher read the story.

Their teacher read the story, ——————————— .

7. Mike's family might attend. Paul's family might attend.

Mike's family might attend, ——————————— .

8. Their gift cost a lot. Our gift cost a lot.

Their gift cost a lot, ——————————— .

9. My car can go very fast. Your car can go very fast.

My car can go very fast, ——————————— .

10. His test was excellent. My test was excellent.

His test was excellent, ——————————— .

Exercise 13   (E, pp. 154–55)
Write a question with *whose*. Give a short answer.

Mary's cat likes fish.

Whose cat likes fish ?
Mary's does.

He saw Mary's cat.

Whose cat did he see ?
Mary's.

1. This is Steve's pencil.

——————————————

——————————

2. My car cost ten thousand dollars.

_____

_____

3. Matt's father owns this grocery store.

_____

_____

4. She would like to have my car.

_____

_____

5. John is using Steve's pencil.

_____

_____

6. We met Jack's father.

_____

_____

7. Her letter was on the table this morning.

_____

_____

8. They wanted to read Paul's letter.

_____

_____

9. The teacher corrected George's test first.

_____

_____

10. Mark's dog ran away.

_____

_____

Lesson 14

Exercise 14 (F, pp. 156–57)
Write the expression again. Change the noun to *one, ones*, or *a possessive pronoun* when possible. Do not repeat the noun.

a good book   _____a good one_____

a book   _____one_____

some red books   _____Some red ones_____

1. a red car   _____

2. two red cars   _____

3. two cars   _____

4. an apple   _____

5. a red apple   _____

6. a good red apple   _____

7. my book   _____

8. my green book   _____

9. his books   _____

10. his green books   _____

11. some pencils   _____

12. a new watch   _____

13. a few watches   _____

14. this old pen   _____

15. their house   _____

16. your old radio   _____

17. their money   _____

18. their books   _____

19. their green books   _____

20. many difficult tests   _____

21. many tests   _____

22. several good books ———————————————

23. these green books ———————————————

24. a cheap shirt ———————————————

25. an expensive shirt ———————————————

26. some pencils ———————————————

27. some yellow pencils ———————————————

28. a few pens ———————————————

29. a few red pens ———————————————

30. a nice present ———————————————

Exercise 15 (F, pp. 156–57)
Complete the sentence with a noun substitute. Use a *possessive pronoun* or *one/ones*. Do not repeat the noun.

I lost my book, but he has __**his**__ .

I don't like long stories. I prefer __**short ones**__ .

1. I don't like sour oranges. I prefer ——————————— .

2. We ate our food, but he didn't eat ——————————— .

3. "Do you want five green books?"

   "Yes, I would like five ——————————— ."

4. I don't need a lot of books. I only need a few good ——————————— .

5. I have my ticket, but he doesn't have ——————————— .

6. She hates big cars, but she likes ——————————— .

7. I don't like green apples. I prefer ——————————— .

8. Don't give me a large drink. I'd like ——————————— .

9. This test is bad, but ——————————— is very good.

10. I can't take an early flight. I'll have to take ——————————— .

Lesson 14

Exercise 16: Review Test
A. Answer the questions with complete sentences.

1. How is the weather now? (hot)

   _____

2. What month is it? (May)

   _____

3. Who is at the door? (Rick)

   _____

4. How far is it from New York to Miami? (1,300 miles)

   _____

B. Write a sentence beginning with *it*.

1. To write letters is easy. _____

2. To know English is good. _____

3. To play baseball can be fun. _____

C. Write the correct form of *be*.

1. There _____ a party tomorrow.

2. There _____ a test yesterday.

3. There _____ some cats eating fish now.

D. Write the possessive expression

1. Mr. Miller has a car _____

2. a vacation for a week _____

3. the table has a top _____

4. I ate my dinner, and he ate _____ .

5. She lost her book, and they lost _____ .

E. Write a question with *whose*.

1. John's father speaks English and Spanish. _____ _____ ?

2. We visited John's father yesterday. _____ ?

F. Write *yes* or *no* to tell if the expression is correct.

1. _____ this red one

2. _____ this one

3. _____ these red ones

4. _____ these ones

5. _____ some ones

6. _____ a few good ones

7. _____ mine green one

8. _____ mine green ones

9. _____ several ones

10. _____ those cheap ones

Exercise 17: Review Test
Choose the correct answer. Put a circle around the letter of the answer.

1. "Do you need any books?"
   "Yes, I would like _____ ones."
   a) a few
   b) many
   c) some good
   d) some those

2. " _____ car does he usually drive?"
   "Hers."
   a) Who
   b) Whom
   c) Whose
   d) Where

3. " _____ a party tonight. Do you want to go?"
   "Yes, I do. I'll be ready at eight o'clock."
   a) It
   b) There
   c) It's
   d) There's

4. Our cat likes fish, and _____ does too.

   a) of Mary

   b) of Mary's

   c) her

   d) hers

5. That boy has two books. They're _____ .

   a) books of the boy

   b) boy of the books

   c) the boy's books

   d) the boys' books

6. "How is the weather now?"

   " _____ snowing."

   a) Is

   b) It

   c) It's

   d) There's

7. _____ polite to say "thank you."

   a) Whose is

   b) There is

   c) It is

   d) There

8. We have _____ .

   a) the dog of Mary

   b) the store's address

   c) today's newspaper

   d) a vacation of a week

9. We want _____ ones.

   a) several

   b) a few

   c) green

   d) their

10. "Who was on the phone?"

    " _____ my sister."

    a) She was

    b) Who were

    c) It was

    d) He was

Lesson 15

Expressions of comparison

A. *the same as; different from; like; the same . . . as; as . . . as*

B. *more . . . than; -er than*

C. *the most; the . . . -est*

Vocabulary List

age	feather	lazy	soon
badly	fresh	length	speed
beet	gallon	like	strong
best	gray	long	thick
better	hardness	more	thickness
cheap	height	most	times
deep	high	quality	wide
depth	hill	same	width
distance	honey	shape	wink
farther	joke	size	worse

Exercise 1   (A.1, pp. 158–59)

Write *the same as, different from,* or *like*.

My book and your book are the same. There is no difference.

My book is ___the same as___ yours.

Mike's car is small and red. Scott's car is big and green.

Mike's car is ___different from___ Scott's.

This pencil is very similar to that one.

This pencil is ___like___ that one.

1. Peter looks similar to his grandfather.

   Peter looks _____ his grandfather.

2. Paul's notebook is old and blue. My notebook is new and yellow.

   Paul's notebook is _____ mine.

3. This book is big and heavy. That one is too. There is no difference.

   This book is _____ that one.

211

4. Pamela eats a lot, and a horse does too.

   Pamela eats _____ a horse.

5. Two times three is six, and three times two is too.

   Two times three is _____ three times two.

6. My coat is almost the same as my sister's coat.

   My coat is _____ my sister's.

7. Alina's address is 225 Church Street. Martha lives there too.

   Alina's address is _____ Martha's.

8. This book cost two dollars, and yours did too.

   The price of this book is _____ the price of yours.

9. My car is similar to your car.

   My car is _____ yours.

10. George has a small yellow car. Sue has a new red car.

    His car is _____ hers.

Exercise 2   (A.1, pp. 158–59)
Write a new sentence using *the same as, different from*, or *like*.

   My test grade was 85, and yours was too.

   My test grade was the same as yours.

1. Your watch is very similar to my watch.

   _____

2. My shirt is blue and size 15, and yours is too. There is no difference.

   _____

3. This house is very small, but that one is very large.

   _____

4. My sister is young and pretty. Your sister is young and pretty. They look very similar.

   _____

5. My uncle's address is 887 Palm Street, and my aunt lives there too.

_____

6. Mary's purse is brown. Jane's purse is green.

_____

7. Your age is twenty. My age is twenty.

_____

8. She has a small dog. I have a small dog. They are very similar.

_____

9. Your passport is Venezuelan. Her passport is French.

_____

10. This restaurant is small and inexpensive. That restaurant is large and expensive.

_____

Exercise 3 (A.2, pp. 159–63)
Write the correct noun for the adjective.

    big / small ___**size**___

    old / young ___**age**___

1. expensive / cheap _____

2. thick / thin _____

3. fast / slow _____

4. wide / narrow _____

5. far / close _____

6. deep / shallow _____

7. high / low _____

8. tall / short _____

9. hard / soft _____

10. long / short _____

Exercise 4 (A.2, pp. 159–63)
Underline the correct word in each sentence.

This street is as (<u>narrow</u>, width) as that one.
This man is the same (tall, <u>height</u>) as that one.

1. This shirt is the same (expensive, price) as that one.
2. My brother is as (old, age) as your brother.
3. This steak is as (thick, thickness) as that steak.
4. Peter's car is as (fast, speed) as my car.
5. This table is the same (big, size) as the one in my room.
6. Your pencil is the same (long, length) as mine.
7. This box is as (heavy, weight) as that box.
8. Our swimming pool is the same (deep, depth) as theirs.
9. My problem is as (hard, hardness) as yours.
10. John is the same (tall, height) as Mary.
11. I'm the same (old, age) as Martha.
12. What is the (deep, depth) of the pool?
13. This pool is very (deep, depth).
14. This street is not very (wide, width).
15. This pencil is the same (long, length) as that one.

Exercise 5 (A.2, pp. 160–61)
Write *many* or *much* with these expressions of quantity.

John drank four glasses of milk, and I did too.

John drank as __many__ glasses of milk as Tim.

John drank as __much__ milk as Tim.

1. Susan would like two cups of coffee, and Mary would too.

   Susan would like as _____ cups of coffee as Mary.

   Susan would like as _____ coffee as Mary.

2. They bought six shirts, and we did too.

   They bought as _____ shirts as we did.

3. My sister made two cakes, and my mother did too.

   My sister made as _____ cakes as my mother.

4. My car used seven gallons of gasoline, and yours did too.

   My car used as _____ gasoline as yours.

   My car used as _____ gallons of gasoline as yours.

5. Peter always drinks three glasses of tea at lunch, and Mike does too.

   Peter always drinks as _____ tea as Mike.

   Peter always drinks as _____ glasses of tea as Mike.

6. Mary ate two slices of cake, and Paul did too.

   Mary ate as _____ slices as Paul.

   Mary ate as _____ cake as Paul.

7. I used one cup of flour, and Anne did too.

   I used as _____ flour as Anne.

   I used as _____ cups of flour as Anne.

8. He missed four questions, and she did too.

   He missed as _____ questions as she did.

9. He wrote three pages, and I did too.

   He wrote as _____ as I did.

   He wrote as _____ pages as I did.

10. Jack lost five pounds, and George did too.

   Jack lost as _____ pounds as George.

   Jack lost as _____ as George.

Exercise 6 (A.2, pp. 161–63)
Write a new sentence with *as . . . as*.

John drives very carefully, but Jill doesn't.

_____Jill doesn't drive as carefully as John._____

Mike speaks slowly, and Linda does too.

_____Mike speaks as slowly as Linda._____

1. Paul swims very well, but Joe doesn't.

   _____

2. John can run very fast, but Peter can't.

   _____

3. Mr. Smith works very hard, and his wife does too.

   _____

4. Mary cooks well, but George doesn't.

   _____

5. Ann swims very quickly, and Jan does too.

   _____

Exercise 7 (A.1–2, pp. 158–63)
Write new sentences using *the same . . . as* and *as . . . as*.

That car is expensive, and this one is too.

That car is the same price as this one.
That car is as expensive as this one.

John is twenty years old, and Mary is too.

John is the same age as Mary.
John is as old as Mary.

1. Bill is five feet tall. Joe is five feet tall.

_____

_____

2. I ate two sandwiches. Joe ate two sandwiches.

_____

_____

3. Joe is seventeen years old. Peter is fifteen years old.

_____

_____

4. Mark drank three glasses of milk. Nancy drank three glasses of milk.

_____

_____

5. This steak is an inch thick. That steak is an inch thick.

_____

_____

Exercise 8   (B, pp. 164–66)
Put a check mark in the parentheses (✓) by the correct comparative form.

(✓) more careful

( ) oftener

(✓) quicker

1. ( ) taller
2. ( ) more important
3. ( ) earlier
4. ( ) clearlier
5. ( ) more rapidly

6. ( ) better
7. ( ) more nice
8. ( ) necessarier
9. ( ) badder
10. ( ) sooner

Exercise 9   (B, pp. 164–66)
Write the correct comparative adjective form.

Gary is rich. Joe is very rich.

Joe is ___richer___ than Gary.

1. Jill is five feet tall. Martha is six feet tall.

   Martha is _____ than Jill.

2. This book is expensive. That book is cheap.

   This book is _____ than that one.

3. Greg's score was good. Paul's score was very good.

   Paul's score was _____ than Greg's.

4. Ken drives carefully. Matt drives very carefully.

   Matt drives _____ than Ken.

5. George is twenty-one years old. Steve is nineteen years old.

   George is _____ than Steve.

6. Our cat is bad. Their cat is very bad.

   Their cat is _____ than ours.

7. Mike is intelligent. His sister is very intelligent.

   Mike's sister is _____ than he is.

8. The length of this table is four feet. The length of that table is eight feet.

   That table is _____ than this table.

9. Judy's coffee is delicious. Martha's coffee is very delicious.

   Martha's coffee is _____ than Judy's.

10. This box is heavy. That box is light.

   This box is _____ than that box.

Exercise 10   (A–B, pp. 158–66)
Write *as . . . as*, *more . . . than*, or *-er . . . than* for the correct comparative form.

   Mary is the same height as Paul.

   Mary is __as tall as__ Paul.

   Joe is nice, but Peter isn't.

   Joe is __nicer than__ Peter.

1. John drives very quickly, but Ann doesn't.

   John drives _____ Ann.

2. Mr. Smith is happy. Mrs. Smith is very happy.

   Mrs. Smith is _____ Mr. Smith.

3. Mike is the same age as Gary.

   Mike is _____ Gary.

4. The grammar test was very difficult, but the reading test wasn't.

   The grammar test was _____ the reading test.

5. This ice cream is very good, and that ice cream is too.

   This ice cream is _____ that ice cream.

Lesson 15

Exercise 11 (C, pp. 166–68)
Put a check mark in the parentheses (✓) by the correct superlative form.

(   ) the most happy
(✓) the most careful
(✓) the quickest

1. (   ) the most necessary
2. (   ) the goodest
3. (   ) the worst
4. (   ) the laziest
5. (   ) the most expensive

6. (   ) the most busy
7. (   ) the easiliest
8. (   ) the fastest
9. (   ) the saddest
10. (   ) the most rapidly

Exercise 12 (B–C, pp. 164–68)
Write the correct adjective or adverb forms. Follow the examples.

He is ___ .	I am _____ .	She is _____ .
1. tall	_taller_	_the tallest_
2. careful		
3. good		
4. nice		
5. intelligent		

He runs ___ .	I run _____ .	She runs _____ .
6. fast		
7. slowly		
8. rapidly		
9. badly		
10. quickly		

Exercise 13 (B–C, pp. 164–68)
Write the correct form of the word on the line.

(old) John is ___older___ than Pete, but Mary is **the oldest** .

(quickly) She drives very ___quickly___ .

1. (tall) Mary is _____ than Paul.

2. (good) She is _____ student in the class.

3. (happy) She is usually _____ than Joe, but Jack is always _____ .

4. (interesting) The book on the table is _____ than the book on the student's desk.

5. (difficult) My grammar test was _____ than my reading test, but my writing test was _____ .

6. (pretty) Jane is _____ girl in her class.

7. (nice) Jane is very _____ , but her brother is _____ than she is.

8. (bad) My test was _____ in the class.

9. (easy) The reading exam was very _____ .

10. (cold) It is too _____ to go swimming today.

Exercise 14 (C, pp. 167–68)
Write *more* or *the most* with the nouns.

Mary has **more** pencils than Joe.

Jack has **the most** books in the class.

1. Paul usually has _____ money than his brother.

2. Joe ate _____ hamburgers than I did.

3. Susan has _____ watches than Mary does.

4. Mary spent _____ money of all the students.

5. This room has _____ space than the living room, but my bedroom has _____ space.

Lesson 15

6. We will need _____ time for the test than your class did, but my sister's class will

   need _____ .

7. John is friendlier than Peter. John has _____ friends than Peter does.

8. Who has _____ cars—Mr. Jones or Mr. Green?

9. Which student in your class had _____ mistakes on the test?

10. Which player on your team made _____ points last night?

Exercise 15: Review Test
A. Write the correct noun.

1. as tall as   = the same _____ as

2. as old as   = the same _____ as

3. as big as   = the same _____ as

4. as thick as = the same _____ as

5. as long as = the same _____ as

B. Write the forms of these adjectives and adverbs.

	comparative	superlative
1. careful	_____	_____
2. tall	_____	_____
3. good	_____	_____
4. fast	_____	_____
5. quickly	_____	_____
6. busy	_____	_____

C. Underline the correct answer.

1. John is the same (heavy, weight) as Paul.
2. We are as (height, tall) as they are.
3. His test was the (better, best) in our class.
4. He is the (worst, worse) worker here.
5. I have two sisters. Mary is the (taller, tallest) person in our family.

Exercise 16: Review Test
Choose the correct answer. Put a circle around the letter of the answer.

1. "How tall is John?"
   "He's _____ as Mike."
   a) as large
   b) as high
   c) the same height
   d) the same tall

2. Mary is _____ student in the class.
   a) better
   b) very good
   c) the best
   d) the better

3. Peter is more _____ than Paul is.
   a) hungry
   b) careful
   c) better
   d) tall

4. My shirt is _____ as yours.
   a) as price
   b) as big
   c) the same soft
   d) the same small

5. She is _____ than her sister.
   a) taller
   b) gooder
   c) more tall
   d) more good

6. "Did Bill buy the same number of books as Sue did?"
   "Yes, Bill bought _____ as Sue did."
   a) as books
   b) as many
   c) the same books
   d) the same many

7. Their car is small and inexpensive. Our car is large and expensive. Their car is ____ our car.
   a) as size as
   b) as same as
   c) different from
   d) different than

8. "None of the boys wants to work."
   "Yes, but Paul and John are ____ ."
   a) more lazy
   b) same lazy
   c) the most lazy
   d) the laziest

9. John is six feet tall, but Mary is only five feet tall. John is _____ Mary.
   a) tallest as
   b) taller than
   c) as tall as
   d) different tall than

10. John reads quickly, and Mary does too. John reads _____ Mary.
    a) as quickly as
    b) quicklier than
    c) the same quick as
    d) more quickly than

Lesson 16

A. Embedded statements: I know that he lives here.

B. Embedded wh-clauses: I know who lives here.

Vocabulary List

admit	discover	hope	remind
assume	doubt	imagine	reply
assure	dream	notice	suppose
believe	feel	point out	surround
convince	find out	realize	warn
degree	guess	regret	wonder

Exercise 1 (A, pp. 169–70)

Write a complete sentence to answer the questions. Put parentheses ( ) around the word *that* to show that this word is optional.

Which do you think is bigger—New York or Miami?

    I think (that) New York is bigger.

Which do you believe is colder—Florida or Alaska?

    I think (that) Alaska is colder.

1. Which do you think is more expensive—a pencil or a book?

   _____

2. Which did you learn was correct—more tall or taller?

   _____

3. Which do you know is correct—2 + 2 = 4 or 2 + 2 = 5?

   _____

4. Which do you think is heavier—a car or a wallet?

   _____

5. Which do you think is the biggest state in the United States—Alaska, California, or Texas?

   _____

6. Which do you think is more difficult to pronounce—kitchen or chicken?

   _____

7. Which do you think is faster—a cat or a turtle?

   _____

8. Which do you think is more expensive—a plane ticket or a bus ticket?

   _____

9. Which do you think is better for a picnic—steak or fried chicken?

   _____

10. Which do you think is easier to cook—scrambled eggs or toast?

   _____

Exercise 2   (B, pp. 172–74)
Make a question from the statement.

Paul remembers who wanted to buy his car.

   Does Paul remember who wanted to buy his car?

John told us where he was from.

   Did John tell us where he was from?

1. Beth knows who answered the phone.

   _____

2. Ron knows whom John called.

   _____

3. He can explain why his tests were bad.

   _____

4. George knew when the party was.

   _____

5. She asked who was coming to the party.

   _____

6. The teacher would like to know what time it is.

_____

7. Pedro explained where his country is.

_____

8. Rob will tell us whose books he has.

_____

9. The teacher will tell us which answer is correct.

_____

10. Bill told you where the party was.

_____

Exercise 3 (B, pp. 175–77)
Complete the answers to the questions.

When is our test?

I'm not sure _____ when our test is _____ .

What did he say?

I don't know _____ what he said _____ .

1. Why was Greg late?

We don't know _____ .

2. Which shirt does she prefer?

I'm not sure _____ .

3. Where is the new television?

I want to know _____ .

4. What is the boy's name?

She doesn't know _____ .

5. Whose keys did he find?

   He doesn't remember _____ .

6. Whom did they call?

   They didn't say _____ .

7. What time is it?

   We need to know _____ .

8. How far is the post office?

   Do you know _____ ?

9. Where did he go?

   Does his mother know _____ ?

10. What does this word mean?

    I'm not sure _____ .

11. Where is he from?

    No one knows _____ .

12. Who is that girl in the red dress?

    Do you know _____ ?

13. What did he lose?

   I don't know _____ .

14. What did Pete eat?

   Do you know _____ ?

15. When do we have a test?

   Do you know _____ ?

16. What is her phone number?

   I'm not sure _____ .

17. How many students passed the test?

   The teacher will tell us _____ .

18. How did he go to France?

   He didn't tell us _____ .

19. Why did he go to France?

   He didn't tell us _____ .

20. How much did he spend?

   He didn't tell us _____ .

Exercise 4 (B, pp. 172–77)
Complete the answers to these questions.

Was Mary at home or in class?

I'm not sure ___ where Mary was _____ .

Is that Paul or Peter?

I wonder ___ who that is _____ .

1. Do they speak English or French?

   I don't know _____ .

2. Is the post office five blocks or a mile from here?

   I wonder _____ .

3. Did Paul go to France by ship or by plane?

   We're not sure _____ .

4. Do you have grammar class at eight or at nine?

   I always forget _____ .

5. Can John or Joe drive a car?

   I'm not sure _____ .

6. Does the party begin now or later?

   Can you tell me _____ ?

7. Is this John's book or Peter's book?

   I need to know _____ .

8. Will the Smiths go to England or France?

   I'm not sure _____ .

9. Is the new boy's father a doctor or a teacher?

   No one knows _____ .

10. Does that new car cost nine or ten thousand dollars?

    I don't know _____ .

Exercise 5 (B, p. 178)
Complete the answers to these questions. Use *if* in your answers.

Is the dog under the bed?

I wonder ___if the dog is under the bed___ .

Does John speak Japanese?

We'll ask ___if John speaks Japanese___ .

1. Did she bake some bread?

   I wonder _____ .

2. Did George go to the doctor?

   Do you know _____ ?

3. Does he like ice cream?

   Do you know _____ ?

4. Are they going home now?

   Can you tell me _____ ?

5. Am I in the right room?

   I'm not sure _____ .

6. Are you in the right room?

   You aren't sure _____ .

7. Was their baby born in December?

   I don't remember _____ .

8. Did the new student buy his books?

   Paul doesn't know _____ .

9. Will they arrive soon?

   I wonder _____ .

10. Can we go to Florida?

    We would like to know _____ .

Lesson 16

Exercise 6 (B, pp. 172–78)
Put a check mark in the parentheses (✓) by the correct sentences. If the sentence is not correct, write it correctly.

(✓) Do you know when the party is?

_____

( ) I'm not sure what time is it.

I'm not sure what time it is .

( ) I wonder where do they live.

I wonder where they live .

1. ( ) Do you remember what his name is?

_____

2. ( ) We'll ask where are they going.

_____

3. ( ) Can you tell me if John's home now?

_____

4. ( ) Where do they have class in the morning?

_____

5. ( ) We'd like to know where our money is.

_____

6. ( ) You must ask how much does a ticket cost.

_____

7. ( ) He didn't say why wasn't he there.

_____

8. ( ) Do you know how he got there?

_____

9. ( ) I'll ask whether he has enough money.

_____

10. ( ) Do you know what time is it?

_____

Exercise 7: Review Test

A. Write a complete answer to these questions.

1. Which do you think is heavier—a car or a bicycle?

   _____

2. Which do you believe is more expensive—a pen or a diamond?

   _____

3. Which do you think is sweeter—a tomato or chocolate?

   _____

4. Which do you suppose is stronger—a man or a cat?

   _____

B. Complete the answers to these questions.

1. When did Joe call?

   I don't remember _____ .

2. How far is New York?

   I don't know _____ .

3. Is John coming by plane or by bus?

   I'm not sure _____ .

4. Were they here yesterday or last week?

   Do you recall _____ ?

5. Who is that lady?

   I'm not sure _____ .

6. Do they understand English?

   I don't know _____ .

7. Did Joe call last night?

   Do you know _____ ?

Exercise 8: Review Test
Choose the correct answer. Put a circle around the letter of the answer.

1. I don't know _____ .
   a) how came he
   b) when he go
   c) if he called
   d) whether spoke he

2. "Do you remember _____ ?"
   "No, I don't."
   a) why they left
   b) how left they
   c) when left they
   d) that left they

3. "Which do you think is bigger—a car or a
   cat?" "I think _____ ."
   a) a car is more big
   b) that a car is big
   c) a car is bigger
   d) is bigger a car

4. I don't remember _____ .
   a) when did John call
   b) where Mary did eat
   c) if he called her
   d) than he called

5. John knows _____ .
   a) what time is it
   b) where the dog is
   c) how did they call
   d) that is it raining

6. They don't know _____ to New York.
   a) when they will go
   b) where they're going
   c) if will they go
   d) how are they going

7. "Did we do lesson 15 last week?"
   "I don't recall _____ it."
   a) did we do
   b) we didn't
   c) if we did
   d) if did we do

8. "Did he say _____ ?"
   "I don't recall."
   a) what his name is
   b) where is he from
   c) that did he understand
   d) if was very hungry now

9. "Does Mr. Jones remember _____ book
   we want?" "Yes, he does."
   a) when
   b) why
   c) whose
   d) where

10. "Which do you believe is smaller—a
    nickel or a quarter?"
    "I _____ a nickel is smaller."
    a) think
    b) don't think
    c) think if
    d) don't think if

Lesson 17

A. Relative clauses

B. *For, during, when, while, before, after, until*

Vocabulary List

after	contain	for	prescription
afterwards	dark	kick	serve
bake	drop	laugh at	storm
before	during	poem	until
bore	fall down	point	while
colorful			

Exercise 1   (A.1, pp. 179–84)

Read the two sentences, and then write a new sentence by including the second one within the first.

I see the man. The man helped us.

I see the man that helped us.

I see the man. We helped the man.

I see the man that we helped.

1. This is the letter. The letter was in my book.

   _____

2. This is the letter. John wrote the letter.

   _____

3. We read the book. The book discusses Kennedy.

   _____

4. We read the book. Peter owns the book.

   _____

5. They ate the food. The food was in the refrigerator.

   _____

6. They ate the food. I cooked the food.

   _____

7. Did you find the pen? The pen was on the floor.

   _____

8. Did you find the pen? I needed the pen.

   _____

9. That is the car. The car costs four thousand dollars.

   _____

10. That is the car. We saw the car yesterday.

    _____

11. Does Mary have the pen? The pen writes green.

    _____

12. Does Mary have the pen? John gave the pen to her.

    _____

13. This is the television. The television was on sale.

    _____

14. This is the television. I bought the television.

    _____

15. Did you watch the movie? The movie was on television last night.

    _____

16. Did you watch the movie? We watched the movie.

    _____

17. I know the girl. The girl has a new green car.

    _____

18. I know the girl. You know the girl.

    _____

19. We helped the man. The man had a car accident.

_____

20. We helped the man. You know the man.

_____

Exercise 2   (A.1, pp. 179–84)
Read the two sentences, and then complete the new sentence.

The man wrote a famous book. He was here last week.

The man **that wrote a famous book** was here last week.

I talked to the man. He won a new car.

The man **that I talked to** won a new car.

1. The house is on Main Street. It costs $65,000.

   The house _____ costs $65,000.

2. The boy has a broken arm. He is my brother.

   The boy _____ is my brother.

3. The student sent her a letter. He is her boyfriend.

   The student _____ is her boyfriend.

4. The girl is riding a red bicycle. She is my sister's friend.

   The girl _____ is my sister's friend.

5. We saw the man. He works at the bank.

   The man _____ works at the bank.

6. She bought the dog. It is brown and black.

   The dog _____ is brown and black.

7. I wrote a letter. It was too long.

   The letter _____ was too long.

8. Mary made a phone call. It cost two dollars.

   The phone call _____ cost two dollars.

9. The test had thirty questions. It was too hard.

   The test _____ was too hard.

10. Mrs. Jones made the food. It was delicious.

   The food _____ was delicious.

Exercise 3   (A.1, pp. 179–84)
Answer the questions with complete sentences.

The cat went up the tree. Did you see the cat?

Yes, _I saw the cat that went up the tree._

John read a book. Was the book interesting?

Yes, _the book that John read was interesting._

Mary likes the car. Is the car expensive?

Yes, _the car that Mary likes is expensive._

1. Mary baked a cake. Did John eat the cake?

   Yes, _____ .

2. John ate a cake. Was the cake delicious?

   Yes, _____ .

3. The student speaks German. Do you know the student?

   Yes, _____ .

4. We called the store. Did it close at nine o'clock?

   Yes, _____ .

5. Mary spoke to the doctor. Did you speak to him?

   Yes, _____ .

6. The boys bought the book. Did you look at it?

   Yes, _____ .

7. The boys bought the book. Did the book cost a lot?

   Yes, _____ .

8. Phil wrote a story. Did the teacher like the story?

   Yes, _____ .

9. Phil wrote a story. Was the story very interesting?

   Yes, _____ .

10. She cooked some rice. Did you like the rice?

   Yes, _____ .

Exercise 4 (A.2, pp. 184–85)
Read the two sentences, and then complete the sentence with *whose*.

   I know the student. The student's father is the mayor.

   I know the student **whose father is the mayor** _____ .

1. We visited the man. The man's house is on State Street.

   We visited the man _____ .

2. The man is our friend. The man's house is on State Street.

   The man _____ .

3. I played tennis with the boy. We rode in the boy's car yesterday.

   I played tennis with the boy _____ .

4. The teacher spoke with the student. The student's test grade was poor.

   The teacher spoke with the student _____

   _____ .

5. The teacher only teaches in the morning. The teacher's tests are extremely difficult.

   The teacher _____ .

6. John knows the girl. Her father always says "hello" to us.

   John knows the girl _____ .

7. The girl is always late to class. Her mother was on television last night.

   The girl _____

   _____ .

8. The student studies every night. We would like to borrow his notes.

   The student _____

   _____ .

9. The player was excellent in last night's game. His uniform is almost always dirty.

   The player _____

   _____ .

10. Bob likes the new girl. Her father owns several stores.

   Bob likes the new girl _____ .

Exercise 5   (A.1–2, pp. 179–85)
Read the statement and then answer the question. Write the letter of the correct answer on the line by the number.

   The man talking to the teacher is Mr. Smith.
   __a__ Who is Mr. Smith?
      a) the man
      b) the teacher
      c) the student

_____ 1. Bob likes the girl whose sister is in Sue's class. Who is in Sue's class?
      a) Bob
      b) the girl
      c) the girl's sister
_____ 2. The gentleman who sold that car to Mike works at the bank. Who works at the bank?
      a) the gentleman
      b) Mike
      c) the owner of the car
_____ 3. The man whose son the teacher is talking to is Mr. Miller. Whom is the teacher talking to?
      a) the man
      b) the son
      c) Mr. Miller
_____ 4. Mary would like to meet the girl who was playing tennis with Jack. Which of these statements is true?
      a) Mary was playing tennis with Jack.
      b) The girl was playing tennis with Jack.
      c) Mary was playing tennis with the girl.

_____ 5. Do you think we should invite the girl whose mother is our teacher? Whom should we invite?

    a) our teacher

    b) the girl

    c) the girl's mother

Exercise 6 (A.3, pp. 186–87)
Put parentheses around the words which are optional.

    We bought the large house (that is) on Main Street.
    The man (who is) at the blackboard speaks Greek.

1. The book that is on my desk is very interesting.
2. I asked the boy who was playing baseball what time it was.
3. We ate the cake that was on the table.
4. We need a car that is as pretty as theirs.
5. Who is the girl who is speaking with the teacher?
6. She's going to get a dress that is like Donna's.
7. The child who is playing with the cat is my little sister.
8. The restaurant which is near our school serves delicious food.
9. The man who is going to Miami is a businessman.
10. Our teacher is the lady who is standing by the soft drink machine.

Exercise 7 (B.1, pp. 188–89)
Write *for* or *during* on the line.

    __during__ the school year
    __for__ two hours

1. _____ a few minutes
2. _____ a few years
3. _____ the night
4. _____ one day
5. _____ a long time
6. _____ six years
7. _____ the evening
8. _____ our vacation
9. _____ an hour
10. _____ three hours

Exercise 8 (B.1, pp. 188–89)
Write a complete answer to the question. Use *for* or *during* in your answer.

How long did you study? (two hours)

_____I studied for two hours._____

When did you study? (the afternoon)

_____I studied during the afternoon._____

1. When did you write letters? (my vacation)

   _____

2. How long did you have the flu? (two weeks)

   _____

3. How long did he talk to you? (twenty minutes)

   _____

4. When did she study grammar? (the morning)

   _____

5. How long did they stay with you? (a few days)

   _____

Exercise 9 (B.2, pp. 189–91)
Write *while* or *when* on the line. Remember to use *when* for an action that is of short duration and *while* for an action that is of a longer duration.

She was studying __when____ the phone rang.

The phone rang __while____ she was studying.

1. We were watching television _____ our parents came home.

2. It began to rain _____ we were working in the yard.

3. She was cooking dinner _____ she dropped the plate.

4. The baby woke up _____ we were watching television.

5. I was writing a letter _____ I realized that I didn't have any stamps.

6. Mr. Jones arrived _____ she was eating her dinner.

7. He was smiling _____ they took his picture.

8. Mary was reading _____ Peter was talking to her.

9. We found a dollar _____ we were cleaning the room.

10. I went home _____ Susan came to the party.

Exercise 10 (B.2, pp. 189–91)
Write a sentence with *while* and another sentence with *when*.

John called. I was taking a shower.

> I was taking a shower when John called.
> John called while I was taking a shower.

1. Bill lost his book. He was walking to school.

_____

_____

2. Susan called. I was getting ready to eat.

_____

_____

3. He was writing a letter. His pen ran out of ink.

_____

_____

4. Kay was cooking dinner. She received a telephone call.

_____

_____

5. Tom found a dollar bill. He was cleaning under the sofa.

_____

_____

Exercise 11 (B.3, pp. 191–92)
Write *before, after,* or *until* on the line.

We played tennis. We stopped at four o'clock.

We played tennis __until__ four o'clock.

John ate dinner. Then, he studied.

John ate dinner __before__ he studied.

1. Mr. Miller worked. Then, he went home.

   Mr. Miller went home _____ he worked.

2. The teacher corrected the papers. He handed them out.

   The teacher handed out the papers _____ he corrected them.

3. Rosemary took a shower. Then, she ate breakfast.

   Rosemary ate breakfast _____ she took a shower.

4. The boys watched television. They fell asleep at eight o'clock.

   The boys watched television _____ they fell asleep at eight o'clock.

5. Mike looked up the words. Then, he tried to pronounce all of them.

   _____ Mike looked the words up, he tried to pronounce all of them.

Exercise 12 (B.3, pp. 191–92)
Write a new sentence that begins with *before, after,* or *until*. Be sure to use a comma in your new sentence.

We studied before we ate dinner.

__Before we ate dinner, we studied.__

1. We ate dinner after we studied.

   _____

2. She was studying until they arrived.

   _____

3. I called John up after I got his letter.

   _____

4. You should put the food on the table before the party begins.

_____

5. Ken studied grammar before he did his other homework.

_____

Exercise 13   (B.3, p. 192)
Write *after* or *afterwards*.

He ate dinner. __Afterwards__ , he called me up.

He called me up __after__ he ate dinner.

1. _____ , he ate dessert.

2. _____ class, he went to the library.

3. _____ he takes a shower, he eats breakfast.

4. Please don't call me _____ ten o'clock.

5. Matt went to France _____ he visited England.

6. Matt visited England. _____ , he went to France.

7. Maybe I'll call you up _____ I finish my work.

8. Pat ate dinner. _____ that, she went out.

9. _____ , we had a cup of coffee.

10. I won't be able to help you _____ .

Exercise 14: Review Test
A. Read the two sentences, and then write a new sentence or answer with *who, whom, which, that,* or *whose*.

1. We saw the man. The man wrote a book.

   We saw _____ .

2. We saw the man. Mary and John know the man.

   We saw _____ .

3. Mary baked a cake. Was the cake delicious?

   Yes, _____ .

4. The cake was on the table. Was the cake delicious?

   Yes, _____ .

5. I talked to the boy. The boy's mother is my teacher.

   I talked _____ .

6. The boy lent us his bicycle. The boy's mother is our teacher.

   The boy _____ .

B. Write a new sentence using *before, after, until, when,* or *while*.

1. John was reading. Mary was writing.

   John _____ .

2. I ate my dinner. Then, I did my homework.

   I ate _____ .

3. I did my homework. Then, I ate my dinner.

   I did _____ .

4. We studied grammar. We stopped at 7:30.

   We studied _____ .

5. He was eating. The telephone rang.

   He _____ .

6. The phone rang. He was eating.

   The phone _____ .

Exercise 15: Review Test
Choose the correct answer. Put a circle around the letter of the answer.

1. She eats breakfast immediately
   _____ she wakes up.
   a) after
   b) before
   c) until
   d) while

2. "Did you read Peter's letter?"
   "No, I didn't read _____ ."
   a) the letter he wrote
   b) he wrote the letter
   c) whom Peter wrote
   d) whose Peter wrote

3. _____ we were studying, they
   were studying, too.
   a) Until
   b) During
   c) Whose
   d) While

4. We played tennis until _____ .
   a) tomorrow
   b) tonight
   c) noon
   d) that it rained

5. The boy _____ is our friend.
   a) whose
   b) who
   c) who is our friend
   d) that we spoke to

6. Please come to class _____ eight o'clock.
   a) until
   b) whose
   c) while
   d) before

7. We might study _____ two or three hours.
   a) for
   b) until
   c) while
   d) during

8. _____ the telephone rang, I answered it.
   a) For
   b) Until
   c) During
   d) When

9. The people _____ for the bus are tired.
   a) who is waiting
   b) who waits
   c) waiting
   d) whom waits

10. _____ the time we were in
    France, we learned a lot of French.
    a) For
    b) When
    c) While
    d) During

247

Lesson 18

A. The present perfect: *have studied*

B. The present perfect progressive: *have been studying*

C. The past perfect: *had studied*

D. Short answers: Yes, I have; No, I haven't.

E. Irregular verbs: *go, went, gone*, etc.

Vocabulary List

bend	dig	lie	smoothly
billfold	draw	lose	so far
bind	fight	owe	steal
bite	gain	ride	strike
bleed	hit	run	swear
blow	hold	set	sweep
borrow	hurt	shoot	swing
break down	just	shrink	tear
chess	keep	since	weight
choose	lead	sink	wind
deal	let	slide	wring

Exercise 1 (A.1, pp. 193–95; p. 11; p. 26)

Write the forms of *work* in *present, past,* and *present perfect*. Follow the examples.

verb

1. I __work__ every day.

2. You _____ every week.

3. He _____ every Monday.

4. She _____ every summer.

5. It _____ all of the time.

6. We _____ most of the time.

7. They _____ every morning.

verb + *ed*

8. I __worked__ last week.

9. You _____ in 1960.

10. He _____ last night.

11. She _____ yesterday.

12. It _____ a month ago.

13. We _____ last Monday.

14. They _____ a few days ago.

have + past participle

15. I __have worked__ for two years.

16. You _____ since 1965.

17. He _____ one week so far.

18. She _____ recently.

19. It _____ many times before.

20. We _____ this semester.

21. They _____ this year.

Exercise 2   (A.1, pp. 193–95)
Put a check mark in the parentheses (✓) by the expressions that are possible with *present perfect* tense.

(✓) today
( ) yesterday
(✓) this morning

1. ( ) last week
2. ( ) this week
3. ( ) tomorrow
4. ( ) a few minutes ago
5. ( ) before class

6. ( ) just
7. ( ) so far
8. ( ) recently
9. ( ) in 1965
10. ( ) today

Exercise 3   (A.1, pp. 196–97)
Underline the correct tense of the verb. Use the *present perfect* whenever possible.

We (<u>studied,</u> have studied) last week.
We (studied, <u>have studied</u>) today.

1. They (worked, have worked) last month.
2. The men (talked, have talked) to us this week.
3. Mr. Brown (answered, has answered) all our questions last night.

4. Mary (ate, has eaten) a lot at lunch today.
5. I (read, have read) two of the books so far.
6. Before he went to class, John (ate, has eaten) breakfast.
7. Susan and Joe (bought, have bought) a lot of clothes this week.
8. The children (studied, have studied) in that school two years ago.
9. (Did you work, Have you worked) here in 1970?
10. (Did you study, Have you studied) the lesson today?

Exercise 4   (A.1–2, pp. 193–98)
Write the verb in the correct tense. Use *present perfect* or simple *past* tense. Use *present perfect* whenever possible.

(study) We ___studied___ before the test.

(work) They ___have worked___ here since 1972.

1. (call) She _____ us after the meeting.

2. (work) I _____ there last year.

3. (be) She _____ a teacher when they _____ students at that school.

4. (have) Bob _____ a headache during the last class.

5. (want) He _____ to buy that car since he saw it.

6. (play) You _____ tennis since you were a child.

7. (visit) They _____ us for a few hours last Sunday.

8. (listen) She _____ to the song, and then she began to cry.

9. (call) _____ she _____ you last night?

10. (want) _____ she _____ a car for a long time?

11. (work) _____ he _____ there in 1965?

12. (visit) _____ James _____ you yesterday?

13. (open) Paul _____ the window a few minutes ago.

14. (answer) I _____ half of the questions so far.

15. (answer) _____ you _____ all the questions yesterday?

Exercise 5 (A.1–2, pp. 193–98)
Read the statement, and then write the verb in parentheses in the correct tense. Use simple *past* or *present perfect*.

(go) I ___**have gone**___ to France several times.

(go) I ___**went**___ to France in 1975.

1. (be) He _____ in Italy three times.

   (be) He _____ there in 1965, 1968, and 1972.

2. (live) I _____ in Miami from 1970 to 1980.

   (live) I _____ here since 1980.

3. (eat) He _____ a lot of French food last week.

   (eat) He _____ a lot of Mexican food this week.

4. (fly) She _____ on Great Airlines the last time she went to New York.

   (fly) She _____ on many different airlines.

5. (read) He _____ a good book last week.

   (read) He _____ many good books recently.

6. (have) They _____ a lot of parties at their house this year.

   (have) They _____ one last night.

7. (go) I _____ there in 1962.

   (go) I _____ many times.

8. (write) I _____ many letters to famous people.

   (write) I _____ a letter to the president a long time ago.

9. (see) We _____ that movie last night.

   (see) It is the best movie that we _____ ever _____ .

10. (work) He _____ here in 1965.

    (work) He _____ here since 1965.

Lesson 18

Exercise 6   (A.2, pp. 195–98)
Write *since* or *for* on the line.

_since_____ yesterday

_for_____ a few days

1. _____ last week

2. _____ a week

3. _____ six o'clock

4. _____ six hours

5. _____ this morning

6. _____ early this morning

7. _____ last month

8. _____ one minute

9. _____ Wednesday

10. _____ 1976

Exercise 7   (A.2, pp. 195–98)
Read the two sentences, and then write a new sentence with *since* or *for*.

I live on Green Street. I moved there five months ago.

I have lived on Green Street for five months.

I lived on Green Street in 1970. I live there now.

I have lived on Green Street since 1970.

1. Mr. Brown works at the bank. He began to work there in May.

   _____

2. Peter had a big car two months ago. He has one now.

   _____

3. I am in class now. I arrived here ten minutes ago.

   _____

4. Paul and I know you. We met you last week.

   _____

5. I began to go to high school two years ago. I go there now.

   _____

252

6. She stopped speaking Spanish in class last week. She hasn't spoken Spanish again.

_____

7. We like television. We began to like it when our radio broke.

_____

8. They began to hear that noise an hour ago. They hear it now.

_____

9. I know his name. My sister told me his name last week.

_____

10. I like tennis. My father introduced me to the game a few years ago.

_____

Exercise 8   (A.1–2, pp. 193–98)
Read the sentence, and then write *yes* or *no* to tell if the sentence is correct.

   yes I was in France in 1962.

   _no_ I have been there yesterday.

1. _____ He has been sick a lot this winter.

2. _____ He was sick a lot last winter.

3. _____ Mike has called me last night.

4. _____ They have been here since noon.

5. _____ He has just finished the work.

6. _____ She is sick since yesterday.

7. _____ She was sick since yesterday.

8. _____ I wrote to him twice.

9. _____ I have written to him twice.

10. _____ How long are you here in this country?

11. _____ How many pages have you written so far?

12. _____ Joe ate in that restaurant a few days ago.

Lesson 18

13. _____ I was late to class today.

14. _____ I have been late to my reading class today.

15. _____ Matt knows French for five years.

16. _____ I have met Pat for a year.

17. _____ I had that car since 1962.

18. _____ She has gone to France several times.

19. _____ I have had that green car in 1962.

20. _____ Pat has been in many countries.

21. _____ He has begun to study since six o'clock.

22. _____ He has begun to study a few hours ago.

23. _____ He has just begun to study.

24. _____ She has arrived here five minutes so far.

25. _____ They have studied a lot.

Exercise 9 (B, pp. 198–99; p. 36)
Write the forms of *work* in *present progressive* tense and *present perfect progressive* tense. Follow the examples.

   be + **verb** + *ing*

1. I __am working__ now.

2. You _____ right now.

3. He _____ at this moment.

4. She _____ now.

5. It _____ right now.

6. We _____ at the present moment.

7. They _____ at this moment.

254

have + *been* + verb + *ing*

8. I __*have been working*__ for a month.

9. You _____ since 1965.

10. He _____ this week.

11. She _____ today.

12. It _____ so far.

13. We _____ for a week.

14. They _____ recently.

Exercise 10   (B, pp. 198–99)

Read the first sentence. Change the verb from the first sentence to *present perfect progressive* tense in the second sentence.

She is studying grammar now. She __*has been studying*__ grammar for an hour.

The boys are playing tennis right now. The boys __*have been playing*__ since noon.

1. Joe is reading a book now. Joe _____ a book since last week.

2. We are eating lunch. We _____ lunch since noon.

3. Our class is studying the history of Greece. Our class _____ the history of Greece for two weeks.

4. That cat is making a lot of noise. That cat _____ a lot of noise for more than an hour.

5. Mike and Sue are writing letters. Mike and Sue _____ letters every day this week.

6. Jane is talking to her mother. Jane _____ to her mother for a long time now.

7. We aren't studying now. We _____ this semester.

8. My television is working very well. My television _____ very well since I bought it.

9. The water is boiling. The water _____ for almost five minutes.

10. Somebody is knocking on the door. Somebody _____ on the door for two minutes.

Lesson 18

Exercise 11   (C, pp. 199–200)
Write the forms of *work* in *past* tense and *past perfect* tense. Follow the examples.

verb **+ ed**

1. I __worked__ yesterday.

2. You _____ last year.

3. He _____ last night.

4. She _____ last week.

5. It _____ a few minutes ago.

6. We _____ in 1970.

7. They _____ last summer.

had **+ past participle**

8. Before I started to work here, I __had worked__ in Miami.

9. You got more money because you _____ many extra hours.

10. He was tired at noon because he _____ all morning.

11. Before Anne went to college, she _____ in a grocery store.

12. John told me that his old stereo _____ perfectly at his party.

13. We arrived home late because we _____ after our normal quitting time.

14. I didn't meet the man that they _____ with.

Exercise 12   (C, pp. 199–200)
Underline the correct verb tense.

John (<u>did</u>, had done) well on the test because he (studied, <u>had studied</u>) very hard.

1. We (worked, had worked) for two hours before John (called, had called).
2. John (called, had called) after we (worked, had worked) for two hours.
3. My friend (arrived, had arrived) late because he (had, had had) problems with his car.
4. I (lived, had lived) in New York before I (moved, had moved) here.

256

5. Because George (saved, had saved) his money, he (was, had been) able to go to South America.

6. The telephone (was, had been) ringing for two minutes before I (answered, had answered) it.

7. The new student (understood, had understood) the lesson yesterday because the teacher (explained, had explained) it to him two days ago.

8. Because it (was, had been) raining very hard all night, we (weren't, hadn't been) able to go on our trip today.

9. Peter (said, had said) that his vacation (was, had been) very bad.

10. James (knew, had known) the answer because he (was, had been) studying.

Exercise 13   (D, pp. 200–201)
Write a short answer to these questions.

Have you eaten breakfast this morning?

Yes, __I have__ .

Had they eaten breakfast before we arrived?

Yes, __they had__ .

1. Has Peter written a letter to his parents?

   Yes, _____ .

2. Have they called him?

   No, _____ .

3. Had she thought about her decision before she made it?

   Yes, _____ .

4. Have you seen Paul today?

   No, _____ .

5. Has Sue done all the work?

   Yes, _____ .

6. Have you heard from Mary?

   No, _____ .

7. Have you and Mary studied for the test?

   Yes, _____ .

257

Lesson 18

8. Had his car broken down before he went on vacation?

No, _____ .

9. Have I been very angry recently?

Yes, _____ .

10. Have the children ever had a bad cold?

No, _____ .

Exercise 14 (E.1–2, pp. 202–3)
Write the verb forms that are not given (*present, past, past participle*).

go __went__ __gone__

__say__ __said__ said

present	*past*	*past participle*
1. read	_____	_____
2. _____	_____	slept
3. _____	chose	_____
4. _____	left	_____
5. lend	_____	_____
6. speak	_____	_____
7. build	_____	_____
8. know	_____	_____
9. _____	sang	_____
10. _____	_____	flown
11. _____	_____	made
12. _____	understood	_____
13. give	_____	_____
14. come	_____	_____
15. fall	_____	_____

258

16. meet	_____	_____
17. lose	_____	_____
18. cost	_____	_____
19. drink	_____	_____
20. take	_____	_____
21. _____	cut	_____
22. begin	_____	_____
23. _____	_____	wrung
24. _____	found	_____
25. run	_____	_____
26. win	_____	_____
27. get	_____	_____
28. _____	_____	thought
29. _____	forgot	_____
30. buy	_____	_____

Exercise 15   (E.1–2, pp. 202–3)

Write the verb forms that are not given (*present*, *past*, past participle).

go	_went_	_gone_
say	_said_	said

present	*past*	*past participle*
1. write	_____	_____
2. sit	_____	_____
3. _____	_____	sold
4. _____	showed	_____
5. see	_____	_____

present	past	past participle
6. bite	_____	_____
7. teach	_____	_____
8. _____	broke	_____
9. _____	_____	grown
10. bring	_____	_____
11. freeze	_____	_____
12. send	_____	_____
13. _____	_____	driven
14. be	_____	_____
15. do	_____	_____
16. _____	told	_____
17. _____	spent	_____
18. ring	_____	_____
19. _____	had	_____
20. eat	_____	_____

Exercise 16   (E.1–2, pp. 202–4)

Write the verb forms that are not given (*present, past,* past participle).

go	_went_	_gone_
say	_said_	said

present	past	past participle
1. sink	_____	_____
2. _____	_____	fed
3. _____	put	_____
4. shrink	_____	_____
5. _____	hung	_____

	present	*past*	*past participle*
6.	_____	set	_____
7.	wear	_____	_____
8.	shoot	_____	_____
9.	_____	swung	_____
10.	_____	_____	torn
11.	_____	_____	caught
12.	fight	_____	_____
13.	lie	_____	_____
14.	_____	_____	kept
15.	wake	_____	_____
16.	_____	_____	thrown
17.	_____	_____	let
18.	bend	_____	_____
19.	hide	_____	_____
20.	slide	_____	_____
21.	_____	blew	_____
22.	hurt	_____	_____
23.	ride	_____	_____
24.	_____	_____	led
25.	_____	said	_____
26.	bleed	_____	_____
27.	strike	_____	_____
28.	_____	_____	felt
29.	_____	swore	_____
30.	_____	meant	_____

Lesson 18

Exercise 17 (E.1–2, pp. 202–3)
Read the sentence, and then use the correct verb tense. Make the verb negative when necessary.

(go) I _____ **went** _____ to class yesterday.

(make) She _____ **made** _____ some cookies last month, but she **hasn't**

_____ **made** _____ any since.

1. (work) They _____ here since 1969.

2. (do) She _____ the homework last night.

3. (write) He _____ a letter last week, but he _____
   any this week.

4. (watch) I _____ some movies on television yesterday.

5. (move) We heard that the Smiths _____ to another state.

6. (lose) She _____ her keys a month ago, but she _____
   _____ them since then.

7. (eat) They _____ all the hamburgers before we arrived.

8. (have) The student _____ any more colds or fever since last month

   when he _____ to go to the doctor.

9. (tell) The teacher _____ them to do their homework many times this
   semester.

10. (begin) Our class _____ late yesterday. It _____
    late several times in this course.

11. (buy) I _____ a new shirt last week, but I _____
    any since.

12. (give) Susan _____ me some paper a few minutes ago.

13. (speak) Paul _____ to me several times this week.

14. (drink) He _____ any tea at the meeting because he doesn't like it.

15. (study) Brian passed all his exams this week because he _____ every
    night last week.

Exercise 18: Verb Discrimination—Past, Present Perfect, Past Perfect
Underline the correct form of the verb.

He (<u>arrived</u>, has arrived, had arrived) at night.

1. We ate the cake that she (baked, has baked, had baked).
2. Paul (lived, has lived, had lived) there since 1970.
3. Paul (lived, has lived, had lived) there in 1970.
4. Paul (lived, has lived, had lived) there before he came here.
5. She (told, has told, had told) me today that she was not going to be in class tomorrow.
6. This letter (came, has come, had come) for you yesterday.
7. Pat (wrote, has written, had written) me a letter a few days ago.
8. I (had, have had, had had) a cold since yesterday.
9. She (was, has been, had been) in Europe a few weeks ago.
10. They (saw, have seen, had seen) that movie twice so far.

Exercise 19: Review Test
A. Read the two sentences, and then combine them using *since* or *for*.

1. John speaks French. He learned it two years ago.

   _____

2. We are studying. We began to study at ten o'clock.

   _____

3. I had a cold last month, and I have one now.

   _____

4. She is learning English. She began in June.

   _____

B. Write the past tense and past participle form of the verbs.

1. go   _____   _____

2. do   _____   _____

3. begin   _____   _____

4. eat   _____   _____

Lesson 18

5. study   _____   _____

6. send   _____   _____

7. give   _____   _____

8. write   _____   _____

9. break   _____   _____

10. find   _____   _____

C. Read the sentence, and then write the correct tense of the verb.

1. (go) We _____ yesterday.

2. (be) She _____ here since yesterday.

3. (do / study) He _____ well on the test yesterday because he _____ very hard.

4. (talk) I _____ on the phone last night.

5. (see) My teacher _____ the boy copying on the test.

Exercise 20: Review Test
Choose the correct answer. Put a circle around the letter of the answer.

1. "Have Mary and John called you?"
   "Yes, _____ ."
   a) they did
   b) they have
   c) I did
   d) I have

2. She _____ a car since January.
   a) doesn't have
   b) didn't have
   c) hasn't had
   d) hadn't has

3. It _____ raining before I woke up.
   a) has
   b) had
   c) has been
   d) had been

4. We studied _____ one hour last night.

   a) for

   b) during

   c) whilc

   d) since

5. John Kennedy _____ President in 1962.

   a) was

   b) wcnt

   c) has been

   d) had been

6. The teacher didn't teach our class today, but he _____ us yesterday.

   a) teaches

   b) taught

   c) has taught

   d) had taught

7. I _____ that movie twice so far.

   a) see

   b) am seeing

   c) have seen

   d) had seen

8. They're hungry because they _____ dinner last night.

   a) don't eat

   b) didn't eat

   c) hadn't eaten

   d) havent' eaten

9. "When did Alina go to the hospital?"

   "I'm not sure. I think that she _____ in the hospital since last Thursday."

   a) went

   b) has gone

   c) was

   d) has been

10. "Does your father work at the post office?"

    "No, my father _____ at the bank since I was born."

    a) works

    b) is working

    c) worked

    d) has been working

Lesson 19

A. Passive sentences: The letters were written.

B. The use of *still, any more, already,* and *yet*

C. Past participles as modifiers: John is interested.
   Adjectives ending in *-ing*: The story is interesting.

D. Adjective + preposition combinations: interested in music, excited about music

Vocabulary List

action	construct	interest	still
already	disappoint	invent	surprise
amaze	disgust	perform	tire (verb)
any more	excite	pleased	used to
complain	frighten	sharpen	yet
compose	inflation		

Exercise 1   (A, pp. 206–9)
Write the correct form of *write*. Follow the examples.

Present **tense,** *active* **voice (verb)**

1. I __write__ business letters every day.

2. You _____ long letters at night.

3. He _____ a few letters every week.

4. She _____ a business letter every day.

5. We _____ polite letters every day.

6. They _____ a short letter every day.

Present tense, *passive* voice (*be* + past participle)

7. Business letters __are written__ every day.

8. Long letters _____ at night.

9. A few letters _____ every week.

10. A business letter _____ every day.

11. Polite letters _____ every day.

12. A short letter _____ every day.

Past tense, *active* voice (verb)

13. I __wrote__ business letters yesterday.

14. You _____ long letters last night.

15. He _____ a few letters last week.

16. She _____ a business letter last Monday.

17. We _____ polite letters two days ago.

18. They _____ a short letter yesterday.

Past tense, *passive* voice (*be* + past participle)

19. Business letters __were written__ yesterday.

20. Long letters _____ last night.

21. A few letters _____ last week.

22. A business letter _____ last Monday.

23. Polite letters _____ two days ago.

24. A short letter _____ yesterday.

Lesson 19

Present progressive tense, *active* voice (*be* + verb + *ing*)

25. I ___am writing___ business letters now.

26. You _____ long letters this week.

27. He _____ a few letters today.

28. She _____ a business letter right now.

29. We _____ polite letters now.

30. They _____ a short letter right now.

Present progressive tense, *passive* voice (*be* + *being* + **past participle**)

31. Business letters ___are being written___ now.

32. Long letters _____ this week.

33. A few letters _____ today.

34. A business letter _____ right now.

35. Polite letters _____ now.

36. A short letter _____ right now.

Be + *going to*, *active* voice (*be* + *going to* + **verb**)

37. I ___am going to write___ business letters tomorrow.

38. You _____ long letters next week.

39. He _____ a few letters tomorrow.

40. She _____ a business letter later.

41. We _____ polite letters in the future.

42. They _____ a short letter next Monday.

Be + going to, passive voice (*be + going to + be + past participle*)

43. Business letters <u>are going to be written</u> tomorrow.

44. Long letters _____ next week.

45. A few letters _____ tomorrow.

46. A business letter _____ later.

47. Polite letters _____ in the future.

48. A short letter _____ next Monday.

Modals, active voice (**modal + verb**). Use *will* for 49–51 and *should* for 52–54.

49. I <u>will write</u> business letters tomorrow.

50. You _____ long letters next week.

51. He _____ a few letters tomorrow.

52. She <u>should write</u> a business letter to Mr. Jones.

53. We _____ polite letters to the customers.

54. They _____ a short letter immediately.

Modals, passive voice (**Modal + be + past participle**). Use *will* for 55–57 and *should* for 58–60.

55. Business letters <u>will be written</u> tomorrow.

56. Long letters _____ next week.

57. A few letters _____ tomorrow.

58. A business letter <u>should be written</u> to Mr. Jones.

59. Polite letters _____ to the customers.

60. A short letter _____ immediately.

Lesson 19

Present perfect tense, *active* voice (*have* + **past participle**)

61. I ___have written___ business letters this week.

62. You _____ long letters many times.

63. He _____ a few letters since yesterday.

64. She _____ a business letter every day.

65. We _____ two polite letters so far.

66. They _____ a short letter every day this week.

Present perfect tense, *passive* voice (*have* + *been* + **past participle**)

67. Business letters ___have been written___ this week.

68. Long letters _____ many times.

69. A few letters _____ since yesterday.

70. A business letter _____ every day.

71. Two polite letters _____ so far.

72. A short letter _____ every day this week.

Exercise 2   (A, pp. 206–9)
Write the verb in the passive voice.

Mr. Brown wrote that book. That book ___was written___ by Mr. Brown.

You should do the work immediately. The work ___should be done___ immediately.

1. We are going to do all of the work tomorrow. All of the work _____ tomorrow.

2. Martha has to write those letters. Those letters _____ by Martha.

3. The maid cleans our rooms every day. Our rooms _____ by the maid every day.

4. Everyone should eat more green vegetables. More green vegetables _____ by everyone.

5. Mark has done most of the work this week. Most of the work _____ by Mary this week.

270

6. All of the boys painted the kitchen. The kitchen _____ by all of the boys.

7. We had called the police before Paul called them. The police _____ by us before they _____ by Paul.

8. Mr. Todd will give the final exam. The final exam _____ by Mr. Todd.

9. They found the keys last night. The keys _____ last night.

10. The maid is cooking the potatoes now. The potatoes _____ by the maid now.

Exercise 3 (A, pp. 206–9)
Write a sentence with a verb in the passive voice.

That student wrote the story.

The story was written by that student.

1. Mary is making tonight's dinner.

_____

2. Mr. Smith will give the grammar and vocabulary tests.

_____

3. The president made many new laws.

_____

4. Susan washes the dishes every night.

_____

5. My brother bought that car a long time ago.

_____

6. All of the people must do the work.

_____

7. Susan has telephoned Mrs. Smith.

_____

8. The grammar teacher will grade our test papers.

_____

9. The secretary should write those letters immediately.

_____

10. Someone has to call the police immediately.

_____

Exercise 4: Verb Discrimination—Active/Passive Voice
Underline the correct verb form.

He (<u>writes</u>, is written) long letters most of the time.
Most small cars (make, <u>are made</u>) in Japan.

1. All the letters (signed, were signed) yesterday.
2. They (watched, were watched) the movie.
3. John (has studied, has been studied) for the test.
4. Our car (shouldn't use, shouldn't be used) a lot of gasoline.
5. The people (saw, were seen) the president.
6. She (has sharpened, has been sharpened) the pencils.
7. The new hospital (is building, is being built) this year.
8. My friends (are going to bring, are going to be brought) their parents.
9. That letter (was writing, was written) several years ago.
10. She (is made, is making) a cake.

Exercise 5   (B.1, pp. 209–10)
Write *still* or *any more* on the line.

We ___**still**___ don't have enough money.

We can't sing well ___**any more**___ .

1. I studied French in high school a long time ago, but I can't speak it _____ .

2. She is _____ in New York. She won't return until next week.

3. Richard took the medicine. He isn't sick _____ .

4. Bill took some medicine, but he is _____ sick.

5. I worked at the bank last year, and I _____ work there.

6. I worked at the bank last year, but I don't work there _____ . Now I work in a supermarket.

7. When I ate dinner in that restaurant last night, the food was very bad. I won't go there

_____ .

8. They didn't pay their telephone bill from last month. They don't have a telephone

_____ .

9. I don't like other people to use my car. Please don't use it _____ .

10. The teacher has explained the lesson several times, but Pamela _____ doesn't understand.

Exercise 6   (B.1, pp. 209–10)
Read the two sentences, and then write a new sentence with *still* or *any more*.

We didn't have enough money yesterday. We don't have enough money now.

We still don't have enough money .

1. We could speak French last year. We can't speak French now.

_____

2. They didn't have a telephone last month. They don't have a telephone now.

_____

3. I was sick last week. I am sick now.

_____

4. Joe worked here last year. He is working here now.

_____

5. She isn't hungry now. She was hungry a few minutes ago.

_____

Lesson 19

Exercise 7 (B.2, pp. 210–11)
Write *already* or *yet* on the line.

She hasn't called me ___yet___ .

He has __already__ called me.

1. We were expecting him to arrive at noon. It's only eleven o'clock, and he has _____ arrived.

2. The teacher is asking for the test papers, but those students haven't finished _____ _____ .

3. They were supposed to be here an hour ago, but they haven't arrived _____ .

4. Her boss is very angry because she hasn't arrived at the office _____ .

5. I have a big test tomorrow, but I haven't studied _____ .

6. She has only been in the United States for a few weeks, but she _____ speaks English very well.

7. "Have you written that letter?"

   "Yes, I have _____ written it."

8. "Have you _____ studied for the final exam?"
   "Yes, I have."

9. Mr. Johnson usually gets home at six o'clock, but he is home _____ and it's only five-thirty.

10. Pete usually loses things very easily. I gave him a pencil a few minutes ago, and he

    has _____ lost it.

Exercise 8   (B.2, pp. 210–11)
Read the sentences, and then write a new sentence using *already* or *yet*.

It's only seven-thirty, but they have arrived.   <u>They have already arrived.</u>

It's seven-thirty, but they haven't arrived.   <u>They haven't arrived yet.</u>

1. The weather is very hot, but it isn't summer.

   _____

2. They are waiting for the bus, but it hasn't come.

   _____

3. It's only eleven-thirty, but John has eaten lunch.

   _____

4. Today is only the first day of December, but we have bought our Christmas gifts.

   _____

5. The store usually closes at six o'clock. It's only five-thirty, but that store is closed.

   _____

Exercise 9 (B.1–2, pp. 209–11)
Write *still, any more, already,* or *yet* on the line.

The test is tomorrow, but John hasn't studied for it __yet__ .

I called his office, but he __still__ hasn't returned my call.

1. The teacher explained the lesson just a few minutes ago. Mike has _____ forgotten what the teacher explained.

2. The teacher has told them that they must do their work. They won't listen to him. They _____ won't do their work.

3. Paul didn't mail his letter yesterday, but he will mail it soon. He hasn't mailed it _____ .

4. The history class begins too early in the morning for Peter. He went to class during the first week of the semester, but he hasn't gone back _____ .

5. Grammar class begins at eight o'clock sharp. It's _____ eight-ten, and class hasn't started _____ .

6. Marco hasn't received his visa _____ . He has been waiting for it for more than a month.

7. American passports are good for five years. I've had mine for just a year. My passport is _____ good.

8. "Did the plane arrive early?"

   "Yes, it has _____ arrived."

9. "Where are the passengers from Flight 449?"

   "They haven't left the airplane _____ ."

10. "Is Jack there?"

   "No, he isn't. He has _____ gone home."

Exercise 10 (C, pp. 211–13)
Write the correct past participle / -ing verb form.

The movie interests Peter.

The movie is __interesting__ .

Peter is __interested__ .

1. That class always bores the students.

   That class is _____ .

   The students are _____ .

2. The movie frightened us.

   We were _____ .

   The movie was _____ .

3. The news surprised the people.

   The people were _____ .

   The news was _____ .

4. The clown entertained the children.

   The clown was _____ .

   The children were _____ .

5. Paul's decision disappointed his family.

   His family was _____ .

   Paul's decision was _____ .

Exercise 11 (C, pp. 211–13)
Underline the correct adjective form.

The news was (excited, <u>exciting</u>).

1. The (shocked, shocking) people began to cry when they heard the news.
2. That man was (disgusted, disgusting) by the movie.
3. The movie was (disgusted, disgusting).
4. The answer was very (confused, confusing). It confused everyone in class.

5. His new book is (interested, interesting) and all of the people are (interested, interesting).
6. His explanation was not (convinced, convincing).
7. The (frightened, frightening) little boy began to cry.
8. My trip was very (excited, exciting).
9. The history lesson today was very (bored, boring).
10. He explained the lesson again, but I was still (confused, confusing).
11. Were the students (bored, boring) in class yesterday?
12. The people were very (surprised, surprising) when they read the newspaper.
13. He is very (worried, worrying) about his test grade.
14. The movie that I saw last night was (interested, interesting).
15. His dogs can jump very high. They are really (amazed, amazing).

Exercise 12 (D, pp. 213–14)
Write the correct preposition on the line.

He is unhappy __about__ leaving his family.

1. She's tired _____ eating this food.
2. They were surprised _____ his new clothes.
3. Are you pleased _____ your new doctor?
4. I'm very worried _____ my grandmother.
5. The children are accustomed _____ waking up very early.
6. Joe is in favor _____ the new law.
7. Peter is always bored _____ his classes.
8. I was very disappointed _____ my test grade.
9. He's used _____ American food.
10. We are very interested _____ going on vacation in Florida.

Exercise 13 (D, pp. 213–14)
Read the sentences, and then write a new sentence using an *adjective + preposition* structure. Be sure that the *-ing* form of the verb is used to describe the action.

Mary received a good grade. She's very happy.

She's very happy about receiving a good grade.

Bess doesn't have enough money. She is worried.

She is worried about not having enough money.

1. John made the best grade. He was surprised.

2. Mike eats hamburgers all of the time. He's tired of it.

3. George doesn't have a car. He's unhappy.

4. They want to learn English. They are interested.

5. I am spending too much money. I am worried.

6. Dave wakes up at six in the morning. He is accustomed to it.

7. Bill and Frank go to the park every Sunday. They are bored with it.

8. Maria eats American food now. She is used to it.

9. Mr. Jones pays a lot of taxes. He is not in favor of it.

10. Mark is going to Europe. He's excited about it.

Lesson 19

Exercise 14   (D, p. 214)
Write the correct structure with *read*. Follow the examples.

    be + used to + verb + ing

1. I __am used to reading__ a lot.

2. You _____ a lot.

3. He _____ a lot.

4. She _____ a lot.

5. We _____ a lot.

6. They _____ a lot.

    used to + verb

7. I __used to read__ a lot.

8. You _____ a lot.

9. He _____ a lot.

10. She _____ a lot.

11. We _____ a lot.

12. They _____ a lot.

Exercise 15   (D, p. 214)
Read the situation, and then complete the sentence with *be + used to + verb + ing* or *used to + verb.*

I am accustomed to waking up early.

I __am used to waking up__ early.

I studied a lot last semester, but I don't study any more.

I __used to study__ a lot.

1. Matt is accustomed to eating American food now. He hated it when he first arrived in the United States.

He _____ American food.

He _____ only food from his country.

2. Ted is accustomed to attending five classes now. Last semester he only had one class.

Ted _____ five classes.

Ted _____ one class daily.

3. Mrs. Smith doesn't cook dinner any more. She has a maid.

Mrs. Smith _____ dinner.

Mrs. Smith _____ the food that her maid cooks.

4. The name of this store was "The Toy Store." Now the name has been changed to "The Play Room."

The name of the store _____ "The Toy Store."

5. Sam ate Italian food a long time ago. Now he will not eat it.

Sam _____ Italian food.

Exercise 16: Review Test
A. Underline the correct verb form.

1. That car (made, was made) in Japan.
2. The movie (saw, was seen) by many people.
3. The watch is going to (sell, be sold) soon.
4. The house is (building, being built) this year.
5. They should (do, be done) the work next week.

B. Write *still, any more, already,* or *yet*.

1. We _____ haven't received the check.

2. "Do you have their money?"

   "No, they haven't paid me their money _____ ."

3. "Has Mike _____ called you?"

   "Yes, he has. It's only eight o'clock, but he called a few minutes ago."

4. Mary isn't sick _____ . She feels much better.

5. "Have you called him up?"

   "No, not _____ . I'll do it right away."

Lesson 19

C. Underline the correct answer.

1. John was very (disappointed, disappointing) with the news.
2. After the trip, we were very (tired, tiring).
3. The (excited, exciting) news was nice to hear.
4. That book is (disgusted, disgusting).

D. Write the correct preposition.

1. We were surprised _____ the price of his new car.

2. They are accustomed _____ eating sandwiches for dinner.

3. I am very excited _____ going to Europe.

4. Are you used _____ hearing English all of the time?

5. My parents are always worried _____ me.

Exercise 17: Review Test
Choose the correct answer. Put a circle around the letter of the answer.

1. That house _____ last year.
   a) built
   b) was build
   c) was being built
   d) has been built
2. John's story was very _____ .
   a) bored
   b) excited
   c) surprised
   d) amusing
3. We _____ haven't received today's newspaper.
   a) yet
   b) still
   c) already
   d) any more
4. They are accustomed _____ American food now.
   a) to eat
   b) to eating
   c) of eat
   d) of eating

282

5. The television _____ broken since last week.
   a) was
   b) has
   c) was been
   d) has been

6. We have _____ made our lunch.
   a) yet
   b) still
   c) already
   d) any more

7. John thought that the test was very _____ .
   a) confused
   b) confusing
   c) broken
   d) breaking

8. "Where are the letters?"
   "Those letters _____ already."
   a) mailed
   b) was mailed
   c) had been mailed
   d) have been mailed

9. Kevin _____ his keys all of the time.
   a) lose
   b) losing
   c) loses
   d) is lost

10. Jane and Sue are _____ their new dog.
    a) used of
    b) happy for
    c) unhappy by
    d) worried about

Review Test 3 (Lessons 11–19)

Choose the best answer and put a circle around the letter of the correct answer.

1. We need to know _____ .
   a) where is Boston
   b) when are they coming
   c) what time is it
   d) who the new boy is

2. I was talking to the man _____ .
   a) that Mary knows
   b) which Mary knows
   c) whom knows Mary
   d) who know Mary

3. We have completed five lessons _____ .
   a) since
   b) after
   c) so far
   d) during

4. "Is it raining yet?"
   "It _____ be raining. I saw a lady with a wet umbrella."
   a) should
   b) should to
   c) must
   d) must to

5. " _____ we smoke here?"
   "No, no one is permitted to smoke here."
   a) May
   b) Must
   c) Should
   d) Have

6. Jack needs to pass the final exam in order to pass the course. He _____ study hard.
   a) can
   b) may
   c) might
   d) should

7. "Why aren't they coming to the party tonight?"
   "I don't know. They _____ study."
   a) can have to
   b) have to can
   c) must have to
   d) have to must

8. They studied hard, and we _____ .
   a) studied too
   b) studied either
   c) did too
   d) didn't either

9. These words are very _____ .
   a) difficult of pronounce
   b) difficult to pronouncing
   c) easy for me of pronounce
   d) easy for me to pronounce

10. The man _____ is my uncle.
    a) whom is talking
    b) who talks now
    c) is talking
    d) talking

11. John really needs _____ to the library now.
    a) go
    b) to go
    c) going
    d) has gone

12. Mr. Miller wants _____ a letter for him.
    a) Susan writes
    b) Susan to write
    c) that Susan write
    d) that Susan writes

13. This book is _____ read.
    a) easy enough for
    b) enough easy for
    c) easy enough to
    d) enough easy to

14. The hamburgers _____ yesterday.
    a) ate
    b) were ate
    c) are eaten
    d) were eaten

15. "Where is John?"
    "He doesn't work here _____ ."
    a) too
    b) still
    c) already
    d) any more

16. This machine works well, but the new machine is better because it works _____ .
    a) rapidlier
    b) more rapidly
    c) as rapidly as
    d) the most rapidly

17. Mark was tired last night because he _____ tennis all afternoon.
    a) must play
    b) has played
    c) had played
    d) has playing

18. Mr. Smith is very happy _____ the news.
    a) of
    b) by
    c) for
    d) about

19. Pam _____ hasn't done the work.
    a) too
    b) yet
    c) still
    d) already

20. Yesterday was Friday. I _____ to class.
    a) must go
    b) must went
    c) had to
    d) had to go

21. "How did they get here?"
    "They came _____ ."
    a) for see me
    b) to see me
    c) by bus
    d) by walk

22. I think _____ a party now.
    a) it is
    b) that it's
    c) there is
    d) whose is

23. "Did you enjoy the book?"
    "No, it was _____ read."
    a) hard very to
    b) hard enough to
    c) too hard to
    d) enough hard

24. The new hospital _____ when the government ran out of money for the project.
    a) was building
    b) is building
    c) was being built
    d) is being built

25. "Did George like the movie?"
    "No, he didn't. He was _____ ."
    a) bored
    b) boring
    c) interested
    d) interesting

26. My new shoes are too small. When I get home, I'm going to _____ .
    a) take off them
    b) take them off
    c) took off them
    d) took them off

27. The group arrived _____ car.
    a) with
    b) for
    c) in
    d) by

28. We can't go outside because _____ .
    a) is raining
    b) is too cold
    c) it's cold enough
    d) it's too cold

29. Jill was eating dinner _____ I called her up.
    a) when
    b) while
    c) during
    d) already

30. "Are you going to France?"
    "No, I'm not. The ticket is ____ me."
    a) too expensive to
    b) too expensive for
    c) expensive enough to
    d) expensive enough for

31. Jack's cat likes that brand of cat food, and _____ too.
    a) Mary does
    b) hers does
    c) Mary likes
    d) hers likes

32. "Would you like some onions?"
    "Yes, please. I'd like some _____ ."
    a) one
    b) small one
    c) ones
    d) small ones

33. I can't imagine _____ that is.
    a) of whom car
    b) what car does
    c) that whose car
    d) whose car

34. "Where is my paper?"
    "Maybe she _____ ."
    a) put out it
    b) hand it in
    c) gave back it
    d) threw it away

35. Martha went to the store ____ some milk.
    a) for buy
    b) for buying
    c) to buy
    d) to buying

36. " _____ is this?"
    "It's mine."
    a) Of who
    b) Of whom
    c) Who's
    d) Whose

37. "Have you read _____ ?"
    "No, but I will."
    a) today newspaper
    b) the today newspaper
    c) the newspaper of today
    d) today's newspaper

38. The girls have their books, and we have _____ books.
    a) ours
    b) our
    c) our ones
    d) ours ones

39. I believe I am _____ Bill.
    a) taller than
    b) taller that
    c) more tall than
    d) more tall that

40. "How many of those shirts ____ today?"
    "About thirty."
    a) have sold
    b) are sold
    c) were selling
    d) have been sold

41. I like the red shirt, but I prefer the _____ .
    a) one blue
    b) blues ones
    c) blues one
    d) blue one

42. I know _____ here.
    a) whose lives
    b) whom lives
    c) that he lives
    d) that lives he

43. The man _____ last night.
    a) we saw
    b) that we saw
    c) we will visit called
    d) that we will visit

44. "Did they study a lot?"
    "Yes, they studied _____ ."
    a) afterwards
    b) during five days
    c) for the vacation
    d) until five o'clock

45. "Have all of the students gone home?"
    "Yes, they _____ ."
    a) did
    b) had
    c) have
    d) gone

46. He speaks English well because he
    _____ it since he was a child.
    a) speaks
    b) spoke
    c) has spoken
    d) had spoken

47. He didn't pass the test because he _____ .
    a) must not study
    b) must not studied
    c) hadn't studied
    d) hadn't to study

48. John likes to swim, and Mark _____ .
    a) doesn't either
    b) likes either
    c) does too
    d) likes too

49. John said that all the apples
    _____ yesterday.
    a) was eaten
    b) had been eaten
    c) ate
    d) were ate

50. This book is _____ as that one.
    a) same price
    b) as price
    c) different
    d) as expensive

Review Test 4 (Lessons 11–19)

Choose the correct answer. Put a circle around the letter of the answer.

1. "Where are my papers?"
   "I threw _____ ."
   a) away it
   b) it away
   c) away them
   d) them away

2. "_____ did John send the letter?"
   "He sent it by air mail."
   a) Which
   b) Why
   c) How
   d) Can

3. "Should he study more?"
   "Yes, he _____ study a lot."
   a) must to
   b) needs to
   c) is going
   d) can to

4. "Can I help you?"
   "Yes, I would like _____ help me."
   a) you to
   b) for you
   c) that you
   d) you can

5. "How many people were _____ at the party?"
   "About twenty-five."
   a) those
   b) there
   c) they
   d) we

6. "How did you learn the words?"
   "By _____ them several times."
   a) write
   b) wrote
   c) writing
   d) written

7. "What did he eat?"
   "I'm not sure what _____ ."
   a) did he eat
   b) did eat he
   c) he ate
   d) ate he

8. "Do you know the boy and his father?"
   "Yes, the boy _____ I know used to be in my class."
   a) whose
   b) which
   c) whose father
   d) which father

9. "Did you go to Japan?"
   "No, but I had _____ ."
   a) must
   b) could
   c) planned to
   d) expecting to

10. "What did the doctor say?"
    "He told _____ ."
    a) I resting
    b) that I rest
    c) me to rest
    d) to me rest

11. "Did you study?"
    "Yes, we studied ____ the weekend."
    a) for
    b) while
    c) since
    d) during

12. I passed all my exams because I _____ very hard.
    a) am studied
    b) am studying
    c) had studied
    d) have studied

288

13. "Will you go to the party tonight?"
"No, but I _____ ."
a) hope
b) won't
c) want to
d) must to

14. "Did he receive his check _____ ?"
"No, but he might get it tomorrow."
a) yet
b) since
c) still
d) any more

15. "What were you doing?"
"I was reading ____ she called me up."
a) when
b) while
c) whose
d) during

16. Joseph is ____ waking up very early.
a) unhappy with
b) excited of
c) tired for
d) used to

17. "Did you discuss the problem?"
"Yes, we _____ ."
a) thought of it
b) talked it over
c) asked for it
d) wrote it down

18. "Did you find the book?"
"Yes, we found the book
_____ looking for."
a) what we were
b) what were we
c) we were
d) were we

19. These two pencils are the same ____ .
a) thick
b) length
c) wide
d) cheap

20. "Is that Paul or is that Joe?"
"I don't know _____ ."
a) who is
b) is who
c) who that is
d) who is that

21. "Can you play tennis now?"
"No, I'm ____ to play right now."
a) tired too
b) too tired
c) tiring too
d) too tiring

22. "Is John still working at the bank?"
"Yes, he _____ working
there for a long time."
a) is
b) has
c) has been
d) had been

23. "I can't reach that shelf."
"I'm not _____ either."
a) tall very
b) tall enough
c) short very
d) short enough

24. " _____ test was the best?"
"Mark's was."
a) Whose
b) Whom
c) Why
d) Who

25. "How's the weather now?"
" _____ raining."
a) There is
b) There
c) It is
d) It

26. "Which do you think are sweeter—
bananas or lemons?"
"I think _____ are sweeter."
a) that bananas
b) that lemons
c) which bananas
d) which lemons

27. These books are easy _____ .
a) that I read
b) that me read
c) to me for read
d) for me to read

28. "Who has a watch?"
"I don't, but I know _____ ."
a) whose he does
b) whose does he
c) what time is it
d) what time it is

29. "Did you see John's new car?"
"Yes, I saw the car ____ John bought."
a) whose
b) which
c) whom
d) this

30. "Do you need some maps?"
"Yes, I'd like ____ ones, please."
a) some
b) a few
c) large
d) those

31. "Does Paul have a test tomorrow?"
"Yes, he _____ study tonight."
a) has
b) ought
c) must
d) won't

32. John's cat sleeps under the house, and
_____ too.
a) mine is
b) yours sleeps
c) hers does
d) Mary does

33. "How was your test?"
"Mine was _____ ."
a) the best
b) most good
c) enough easy
d) easy very

34. "Do you think that Mike and John are
Canadian?"
"I know that Mike is from Canada, and
John _____ ."
a) can't be either
b) might be too
c) is either
d) isn't too

35. "Are you hungry?"
"No, I've _____ eaten."
a) already
b) any more
c) still
d) yet

36. "What happened to the letters that I left
on my desk?"
"They _____ yesterday."
a) mailed
b) mailing
c) were mailed
d) were mailing

37. Matt has a new car, and Jill _____ .
a) has too
b) does too
c) has either
d) does either

38. "Will you help me find the pencils?"
"Yes, I'll _____ ."
a) look for them
b) look at them
c) put them away
d) put them out

39. "Are you _____ about the news?"
"Yes, of course."
a) used
b) surprising
c) bored
d) happy

40. "Will you read a lot tonight?"
"Yes, _____ will be very hard."
a) tomorrow's test
b) last week's exam
c) the test of tomorrow
d) the homework of now

41. "Where are _____ ?"
"They're on the table."
a) the pens of Mary
b) John's pencils
c) mine papers
d) the students' book

42. "How many tests have you had ____ ?"
"Only one."
a) last week
b) so far
c) any more
d) recent

43. "Was the book interesting?"
"Yes, the book ____ was very good."
a) was read
b) we read
c) reading
d) interesting

44. This table is _____ that one.
a) the same height
b) the same weight
c) as long as
d) as age as

45. "Do you like coffee?"
"Yes, but tea is more _____ ."
a) delicious
b) carefully
c) better
d) good

46. "Where did Greg go?"
"He went home ____ some money."
a) to get
b) for get
c) by getting
d) with getting

47. "Do you always walk in the park?"
"Yes, this park is pleasant _____ ."
a) for walk
b) for walk in
c) to walk
d) to walk in

48. I conclude that Jane has the correct answer. She _____ right.
a) must have
b) should have
c) must be
d) should be

49. "Whom were you talking to just now on the phone?"
" _____ was Ricky."
a) He
b) It
c) These
d) There

50. "Are you still taking that medicine?"
"The doctor said I ____ take it when I feel a little sick, but it isn't necessary to take it every day."
a) have
b) may
c) ought
d) am able

Lesson 21

A. Verb + noun phrase + verb: See him go.

B. Wish sentences: I wish they knew.

C. *Wh*-word + *to* + verb: They decided when to go.

Vocabulary List

awful	park	sore	tractor
bridge	province	stadium	weak
groceries	relatives	strength	wish
let	skill	throat	wonderful

Exercise 1 (A, pp. 231–34)
Underline the correct verb form.

He saw her (<u>leave</u>, to leave) school.
I want her (leave, <u>to leave</u>) now.

1. Mr. Jones needs someone (help, to help) him.
2. She was watching him (play, to play) baseball.
3. Peter heard the telephone (ring, to ring), but he was too lazy (answer, to answer) it.
4. Mike has (go, to go) to class in a few minutes.
5. I let Mary and Sue (use, to use) my car.
6. I permitted them (use, to use) it for two hours.
7. Have you seen them (sing, to sing) on television?
8. I'll have the maid (make, to make) the beds.
9. We felt the house (shake, to shake) during the storm.
10. Parents should (make, to make) their children (eat, to eat) good food.
11. I'll have my secretary (type, to type) the letter.
12. They want me (help, to help) them.
13. The policeman made the men (go, to go) away.
14. Please help me (learn, to learn) these verbs.
15. Would you permit me (borrow, to borrow) your car?

Exercise 2 (A, pp. 231–34)
Write *to* on the line if it is necessary. If it is not possible to write *to*, then draw a line.

We saw her ⎯⎯ leave.

I want her _to_ leave.

1. I had the man ⎯⎯⎯ fix my car.

2. We are planning ⎯⎯⎯ go tomorrow.

3. They would like ⎯⎯⎯ leave as early as possible.

4. Did you watch that elephant ⎯⎯⎯ eat?

5. The king made the men ⎯⎯⎯ sign the paper.

6. My father had told us not ⎯⎯⎯ go yet.

7. I caught a bird, but I let it ⎯⎯⎯ go.

8. Can you hear the baby ⎯⎯⎯ cry?

9. He often cries ⎯⎯⎯ get our attention.

10. I helped them ⎯⎯⎯ study last night.

11. Would you like us ⎯⎯⎯ help you?

12. I was watching them ⎯⎯⎯ play tennis.

13. Would you permit me ⎯⎯⎯ use your watch?

14. Would you let me ⎯⎯⎯ use your watch?

15. He's planning ⎯⎯⎯ arrive around noon.

16. Did they see you ⎯⎯⎯ take the money?

17. He ordered me ⎯⎯⎯ take the medicine.

18. She made them ⎯⎯⎯ leave.

19. She forced them ⎯⎯⎯ leave.

20. Mark watched the dogs ⎯⎯⎯ play.

21. We felt the plane ⎯⎯⎯ move.

22. I expect ⎯⎯⎯ receive a letter.

Lesson 21

23. I'm expecting _____ receive a letter.

24. Do you often watch her _____ play tennis?

25. Are you going to watch her _____ play tennis?

Exercise 3 (B, pp. 234–36)
Wish for the opposite by supplying the correct answer.

They aren't here. I wish they __were__ here.

1. He doesn't want to help me. I wish he _____ to help me.

2. I don't know that girl. I wish I _____ that girl.

3. She won't arrive early. I wish she _____ early.

4. Peter doesn't speak slowly. I wish that Peter _____ slowly.

5. Susan doesn't speak English. I wish that Susan _____ English.

6. We don't have enough money to buy a car. I wish we _____ enough money to buy a car.

7. You can't come to my party. I wish you _____ come to my party.

8. He won't talk to his sister. I wish he _____ to his sister.

9. I am not tall. I wish I _____ tall.

10. I can't speak French. I wish I _____ speak French.

Exercise 4 (B, pp. 234–36)

Wish for the opposite situation by changing the verb and the italicized word.

John speaks *slowly*. I wish John __**spoke**__ __**rapidly**__ .

1. The test will be *difficult*. I wish the test _____ be _____ .

2. Your sister is *sick*. I wish your sister _____ _____ .

3. They eat *fast*. I wish they _____ _____ .

4. The store is *closed* now. I wish the store _____ _____ now.

5. My answers are *wrong*. I wish my answers _____ _____ .

6. She is *absent* today. I wish she _____ _____ today.

7. I live in the *city*. I wish I _____ in the _____ .

8. Today is *Monday*. I wish today _____ _____ .

9. The teacher gives *difficult* tests. I wish the teacher _____ _____ tests.

10. Those pants are *expensive*. I wish those pants _____ _____ .

Lesson 21

Exercise 5 (B, pp. 234–36)
Wish for the opposite by writing the correct answer on the line.

Coffee is expensive.

I wish coffee **weren't** expensive.

Ann has a bad cold.

I wish Ann **didn't have** a bad cold.

1. A new car costs a lot of money.

   I wish a new car _____ a lot of money.

2. He works six days every week.

   I wish he _____ six days every week.

3. I have to study now.

   I wish I _____ to study now.

4. The grammar test has fifty questions.

   I wish the grammar test _____ fifty questions.

5. Our class begins early in the morning.

   I wish our class _____ early in the morning.

6. I speak with an accent.

   I wish I _____ with an accent.

7. I have a big test tomorrow.

   I wish I _____ a big test tomorrow.

8. The test will be difficult.

   I wish the test _____ be difficult.

9. I need fifty more dollars to buy that radio.

   I wish I _____ fifty more dollars to buy that radio.

10. My car uses a lot of gasoline.

    I wish my car _____ a lot of gasoline.

296

Exercise 6   (B, pp. 234–36)
Read the problem, and then fill in the missing words to wish for the opposite. Follow the examples.

Problem	*Wish*
1. I am not well.	I wish I **were** well.
2. I am sick.	I wish I **weren't** sick.
3. You are not here.	I wish you _____ here.
4. She is sad.	I wish she _____ sad.
5. I speak slowly.	I wish I _____ fast.
6. I speak slowly.	I wish I _____ slowly.
7. He has a cold.	I wish he _____ a cold.
8. You eat fast.	I wish you _____ fast.
9. I have a cold.	I wish I _____ a cold.
10. They work at night.	I wish they _____ at night.
11. She isn't ready.	I wish she _____ ready.
12. I am not tall.	I wish I _____ tall.
13. I don't have a car.	I wish I _____ a car.
14. He doesn't understand.	I wish he _____ .
15. He doesn't write well.	I wish he _____ well.
16. They aren't rich.	I wish they _____ rich.
17. They don't like my food.	I wish they _____ my food.
18. She speaks fast.	I wish she _____ slowly.
19. She speaks fast.	I wish she _____ fast.
20. They don't know her.	I wish they _____ her.

Exercise 7   (B, pp. 234–36)
Wish for the opposite situation by completing the statement with a short response.

I can't go with you, but I wish I ___**could**___ .

I am too tired to go, but I wish I **weren't** .

1. She isn't a good cook, but she wishes she _____ .

2. Mr. Sims will be late, but we wish he _____ .

3. He's never early, but he wishes he _____ .

4. It's raining now, but I wish it _____ .

5. He can't speak English, but I wish he _____ .

6. They don't have a car, but they wish they _____ .

7. They have a big car, but they wish they _____ .

8. She always loses her keys, but she wishes she _____ .

9. I don't understand this homework, but I wish I _____ .

10. They don't read very fast, but they wish they _____ .

11. He has a lot of bills, but he wishes he _____ .

12. It rains every day in the summer, but everyone wishes it _____ .

13. They don't know the answer, but they wish they _____ .

14. He can't go to class tomorrow, but he wishes he _____ .

15. He will not go to the party this afternoon, but we wish he _____ .

Exercise 8   (C, pp. 237–38)
Read the first sentence, and then complete the second one with a question word + *to* + verb.

Should she buy this book or that book?

She doesn't know ___**which to buy**___ .

1. We know what we should do. We know _____ .

2. They don't know if they should leave in the morning or in the afternoon.

They don't know _____ .

3. Should we invite Susan or Mary?

    We don't know _____ .

4. "Do you think they will arrive on time?"

    "Of course. I told them _____ ."

5. I'm not sure if I should stay for five days or one week.

    I must decide _____ .

6. Can I get there better by bus or by plane?

    I'd like to know _____ there.

7. Should we send $50 or $100?

    He told us _____ .

8. "Do you think Joe will make enough food?"

    "Yes, I told him _____ ."

9. "Does Mary know how to cook the food?"

    "Yes, I told her _____ the food."

10. "Did Paul buy the right forks for the dinner?"

    "Yes, he knew _____ ."

Exercise 9: Review Test
A. Underline the correct answer.

1. She asked me (help, to help) her (study, to study).
2. We advised them (go, to go) in August.
3. Those people let us (drive, to drive) their car.
4. I saw them (go, to go) to the airport.

B. Wish for the opposite by writing the missing words.

1. We don't speak English well. We wish we _____ English well.

2. My sister is tall. She wishes she _____ tall.

3. Peter will arrive late. I wish he _____ arrive early.

4. They have to study. They wish they _____ to study.

5. It is expensive. I wish it _____ cheap.

C. Complete the second sentence with a question word + *to* + verb.

1. We don't know if we should arrive at 8 P.M. or 9 P.M. We don't know _____

   _____ .

2. Should they bring $15 or $20? They don't know _____ .

3. Will we invite Joe or his brother? We don't know _____ .

4. What should they do first? They don't know _____ first.

Exercise 10: Review Test
Choose the correct answer. Put a circle around the letter of the answer.

1. "Can you go with us tomorrow?"
   "No, I can't, but I wish I _____ ."
   a) can
   b) could
   c) went
   d) could have

2. "Will they arrive on time?"
   "Yes. I told them _____ to get here."
   a) which
   b) where
   c) when
   d) whom

3. They _____ us to do the work.
   a) wanted
   b) watched
   c) saw
   d) let

4. "Did Mary go to the store?"
   "Yes, but she didn't know _____ buy."
   a) what
   b) what to
   c) when
   d) when to

5. "Did the bus move?"

   "Yes, we felt _____ ."

   a) move it

   b) it move

   c) it to move

   d) to it move

6. "The weather is really bad."

   "Yes, I wish it _____ ."

   a) didn't rain

   b) doesn't rain

   c) weren't raining

   d) wasn't raining

7. "Will he go to France next month?"

   "Yes, but he wishes he _____ to go."

   a) hadn't

   b) hasn't

   c) didn't have

   d) doesn't have

8. We wish we knew _____ French well.

   a) speak

   b) to speak

   c) how speak

   d) how to speak

9. "Do you need more gas in your car?"

   "No, I had the man _____ my car yesterday."

   a) fill

   b) to fill

   c) how fill

   d) how to fill

10. "Are you leaving now?"

    "Yes, I am. I wish I _____ more time to talk, but I must get home now."

    a) have

    b) had

    c) doesn't have

    d) didn't have

Lesson 22

A. *Must have, might have, should have, could have*

B. *Must have* with progressive forms: must have been going

C. Short answers: Did they go? They must have.

D. Wish sentences in the past: I wish you had visited them.

Vocabulary List

cough	karate	mud	souvenir
could have	knock	must have	thief
discourage	lecture	refuse	tools
dorm	mayor	should have	valuable
generous	message	sneeze	wreck
hurricane	might have		

Exercise 1 (A, pp. 239–43)

Read these conversations between two people, and then underline the correct answer.

"Did you know that Mary didn't pass the test?"

"Yes, I did. She really (<u>should</u>, must) have studied more."

1. "Was yesterday's class interesting?"

   "Yes, it was. You (should, might) have been here."
2. "Paul was absent."

   "Yes, he (should, must) have been sick."
3. "Did you go to Europe?"

   "I (could, must) have gone there, but I went to Japan instead."
4. "John didn't answer his telephone when I called, but I'm sure he was at home."

   "Well, he (should, might) have been in the shower."
5. "She didn't pass the test, but she had studied a lot."

   "Well, the test (must, can) have been very difficult."
6. "My father bought two new cars for our family."

   "He (should, must) have spent a lot of money."
7. "John went to a party last night, and he didn't have his report in class today."

   "He (might, should) have been at the library last night."
8. "Did you need this map of the city?"

   "Yes, it (must, might) have helped me to find the building that I was looking for."
9. "My brother has never liked sports, but yesterday he played basketball for a few hours!"

   "He (could, must) have been very tired when he finished."

10. "Does your father already know about the trip?"

"Yes, he does. My mother (must, should) have told him."

11. "Did you help your sister?"

"I (should, could) have helped her, but I wasn't able to."

12. "Jane was very sick."

"She (shouldn't, must not) have gone outside without a coat."

13. "I don't have any money now."

"You (shouldn't, must not) have spent all of your money last night."

14. "He wrote his answers with a pen. The teacher said to use a pencil."

"He (shouldn't, must not) have understood the instructions."

15. "The new student tried to talk to me, but he doesn't speak much English."

"Well, I (couldn't, shouldn't) have helped you because I only speak English."

16. "Where did he lose his passport?"

"He (might, should) have left it on the plane."

17. "Why did he lose his passport?"

"He (might not, should not) have been very careful."

18. "John has a black eye today."

"He (should, must) have had a fight with someone."

19. "My clock is broken, and I woke up late today."

"Why didn't you tell me? I (must, could) have called you this morning."

20. "It's possible that the mailman has already come."

"Yes, he (might, will) have come while we were shopping."

Lesson 22

Exercise 2 (A, pp. 239–43)
Read the sentences, and then write a new sentence with the correct modal.

Does Mary speak Spanish? (I conclude that she does.)

_____ Mary must speak Spanish. _____

Did she do the work? (I conclude that she did.)

_____ She must have done the work. _____

1. Is John a good student? (It's possible.)

_____

2. Was he a good tennis player? (I conclude that he was.)

_____

3. Did Mary study for the test? (It was desirable, but she didn't.)

_____

4. Will Mary study for the test? (She ought to.)

_____

5. Did they eat lunch? (They had the opportunity, but they didn't.)

_____

6. Does Paul like hamburgers? (I conclude that he does.)

_____

7. Did we spend too much money? (It's possible.)

_____

8. Did George eat all of the bread? (I conclude that he did.)

_____

9. Were they here yesterday? (They had the opportunity, but they weren't.)

_____

10. Did it rain last night? (It's possible, but I'm not sure.)

_____

Exercise 3 (B, pp. 244–46)
Write these sentences again with a past modal. Use a progressive verb form with the modal.

It is possible that John was sleeping.

John might have been sleeping.

1. It's possible that it was raining last night.

2. I conclude that she was studying for a long time.

3. It's not possible that John was studying last night.

4. It was desirable for him to go to class every day, but he didn't.

5. I conclude that Paul wasn't doing all of the homework.

6. He ought to have been saving his money, but he wasn't.

7. It's possible that Ben was eating dinner when I called.

8. I conclude that he was eating dinner when I called.

9. Sam wasn't studying last night. He didn't pass the test today.

10. It's impossible that you were talking to Tim at noon.

Exercise 4   (A–B, pp. 239–46)
Read the situation, and write a sentence with a modal to describe the situation. Use *-ing* if it is necessary.

Peter missed class last week. (might)

_____Peter might have been sick._____

She didn't eat breakfast, lunch, or dinner yesterday. (must)

_____She must have been hungry last night._____

1. Jane was putting a stamp on an envelope when I saw her at the post office. (must)

   _____

2. It was cold, but she wasn't wearing a coat. (should)

   _____

3. I understand French, but I didn't help the new students from France. (could)

   _____

4. I had the opportunity to study, but I wasn't studying last night. (could)

   _____

5. Mark didn't have any money because he forgot to go to the bank. (should)

   _____

Exercise 5   (C, pp. 247–48)
Give a short answer to these questions.

Should they have studied more?

Yes, __they should have__ .

1. Might she have lost all the money?

   Yes, _____ .

2. Might she have been studying?

   Yes, _____ .

3. Could they have been sleeping?

   No, _____ .

4. Could they have stolen the money?

    No, _____ .

5. Should Joe have called us sooner?

    Yes, _____ .

6. Should you have been reading your book?

    Yes, _____ .

7. Could you have used another person to help you?

    Yes, _____ .

8. Should I have called you earlier?

    No, _____ .

9. Should he have worked all day?

    Yes, _____ .

10. Should he have been working all day?

    Yes, _____ .

Exercise 6   (C, pp. 247–48)
Read the statement, and then complete the sentence with *but*.

   I didn't study, __**but I should have**__ .
   (*I had the obligation to study*)

1. I thought they hadn't studied last night, _____ .
   (*it was possible*)

2. Sue doesn't believe she spent the money, _____ .
   (*she concludes that she spent it*)

3. We didn't go to Florida, _____ .
   (*we had the opportunity to go*)

4. They said they had been swimming, _____ .
   (*it was not possible*)

5. He wasn't working, _____ .
   (*he had the opportunity*)

Exercise 7 (D, pp. 249–51)
Wish for the opposite by changing the verbs.

They weren't here. I wish they **had been** here.

1. The new car cost a lot of money. I wish the new car _____ a lot of money.

2. I didn't know that girl. I wish I _____ that girl.

3. She arrived late. I wish she _____ late.

4. Peter spoke loudly. I wish Peter _____ loudly.

5. Susan didn't speak English. I wish Susan _____ English.

6. We didn't have enough money. I wish we _____ enough money.

7. You weren't able to come to my party. I wish you _____ able to come to my party.

8. He didn't help us study. I wish he _____ us study.

9. It was raining. I wish it _____ raining.

10. I was too busy to leave home. I wish I _____ too busy to leave home.

Exercise 8 (D, pp. 249–51)
Wish for the opposite by changing the verb to past perfect and then writing the opposite of the adjective/adverb.

Joe *spoke rapidly*. I wish Joe **had spoken slowly** .

1. The test *was difficult*. I wish the test _____ .

2. Your sister *was sick*. I wish your sister _____ .

3. They *ate* dinner *fast*. I wish they _____ .

4. The store *was closed*. I wish the store _____ .

5. I *wrote* the *wrong* answer. I wish I _____ .

6. He *drove fast*. I wish he _____ .

7. They *arrived late*. I wish they _____ .

8. The teacher *explained* the words *rapidly*. I wish the teacher _____

_____ .

9. The homework *was difficult*. I wish the homework _____ .

10. The watches *were expensive*. I wish the watches _____ .

Exercise 9   (D, pp. 249–51)
Wish for the opposite situation. Use the short form of the predicate.

He didn't understand, but he wishes ___**he had**___ .

They are sick, but I wish **they weren't** ___ .

1. He can't help us, but I wish _____ .

2. They don't speak English, but they wish _____ .

3. I wasn't studying, but I wish _____ .

4. She wasn't here, but she wishes _____ .

5. She isn't here, but she wishes _____ .

6. They arrived late, but they wish _____ .

7. She is always hungry, but she wishes _____ .

8. Peter wasn't early, but now he wishes _____ .

9. I bought a new car, but I wish _____ .

10. I never study, but I wish _____ .

11. We like chocolate, but our doctor wishes _____ .

12. He ate chocolate, but he wishes _____ .

13. They won't call me, but I wish _____ .

14. She didn't understand, but now she wishes _____ .

15. We were visiting them, but we wish _____ .

16. We were there, but we wish _____ .

17. We are here, but we wish _____ .

18. He eats a lot, but he wishes _____ .

19. He ate a lot, but he wishes _____ .

20. They can't play well, but they wish _____ .

Exercise 10: Review Test

A. Underline the correct answer.

1. We (should, must) have studied more. Our tests were very bad.
2. They (must, should) have been drinking milk. Here are their glasses, and there is a little milk in them.
3. John (couldn't, must not) have gone to France. It's impossible.
4. They (might, should) have heard us. It's possible.
5. He had the opportunity to go, but he didn't. He (could, should) have gone.
6. I didn't understand him. I (must, should) have listened better.

B. Write the correct short answer.

1. Did you call? (it was desirable)

   No, but I _____ .

2. Did they call you? (it was impossible)

   No, they _____ .

3. Were they eating? (I conclude they were)

   Yes, they _____ .

C. Wish for the opposite. Use the short form.

1. They didn't understand, but they wish _____ .

2. We weren't at the party, but we wish _____ .

3. She went there, but she wishes _____ .

4. It wasn't raining, but I wish _____ .

Exercise 11: Review Test
Choose the correct answer. Put a circle around the letter of the answer.

1. "Did you pass the test?"
   "No, I didn't. I wish I ____ more."
   a) study
   b) studied
   c) was studying
   d) had studied

2. "Did Pete fall asleep in class again today?"
   "Yes, he did. The teacher told him that he ____ gone to bed earlier last night."
   a) must have
   b) must had
   c) should have
   d) should had

3. John read Martha's letters, but he wishes he ____ .
   a) doesn't
   b) didn't
   c) hasn't
   d) hadn't

4. "Is it possible that they were sick?"
   "No, they ____ sick."
   a) could not be
   b) must not be
   c) couldn't have been
   d) must not have been

5. "My brother is in your class. I suppose that you know him."
   "Well, I ____ met him, but I don't remember."
   a) should
   b) must
   c) should have
   d) must have

6. France was very expensive. I wish I ____ to Japan.
   a) went
   b) was
   c) had gone
   d) hadn't went

7. "Is the car clean now?"
   "Yes, someone ____ washed it."
   a) must have
   b) must have been
   c) should have
   d) should have been

8. It was raining very hard, but we wish it ____ .
   a) wasn't
   b) weren't
   c) hadn't been
   d) hasn't been

9. "Did you hear that Mr. Smith was a famous tennis player a few years ago?"
   "Yes, I did. He ____ have been very good."
   a) must
   b) will
   c) should
   d) can

10. "Did you eat dinner twice?"
    "I ____ twice, but I didn't."
    a) might eat
    b) should eat
    c) could have eaten
    d) must have eaten

311

Lesson 23

A. Subordinators: *if, unless, because, although, whether, whenever*

B. *Because of, in spite of, regardless of*

Vocabulary List

although	climate	if	unless
because	freely	in spite of	whenever
because of	hold up	regardless of	whether
carefree			

Exercise 1   (A.1, pp. 252–53)
Read the sentence, and then write *if* or *unless*.

She will arrive on time __**if**__ she doesn't wake up late.

She will arrive on time __**unless**__ she wakes up late.

1. I will pay the rent _____ you don't have enough money.

2. I will pay the rent _____ you have enough money.

3. We won't pass the test _____ we study.

4. We won't pass the test _____ we don't study.

5. They will call us _____ they need our help.

6. They won't call us _____ they need our help.

7. You will be late _____ you don't hurry.

8. You will be late _____ you hurry.

9. We can go _____ the tickets aren't too expensive.

10. It won't snow _____ the weather gets colder.

11. He'll get angry _____ you don't clean his room.

12. I'll stay home _____ they invite me to their party.

13. _____ the food is very good, we'll eat it.

14. _____ everyone can go, I don't want to go.

15. _____ we hurry, we'll be late for sure.

312

Exercise 2 (A.1, pp. 252–53)
Change the sentences with *if* to *unless* and those with *unless* to *if*.

I won't go if they don't invite me.

I won't go unless they invite me.

We'll be late unless we hurry up.

We'll be late if we don't hurry up.

1. They will do the work if they don't go to the party.

_____

2. He can't learn English if he doesn't study.

_____

3. We will call off the party unless the rain stops.

_____

4. She can't buy a new car if she doesn't get a job.

_____

5. I won't study unless it's necessary.

_____

Exercise 3 (A.2, pp. 253–54)
Read the sentence, and then write *because* or *although*.

I called him __because__ he told me to.

1. We didn't eat _____ we were on a diet.

2. They failed the test _____ they had studied.

3. Mary is popular _____ she is very nice.

4. I went by plane _____ I like to fly.

5. She wore a coat _____ it was very cold.

6. He speaks Spanish very well _____ he only studied it for two semesters.

7. He continued to work _____ he was very tired.

8. The girls cried _____ they were sad.

9. We went there by car _____ it was cheaper than going by bus.

10. They need more paper _____ they ran out of it.

11. _____ it's hot, we turned on the air conditioner.

12. _____ it was late, we hurried.

13. _____ she had studied, Jane made an excellent grade on the test.

14. _____ I was sick, I went to work yesterday.

15. _____ I was sick, I didn't go to class.

Exercise 4   (A.2, pp. 253–54)
Read the two sentences, and then write a new sentence with *because* or *although*.

I have to study. I have a big test.

_____ I have to study because I have a big test. _____

1. We don't like the summer. It's too hot.

_____

2. They aren't going to buy the car. They have enough money.

_____

3. She's very tall. All of her brothers are short.

_____

4. She's very tall. Both of her parents are tall.

_____

5. My watch was expensive. It is made of gold.

_____

Exercise 5   (A.3, pp. 254–55)
Read the sentences, and then underline the correct answer.

I will go to New York, but John must go with me.
I'll go to New York (if John goes, whether or not John goes).

1. He always wears a raincoat. The weather isn't important to him.
   He wears a raincoat (if it's raining, whether it's raining or not).
2. Mary usually studies. She studies every night.
   She studies (if she has a test, whether or not she has a test).
3. We are going to play tennis. We don't have to wait for Paul.
   We will play tennis (if Paul comes, whether Paul comes or not).
4. They will cook dinner. They can cook without my help.
   They'll cook dinner (if I help them, whether or not I help them).
5. I would like to open the door. I need my keys.
   I'll open the door (if I find my keys, whether or not I find my keys).
6. John always knows the words. He doesn't have to study.
   He always knows the words (if he looks them over, whether or not he looks them over).
7. I want to eat lunch. I only like steak.
   I'll eat at Bob's house (if he cooks steak, whether or not he cooks steak).
8. They want to take a trip to France. They have a lot of money to spend.
   They'll go to France (if the ticket is cheap, whether or not it is cheap).
9. He likes to read. He only reads good books.
   He'll read the new book (if it's interesting, whether it's interesting or not).
10. He wants to mail a letter. He needs a stamp.
    He'll mail the letter (if he gets a stamp, whether or not he gets a stamp).

Exercise 6   (B, pp. 255–56)
Read the sentence and write *because* or *because of*.

We were tired **because** we had run five miles.

1. We didn't have a picnic _____ it was raining.

2. We didn't have a picnic _____ the rain.

3. I called Bob _____ I had a problem.

4. I called Bob _____ my problem.

5. She asked me _____ she thought I knew the answer.

6. _____ I didn't study, I failed the test.

7. _____ my bad grade, I didn't pass the course.

8. _____ the price, I decided to buy the radio.

9. We like him _____ his nice personality.

10. _____ he is a nice person, we like him a lot.

Exercise 7   (B, pp. 255–56)
Read the sentence and write *although* or *in spite of*.

I went to class **in spite of** my cold.

1. She didn't study _____ she knew about the test.

2. I ate the food _____ it wasn't very good.

3. I ate the food _____ the bad taste.

4. _____ the radio was expensive, I bought it.

5. He sent me a new television _____ it wasn't my birthday or Christmas.

6. He didn't wear a coat _____ the cold weather.

7. He is an excellent basketball player _____ he is very short.

8. My children attend that school _____ the distance they have to walk each morning.

9. She passed the test _____ the difficulty.

10. _____ the test was difficult, she passed it.

Exercise 8   (B, pp. 255–56)
Read the sentence and write *whether or not* or *regardless of*.

We'll travel tomorrow **whether or not** it's snowing.

1. We'll travel _____ the weather.

2. They'll call _____ the time.

3. I plan to buy a car _____ it costs a lot.

4. _____ you can come with me, I'm going to Atlanta.

316

5. _____ the length of the book, I'm sure I won't have any problems reading it.

6. She always makes good grades _____ the subject.

7. He can pronounce a word _____ he has heard it before.

8. We didn't know _____ they had eaten lunch.

9. He'll buy steak for dinner _____ the price.

10. _____ his plans, the other family members will celebrate Christmas at home this year.

Exercise 9 (B, pp. 255–56)

Read the sentence and write *because, because of, although, in spite of, whether or not,* or *regardless of.*

We didn't go **because of** the bad weather.

We didn't go **because** the weather was bad.

1. He gave us more money _____ we didn't need it.

2. The weather is cold, but he'll go outside _____ it.

3. We'll go next week _____ the weather.

4. She ate again _____ she had just eaten dinner.

5. I would like to stop at a restaurant that serves chicken, but I'll stop at the next restaurant _____ the type of food they serve.

6. Mary says that the food is very salty. We'll eat it _____ the taste.

7. We heard the song _____ the batteries were weak.

8. John played tennis yesterday _____ he was very tired.

9. We'll read any book _____ its topic or length.

10. We'll read that book with seven hundred pages _____ its length.

Lesson 23

Exercise 10 (B, pp. 255–56)

Read the first sentence, and then complete the second one with *because of, regardless of,* or *in spite of* and a noun.

We didn't go because the weather was bad.

We didn't go ___because of the bad weather_____ .

1. They will buy a ticket whether or not it's expensive.

   They will buy a ticket _____ .

2. I was late because it was raining.

   I was late _____ .

3. We will read the book whether or not it is long.

   We'll read the book _____ .

4. John was happy although he had made a bad grade.

   John was happy _____ .

5. We took the trip although the ticket was expensive.

   We took the trip _____ .

Exercise 11 (B, pp. 255–56)

Underline the correct answer.

   We didn't go (because, <u>because of</u>) the rain.
   She was studying (<u>although</u>, in spite of) she didn't have a test.
   They eat steak (whether or not, <u>regardless of</u>) the price.

   1. She likes candy (because, because of) it's sweet.
   2. She likes it (because, because of) the taste.
   3. We bought the ticket (although, in spite of) the cost.
   4. We bought it (although, in spite of) it was expensive.
   5. I will go (whether or not, regardless of) John agrees to go.
   6. I will go (whether or not, regardless of) John's decision.
   7. Peter ate the food (because, because of) he was hungry.
   8. Mary walks to class (although, in spite of) the distance.
   9. He will be on time (whether or not, regardless of) the weather.
   10. We left (because, because of) we didn't like the movie.

11. I get up early (whether or not, regardless of) I have to.

12. Bob was laughing (because, because of) John's joke.

13. Students should study (although, in spite of) they don't want to.

14. He'll do the work (whether or not, regardless of) he is paid well.

15. She was crying (because, because of) the onions.

16. (Whether or not, Regardless of) the time, I will call you.

17. I went to class (although, in spite of) I didn't want to.

18. She got sick (although, in spite of) the flight was very pleasant.

19. She got sick (although, in spite of) the pleasant flight.

20. (Because, Because of) the bad weather, we couldn't drive home.

Exercise 12: Review Test
Underline the correct answer.

1. We will go (if, unless) the weather isn't bad.

2. She wore a coat (because, although) it was very cold.

3. They will learn English (if, unless) they always speak Spanish outside of class.

4. She wore a heavy coat (because, although) the weather was warm.

5. I need Paul to go with me. I'll go (whether or not, if) Paul goes.

6. John will call me (if, although) he has time.

7. I always study. I study (whether or not, if) I have a test.

8. She called (because, because of) she had a problem.

9. It is very cold (because, because of) it's winter.

10. They will call (whether or not, regardless of) it's late.

11. They will call (whether or not, regardless of) the time.

12. Suzy came to class yesterday (although, in spite of) she was sick.

13. She ate cake and ice cream (although, in spite of) her diet.

14. Please call me (if, unless) you need to.

15. Please call me (if, unless) it's necessary.

16. They bought a car (because, although) it was expensive.

17. I'll use a pencil (if, although) I can find one.

18. Mary always cooks a lot of food (whether or not, regardless of) she is expecting a lot of guests.

19. The store was still open (although, in spite of) the time.

20. We ate the potatoes (because, although) they didn't taste very good.

Exercise 13: Review Test
Choose the correct answer. Put a circle around the letter of the answer.

1. We were late _____ the weather
   was very bad.
   a) although
   b) because
   c) in spite of
   d) regardless of

2. We will be on time _____ we run.
   a) if
   b) unless
   c) although
   d) whether

3. They bought the car _____ the good price.
   a) in spite of
   b) because of
   c) unless
   d) if

4. I went _____ I didn't have to.
   a) in spite of
   b) regardless of
   c) although
   d) whether

5. "Can you go if it's raining?"
   "I can go _____ it's raining."
   a) whether or not
   b) regardless of
   c) in spite of
   d) because

6. "Did you like the beach?"
   "Yes, I liked it _____ the rainy weather."
   a) although
   b) because
   c) in spite of
   d) whether or not

7. Peter ate the food _____ he was
   very hungry.
   a) because of
   b) because
   c) in spite of
   d) in spite

8. _____ it was late, we went to sleep.
   a) Although
   b) Because
   c) Whether
   d) Unless

9. "That house costs half a million dollars!"
   "Yes, but he's going to buy it
   _____ the price."
   a) because
   b) although
   c) regardless
   d) in spite of

10. "Did you eat the dinner that Mary cooked?"
    "Yes, I ate it _____ I knew that
    Mary's cooking is never good."
    a) because
    b) although
    c) in spite of
    d) regardless of

Lesson 24

A. Conditional sentences:
      If he knows the answer, he will tell her.
      If he knew the answer, he would tell her.
      If he had known the answer, he would have told her.

Vocabulary List

ball-point pen	college	mine (noun)	raise
bill	millionaire	postcard	

Exercise 1 (A, p. 257)
Read the sentence, and then write the correct form of the verbs on the line. Pay close attention to the adverbials of time in the sentences. Follow the examples.

    get   *buy*

1. If he __gets__ his check, he __will buy__ a dog tomorrow.

2. If he _____ his check, he _____ a dog right now.

3. If he _____ his check, he _____ a dog last week.

    come   *be*

4. If Bob _____ to class tomorrow, we _____ surprised.

5. If Bob _____ to class right now, we _____ surprised.

6. If Bob _____ to class yesterday, we _____ surprised.

    have   *take*

7. If he _____ a cold tomorrow, he _____ some aspirin.

8. If he _____ a cold right now, he _____ some aspirin.

9. If he _____ a cold last night, he _____ some aspirin.

Lesson 24

	make		*work*

10. She _____ more money tomorrow if she _____ very hard.

11. She _____ more money this week if she _____ very hard.

12. She _____ more money last month if she _____ very hard.

        study   *pass*

13. If she _____ , she _____ all of her tests next week.

14. If she _____ , she _____ all of her tests this week.

15. If she _____ , she _____ all of her tests last week.

        do   *be*

16. I _____ things better next year if I _____ president.

17. I _____ things better now if I _____ president.

18. I _____ things better last year if I _____ president.

Exercise 2 (A, pp. 257–59)

Complete the verbs in these statements about a student who is thinking about what will happen to him in the future. Follow the examples.

1. (study/pass) If I **study** very hard, I **will pass** the TOEFL.*

2. (pass/enter) If I _____ the TOEFL, I _____ the university.

3. (enter/be) If I _____ the university, I _____ a university student.

4. (be/have) If I _____ a university student, I _____ to study very hard.

5. (have/make) If I _____ to study very hard, I _____ good grades.

6. (make/receive) If I _____ good grades, I _____ a degree with honors.

7. (receive/get) If I _____ a degree with honors, I _____ a good job.

_____

*TOEFL = Test of English as a Foreign Language. This test is required for university admission of students whose native language is not English.

322

Exercise 3 (A, pp. 257–60)
Complete the verbs in these sentences about a person who is thinking about what would happen to him if he received some money right now. Follow the examples.

1. (receive/put) If I **received** $1,000, I **would put** half of it in the bank.

2. (put/have) If I _____ half of it in the bank, I _____ $500.

3. (have/take) If I _____ $500, I _____ a trip.

4. (take/go) If I _____ a trip, I _____ to Canada.

5. (go/visit) If I _____ to Canada, I _____ my friends.

6. (visit/have) If I _____ my friends, I _____ a good time.

7. (have/stay) If I _____ a good time, I _____ as long as possible.

Exercise 4 (A, pp. 257–62)
Complete the verbs in these statements about a student who is thinking about what would have happened to him if he had gone to class yesterday. Follow the examples.

1. (go/know) If I **had gone** to class yesterday, I **would have known** about the composition.

2. (know/do) If I _____ about the composition, I _____ it.

3. (do/write) If I _____ it, I _____ about my family.

4. (write/be) If I _____ about my family, my paper _____ interesting.

5. (be/like) If my paper _____ interesting, the teacher _____ it.

6. (like/get) If the teacher _____ it, I _____ a good grade.

7. (get/be) If I _____ a good grade, I _____ very happy.

Lesson 24

Exercise 5 (A, pp. 257–62)
Answer these questions with complete sentences. Begin your answer with *if*.

What would you do if you were rich?

If I were rich, I would take a big trip.

What will you do if your cat is hungry?

If my cat is hungry, I will feed it.

What would you have done if it had been raining?

If it had been raining, I would have stayed home.

1. What will you do if the ticket is expensive?

   _____

2. What will you do if you have a test?

   _____

3. What would you have done if they had invited you?

   _____

4. What would you buy if you went to Switzerland?

   _____

5. What would you have drunk if you hadn't drunk water?

   _____

6. What would you have studied if you had studied last night?

   _____

7. What will you say if someone tells you "Thank you"?

   _____

8. What would you speak if you lived in France?

   _____

9. What will you do if your car has a flat tire?

   _____

10. What would you have done if you hadn't had enough money?

    _____

Exercise 6 (A, pp. 257–62)
Write the correct verb form on the line.

(see) If I __had seen__ you, I would have told you the news.

1. (get) If I _____ my check, I'll go to the bank.

2. (be) We would begin eating if Joe _____ here.

3. (do) If I _____ my homework, I would have passed the test.

4. (eat) I _____ the cake if I had been hungry.

5. (hear) If I _____ any news, I'll call you.

6. (go) If it weren't raining now, we _____ to the beach.

7. (play) If I had my racket, I _____ tennis with you.

8. (wear) I _____ a suit if I go to the party.

9. (need) If I make a cake, I _____ some sugar.

10. (be) If I _____ you, I wouldn't do that.

Exercise 7 (A, pp. 257–62)
Write the correct verb form on the line.

(see) If I __see__ him, I'll tell him you're looking for him.

1. (be) If you _____ still sick tomorrow, you will have to go to the doctor.

2. (eat) If I _____ that food, I'll get sick.

3. (do) If you _____ your homework, you would have known all the answers.

4. (have) If she _____ a television, she wouldn't have been bored.

5. (get) He will let me know if the cat _____ sick again.

6. (write) If he _____ that letter yesterday, he wouldn't have had to do it today.

7. (cook) If I buy the food, she _____ it.

8. (call) If John had arrived home, he —————————————— me already.

9. (be) If it —————————————— raining, we wouldn't drive to Atlanta.

10. (lend) Susan —————————————— you the money that you need if she had enough.

Exercise 8: Review Test
Write the correct form of the verb on the line.

1. (have) I will study if we —————————————— a test.

2. (buy) I —————————————— some watches if I went to Germany.

3. (eat) I would have spent too much money if I —————————————— more food.

4. (be) If he —————————————— late tomorrow, he —————————————— in trouble.

5. (see) If I —————————————— you, I would have told you the news.

6. (work) If I —————————————— there, I would make a lot of money.

7. (write) If she had remembered, she —————————————— you a letter.

8. (run) Paul would have won the race if he —————————————— faster.

9. (play) She will be tired if she —————————————— tennis tonight.

10. (be) If it —————————————— raining, we wouldn't go.

11. (call) If she had a phone, I —————————————— her now.

12. (go) If they had invited me, I —————————————— with them.

13. (read) If she gives me a book, I —————————————— it.

14. (study) I —————————————— another lesson if I had had more time.

15. (fly) If she —————————————— here, she would have arrived last night instead of this morning.

Exercise 9: Review Test
Choose the correct answer. Put a circle around the letter of the answer.

1. If you were my friends, you _____ me.
   a) helped
   b) will help
   c) would help
   d) would have helped

2. Peter _____ if we invite him.
   a) will come
   b) does come
   c) would have come
   d) might have come

3. If George _____ sick, he would have gone to the doctor.
   a) were
   b) was
   c) would have been
   d) had been

4. We would study if we _____ a test.
   a) had
   b) have
   c) had had
   d) would have had

5. "Can you help me?"
   "I'll help you tomorrow if I _____ enough time."
   a) have had
   b) have
   c) had
   d) will have

6. If she had been sad, she _____ a lot.
   a) cried
   b) will cry
   c) would have cried
   d) would cry

7. "Are you sure that you don't know him?"
   "Well, if he _____ in my class last semester, I would know him."
   a) was
   b) were
   c) had been
   d) would be

8. If it's raining, we _____ have the picnic.
   a) don't
   b) won't
   c) wouldn't
   d) couldn't

9. If you _____ here, you would have had a great time.
   a) were
   b) would be
   c) had been
   d) would have been

10. If I ask my father and he agrees, I _____ his car.
    a) use
    b) uses
    c) will use
    d) would use

Lesson 25

A. *So . . . that:* so busy that he can't go; *such . . . that:* such a busy man that he can't go

B. Negative questions: Isn't the teacher here?

C. Tag questions: John is here, isn't he?

Vocabulary List

across	department	so	such
climb	fall asleep	soldier	ticket
comfortably	invent	speeding	twice

Exercise 1 (A, pp. 263–65)
Change the expressions with *so* to *such*.

The man is so busy. He is ___**such a busy man**___ .

1. The baby is so beautiful. She is _____ .

2. Today is so cold. This is _____ .

3. The car is so expensive. It is _____ .

4. The boy is so tall. He is _____ .

5. The books are so heavy. They are _____ .

6. The movie was so interesting. It was _____ .

7. The cats are so ugly. They are _____ .

8. Mark is so interesting. He is _____ .

9. That watch is so pretty. That is _____ .

10. His sister is so unhappy. She is _____ .

Exercise 2 (A, pp. 263–65)
Change the expressions with *such* to *so*.

He is such a busy man. The man is ___**so busy**___ .

1. This is such a dirty table. This table is _____ .

2. These are such expensive pants. These pants are _____ .

3. It is such a cold day. Today is _____ .

4. He was such a good student. The student was _____ .

5. This is such delicious wine. This wine is _____ .

6. That is such a heavy box. That box is _____ .

7. He is such an intelligent boy. That boy is _____ .

8. This is such a pretty picture. This picture is _____ .

9. These are such heavy boxes. These boxes are _____ .

10. Those are such nice shoes. Those shoes are _____ .

Exercise 3   (A, pp. 263–65)
Read the sentences, and then write *so, such a, such an,* or *such* on the line.

   Mr. Smith is __**so**__ tall that he can reach the ceiling.

   This is __**such a**__ good book.

1. Today is _____ cold day that I won't go to school.

2. You are _____ good friend that I would do anything for you.

3. My father is _____ intelligent that he had a scholarship when he was in college.

4. I'm _____ hungry that I could eat a horse.

5. They're _____ good children.

6. I'm _____ tired that I can't continue walking.

7. She's _____ nice person.

8. It's _____ cold outside that my dogs don't want to go out of the house.

9. You're _____ handsome boy that you must have many girlfriends.

10. They always write _____ good compositions.

Exercise 4 (A, pp. 263–65)
Read the situation, and then write two new sentences. Use *so . . . that* in the first one and *such . . . that* in the second one.

This book is boring. I can't read it.

> *This book is so boring that I can't read it.*
> *This is such a boring book that I can't read it.*

1. The weather is cold. There is ice on our car.

_____

_____

2. This car is too expensive for us to buy.

_____

_____

3. This lesson is easy. Everyone understands it.

_____

_____

4. Mark and Henry are nice. Everyone likes them.

_____

_____

5. The restaurant was good. We want to return as soon as possible.

_____

_____

Exercise 5 (B, pp. 266–67)
Write a negative question.

It's time to leave now. *Isn't it time to leave now?*

1. She is going to France. _____

2. They work in the bank. _____

3. He had a cold during the vacation. _____

4. It was raining when you arrived. _____

5. He speaks French. _____

6. He has been in Austria. _____

7. They had already done their work. _____

8. You ate dinner with John. _____

9. It has been snowing since Monday. _____

10. We should clean our room now. _____

Exercise 6   (B, pp. 266–67)
Give a short answer to the following questions.

Did you study?

Yes, ___I did___ .

1. Weren't you afraid?

   Yes, _____ .

2. Weren't you afraid?

   No, _____ .

3. Didn't he go home?

   Yes, _____ .

4. Don't they understand?

   No, _____ .

5. Aren't they early?

   No, _____ .

6. Isn't she your sister?

   Yes, _____ .

7. Can't he speak English?

   Yes, _____ .

8. Isn't there a test today?

   No, _____ .

9. Doesn't she have a car?

   Yes, _____ .

10. Can't she hear well?

    No, _____ .

Exercise 7 (C, pp. 267–68)

Write a tag question, and then give the expected short answer.

Paul is sick, __isn't he__ ?

__Yes, he is__ .

1. You can go, _____ ?

   _____ .

2. We're all ready, _____ ?

   _____ .

3. They don't have a car, _____ ?

   _____ .

4. We can't go, _____ ?

   _____ .

5. She's happy, _____ ?

   _____ .

6. It isn't raining, _____ ?

   _____ .

7. Bob didn't bring his books, _____ ?

   _____ .

8. She couldn't hear well, _____ ?

   _____ .

9. Peter speaks German, _____ ?

   _____ .

10. She won't call tonight, _____ ?

    _____ .

11. He wrote you another letter, _____ ?

    _____ .

12. You aren't hungry, _____ ?

_____ .

13. Sue will be ready, _____ ?

_____ .

14. She did the work, _____ ?

_____ .

15. I sent you the money, _____ ?

_____ .

16. He hasn't seen that movie yet, _____ ?

_____ .

17. She hadn't been late before, _____ ?

_____ .

18. There isn't much time, _____ ?

_____ .

19. They should study more, _____ ?

_____ .

20. They shouldn't come late, _____ ?

_____ .

Exercise 8: Review Test
A. Write *so* or *such*. Remember to use *a* or *an* when necessary.

1. She is _____ happy that she's crying.

2. He is _____ tall that he can touch the ceiling.

3. It is _____ good day that we might have a picnic.

4. The test was _____ difficult that nobody in my class passed it.

5. Mr. Smith was _____ hungry that he ate lunch twice.

6. That was _____ interesting movie that I want to see it again.

Lesson 25

B. Make negative questions.

1. She went to France. _____

2. They are here. _____

3. It's hot in here. _____

4. She has a car now. _____

C. Write a tag question, and then give the expected answer.

1. She's here, _____ ?

_____ .

2. They ate the rice, _____ ?

_____ .

3. It's been raining, _____ ?

_____ .

4. He didn't go, _____ ?

_____ .

5. We weren't late, _____ ?

_____ .

6. Joe will go with us, _____ ?

_____ .

Exercise 9: Review Test
Choose the correct answer. Put a circle around the letter of the answer.

1. This book is ____ difficult that we can't read it.
   a) such
   b) that
   c) so
   d) too

2. You're going tomorrow, _____ ?
   a) won't you
   b) aren't you
   c) will you
   d) are you

3. Mr. Smith is _____ busy that he is always tired.
   a) so
   b) too
   c) such
   d) such a

4. "Don't they have a new car?"
   "Yes, _____ ."
   a) they do
   b) they don't
   c) it does
   d) it doesn't

5. His hat is _____ small for me to wear.
   a) so
   b) too
   c) such
   d) such a

6. They spoke to you, _____ ?
   a) did they
   b) didn't they
   c) do they
   d) don't they

7. "Won't you be late to class?"
   "Yes, _____ ."
   a) I do
   b) I don't
   c) I will
   d) I won't

8. He's been sick for a long time, _____ ?
   a) isn't he
   b) doesn't he
   c) hasn't he
   d) wasn't he

9. "Will you have more coffee?"
   "Yes, this is _____ good coffee."
   a) too
   b) so
   c) such
   d) such a

10. They didn't go by ship, _____ ?
    a) did they
    b) they did
    c) didn't they
    d) they didn't

Lesson 26

A. *Self* pronouns: *myself, yourself*, etc.

B. Verb expressions in *-ing* after other verbs: I enjoyed singing.

Vocabulary List

alone	finish	itself	package
avoid	get through	keep (on)	sew
can't help	herself	mirror	themselves
consider	himself	myself	yourself
enjoy	insist on	ourselves	yourselves

Exercise 1 (A.1, p. 269)
Write the correct reflexive pronoun.

Mary __herself__

1. I _____ 6. we _____

2. you (sing.) _____ 7. you (pl.) _____

3. he _____ 8. they _____

4. she _____ 9. Bob _____

5. it _____ 10. the boys _____

Exercise 2 (A.1, pp. 269–70)
Read the situation, and then complete the sentences.

John wanted a cake. He made one.

John made __a cake for himself__ .

John made __himself a cake__ .

1. She wanted a chair. She found one.

She found _____ .

She found _____ .

2. I wanted a car. I bought one.

I bought _____ .

I bought _____ .

3. The boy likes to read a short story. He wrote one.

He wrote _____ .

He wrote _____ .

4. Paul needed some aspirin. He got some.

He got _____ .

He got _____ .

5. They needed some skirts. They sewed some.

They sewed _____ .

They sewed _____ .

6. We wanted some pie. We cut a piece.

We cut _____ .

We cut _____ .

7. He was thirsty. He poured a glass of milk.

He poured _____ .

He poured _____ .

8. We were hungry. We fried some fish.

We fried _____ .

We fried _____ .

9. Jack and Sue were hungry. They cooked some eggs.

They cooked _____ .

They cooked _____ .

10. Martha was cold. She got a sweater.

She got _____ .

She got _____ .

Lesson 26

Exercise 3   (A.2, pp. 270–71)
Use a reflexive pronoun for emphasis.

    I'll make lunch ____myself____ .

    She wrote that book ____herself____ .

1. Did you drive all the way here _____ ?

2. They bought a house _____ .

3. Did Joe read the whole book _____ ?

4. We ate the whole cake _____ .

5. Did Mary go to England _____ ?

6. I did the work _____ .

7. Paul saw the accident _____ .

8. We cooked all the food _____ .

9. Did you paint this picture _____ ?

10. He grew those vegetables _____ .

Exercise 4   (A.2, p. 271)
Use *by* + a reflexive pronoun to mean "alone."

    I live ____by myself____ .

    She's going ____by herself____ .

1. He needs to be _____ when he is sad.

2. They work faster when they work _____ .

3. I did all of the work _____ .

4. She answered the questions correctly _____ .

5. I cooked _____ .

6. The boys cleaned their room _____ .

7. Did you wash all the dishes _____ ?

8. Do you live _____ ?

9. Mark and I don't like to be ————————————— .

10. Did he write this ————————————— ?

Exercise 5 (A.1–2, pp. 269–71)
Match the sentences with the meanings. Choose the meaning which is similar to the sentence, and write the letter on the line by the number. Follow the examples.

___a___ 1. I bought a book for myself.

___c___ 2. I bought a book by myself.

_____ 3. I bought myself a book.

_____ 4. I bought a book myself.
       a) I wanted a book, so I bought one.
       b) I bought a book. No other person bought one.
       c) I was alone when I bought a book.

_____ 5. He'll bake himself a cake.

_____ 6. He'll bake a cake by himself.

_____ 7. He'll bake a cake himself.

_____ 8. He'll bake a cake for himself.
       a) He wants a cake, so he'll bake one.
       b) He'll bake a cake. No other person will do it.
       c) He'll be alone when he bakes the cake.

_____ 9. You wrote the note yourself.

_____ 10. You wrote yourself the note.

_____ 11. You wrote the note by yourself.

_____ 12. You wrote the note to yourself.
       a) You wrote a note to remember something.
       b) You wrote the note. No other person wrote it.
       c) You were alone when you wrote the note. No one helped you write it.

Exercise 6 (B, pp. 271–74)
Underline the correct verb form. Some sentences may have two answers.

We wanted (<u>to go</u>, going).
They like (<u>to work</u>, <u>working</u>) here.

1. She prefers (to cook, cooking) her own meals.
2. He insists on (to go, going) by car.
3. They began (to study, studying) about nine o'clock.
4. We started (to eat, eating) dinner around six.
5. You should avoid (to smoke, smoking).
6. I can't help (to eat, eating) bread and butter.
7. He's considering (to move, moving) soon.
8. She planned (to see, seeing) that movie.
9. We finished (to work, working) at four P.M.
10. Bob would like (to write, writing) a letter now, but he doesn't have enough time.

Exercise 7 (B, pp. 271–74)
Write the correct form of the verb.

(eat) I can't help __**eating**__ candy.

1. (go) We'll _____ tomorrow. We plan _____ after lunch.

2. (eat) We're very hungry. Let's stop _____ at the next restaurant that we see.

3. (write) I found a letter that I had written a long time ago. However, I don't remember

_____ it.

4. (stay) He wants _____ . He insists on _____ at home.

5. (swim) I kept on _____ . My sister and I really enjoy _____ .

6. (play) Does he like _____ tennis?

7. (play) Do you want _____ tennis now?

8. (smoke) My doctor told me to stop _____ .

9. (read) When did you get through _____ the book?

10. (speak) She can't help _____ fast.

Exercise 8 (B, pp. 271–74)
Write the correct form of the verb.

(be) We need ___to be___ on time.

(eat) I enjoy ___eating___ spaghetti.

1. (see) I really wanted _____ that movie.

2. (do) He promises _____ the work

3. (think) She kept on _____ about the problem.

4. (watch) I didn't remember _____ the news on television. I was so busy that I forgot.

5. (listen) I don't remember _____ to the news. I might have, but I'm not really sure.

6. (play) She can't _____ tennis very well.

7. (move) I felt the airplane _____ .

8. (sing) Mary enjoys _____ very much.

9. (go) I'm considering _____ to Mexico in May.

10. (eat) I got through _____ at noon.

11. (work) The students kept on _____ until lunch.

12. (eat) I stopped _____ when the telephone rang.

13. (learn) We like _____ other languages.

14. (have) We expect _____ a very good time.

15. (take) Mary must consider _____ her car if I can't take mine.

Lesson 26

Exercise 9: Review Test
A. Match the sentences with the meanings. Write the letter of the meaning on the line by the number.

_____ 1. I bought the picture myself.

_____ 2. I bought the picture by myself.

_____ 3. I bought myself the picture.

_____ 4. I bought the picture for myself.
         a) I wanted a picture, so I bought one.
         b) I was alone when I bought the picture.
         c) I bought the picture. No other person bought it.

B. Write the correct reflexive pronoun.

1. I cut _____ .

2. He saw _____ in the mirror.

3. Mary bought a new book for _____ .

4. The man was talking to _____ .

5. We wrote it by _____ .

C. Write the correct form of the verb.

1. (write) She enjoys _____ letters very much.

2. (help) We must _____ them as much as possible.

3. (go) He insists on _____ to church.

4. (eat) We stopped _____ butter because we are on a diet.

5. (play) Can they _____ football today?

Exercise 10: Review Test
Choose the correct answer. Put a circle around the letter of the answer.

1. "What did the doctor say?"
   "He told her to avoid ____ chocolate."
   a) eat
   b) eats
   c) eating
   d) to eat

2. I got through ____ at five o'clock.
   a) work
   b) works
   c) to work
   d) working

3. We might ____ to Miami next week.
   a) go
   b) goes
   c) to go
   d) going

4. I bought ____ a chair for my apartment.
   a) by myself
   b) for myself
   c) myself
   d) me

5. We made dinner _____ .
   a) ourself
   b) ourselves
   c) for us
   d) for we

6. Mary went home, but Bob kept on ____ .
   a) worked
   b) works
   c) to work
   d) working

7. I cut _____ .
   a) me
   b) my
   c) myself
   d) meself

8. I'm considering ____ the work later.
   a) do
   b) to do
   c) doing
   d) am doing

9. "Did Mary go with him?"
   "No, he went _____ ."
   a) hisself
   b) heself
   c) by himself
   d) by hisself

10. "Will you buy him a car?"
    "No, he must buy _____ ."
    a) one himself
    b) one yourself
    c) one myself
    d) one herself

343

Lesson 27

A. Nouns used as complements after direct objects: They elected Kennedy president.

B. Adjectives used as complements after direct objects: He pushed the door open.

C. Noun + -ing verb expressions used as direct objects: We watched the boys playing.

Vocabulary List

appoint	elect	plain	shovel
barber	mashed	press	smell
boil	medium	push	type
chairman	name	rare	wave
committee	nominate	raw	well-done
designate	pet	shine	wipe
dry-clean			

Exercise 1 (A, pp. 275–77)

Read the situation, and then complete the sentence. Use *as* when it is necessary.

The people elected Johnson. He is president.

The people elected ___Johnson   president___ .

They selected Bill. He is the new representative.

They selected ___Bill as the new representative___ .

1. We chose Bob. He is our new leader.

   We chose _____ .

2. They have a new baby. His name is Paul.

   They named _____ .

3. The people liked Edward. They wanted him to be the king.

   The people made _____ .

4. His name is Joseph. He is called Joe.

   Everyone calls _____ .

5. The students selected the winner. Mark was the winner.

   The students selected _____ .

344

Exercise 2 (A, pp. 275–77)
Answer these questions with complete sentences.

What do you call baby cats?

_____I call baby cats kittens._____

1. What do you call baby dogs?

_____

2. What do you call people from Japan?

_____

3. Whom did the Americans elect as president in the last election?

_____

4. What do you call people from Spain?

_____

5. Whom did the coach select as the best player?

_____

Exercise 3 (B, pp. 277–80)
Read the situation, and then complete the sentence using adjectives and past participles.

I want somebody to clean my room.

I want ____my room cleaned_____ .

He painted the house. It is white now.

He painted ___the house white_____ .

I like coffee. My coffee must be black.

I like ____my coffee black_____ .

1. Mike had someone fix his car.

Mike had _____ .

2. I pulled the curtain. It's closed now.

I pulled _____ .

3. Ann cut her hair. It is short now.

Ann cut _____ .

4. I want you to sell my house.

I want _____ .

5. I want you to take my picture.

I want _____ .

6. I eat potatoes. I like to fry my potatoes.

I like _____ .

7. We need someone to make our beds.

We need _____ .

8. I would like you to repair my car.

I would like _____ .

9. I like soup, but it must be hot.

I like _____ .

10. I need someone to clean my room.

I need _____ .

11. I want somebody to paint my house.

I want _____ .

12. I'm going to have somebody wash my clothes.

I'm going to have _____ .

13. He wants someone to toast his bread.

He wants _____ .

14. I would like someone to correct my mistakes.

I would like _____ .

15. She likes steak. Her steak must be well-done.

She likes _____ .

Exercise 4   (C, pp. 280–81)
Read the two sentences, and then complete the third sentence.

I watched Mary. She was playing tennis.

I watched ___Mary playing tennis_____ .

1. They saw me. I was swimming.

   They saw _____ .

2. He watched the cat. It was eating its food.

   He watched _____ .

3. I caught John. He was copying my homework.

   I caught _____ .

4. We heard the girls. They were singing.

   We heard _____ .

5. We found our brother. He was sleeping on the sofa.

   We found _____ .

6. Mary felt her face. It was getting hot and turning red.

   Mary felt _____ .

7. I was able to smell the cake. It was burning in the oven.

   I was able to smell _____ .

8. Paul saw us. We were leaving school.

   Paul saw _____ .

9. She left her son. He was studying in his room.

   She left _____ .

10. They heard the dog. It was barking all night.

    They heard _____ .

Exercise 5: Discrimination of Verb Forms   (11/A.1, 13/A.1, 13/A.4, 21/A, 26/B, 27/C)
Write the correct form of the verb on the line.

(stop / eat) He told me _to stop eating_ fatty foods.

(use) I let him _use_ my pen.

1. (stop / smoke) He told me _____ _____ immediately.

2. (try / catch / steal) The police should _____ _____ the man _____ the money.

3. (have / arrive) The boss insists on _____ his employees _____ at eight in the morning.

4. (watch / play) We found the boys _____ some people _____ baseball.

5. (consider / let / use) Do you plan _____ _____ John _____ your car?

6. (do) She persuaded Mark _____ the work.

7. (try / avoid / eat) I will _____ _____ _____ fried foods.

8. (cook / cook) We began _____ dinner around two o'clock, and we didn't stop _____ until eight o'clock.

9. (promise / help) You must _____ not _____ him.

10. (try / call) I continued _____ _____ Mark.

11. (watch / land / take) We went to the airport _____ the airplanes _____ and _____ off.

12. (go / try / buy) Martha asked me _____ to the store _____ _____ some fresh apples.

13. (study / study) I didn't get through _____ until midnight although I began _____ in the afternoon.

14. (drive / travel) He stopped _____ because he was too tired to keep on _____ .

15. (let / watch) Will he _____ you _____ the game on his television set?

16. (eat) They invited me _____ dinner at their house.

17. (smell / burn) We could _____ the fish _____ .

18. (remember) He wrote the words several times in order to help him _____ them.

19. (avoid / drive) They would like _____ _____ in the noon traffic.

20. (get / sleep) Joe is used to _____ _____ up early now, but he used to _____ until ten or cleven every morning.

Exercise 6: Review Test
A. Read the sentences, and then write a new sentence.

1. The people elected Jackson. He's president.

   _____

2. I like soup. My soup must be hot.

   _____

3. Mary swept the floor. It is clean now.

   _____

4. I want someone to clean the floor.

   _____

5. She cut her hair. It's short now.

   _____

6. The man painted the room. It's pink now.

   _____

7. I want someone to wash the dishes now.

   _____

8. They saw us. We were taking the money.

   _____

9. He heard her. She was singing a song.

   _____

10. John found them. They were studying grammar.

   _____

B. Underline the correct word.

1. I smelled the fish (fried, frying).
2. I want my room (clean, cleaned) by the maid.
3. I like my bread (toast, toasted).
4. I need my house (sell, sold) as soon as possible.

Exercise 7: Review Test
Choose the correct answer. Put a circle around the letter of the answer.

1. I found the lesson _____ .
   a) difficult
   b) as easy
   c) wrote
   d) finish

2. We can smell the food _____ .
   a) cooks
   b) to cook
   c) cooked
   d) cooking

3. The teacher selected _____ as the best student.
   a) I
   b) he
   c) you
   d) she

4. "What color did you paint the kitchen?"
   "We painted _____ ."
   a) the room yellow
   b) the yellow room
   c) the yellow
   d) yellow it

5. "Is John the new secretary?"
   "Yes, the members elected _____ ."
   a) secretary John
   b) John secretary
   c) secretary
   d) John it

6. "Didn't his parents give him the name Michael?"
   "Yes, but everyone calls _____ ."
   a) Mike
   b) him
   c) him Mike
   d) Mike to him

7. "What happened to your hair?"
   "I had it _____ ."
   a) short to cut
   b) cutting short
   c) short cut
   d) cut short

8. "Did you find the dog?"
   "Yes, I found _____ ."
   a) it to eat
   b) it eat
   c) it eating
   d) it eats

9. "Are you going to sell your house?"
   "Yes, I want _____ immediately."
   a) it sold
   b) sold it
   c) it selling
   d) selling it

10. "What do you call young cats in English?"
    "I call _____ ."
    a) them kittens
    b) kittens to them
    c) it kittens
    d) kittens to it

Lesson 28

A. Verb expressions in *-ing* functioning as noun phrases: Traveling is fun.

B. Verb expressions in *-ing* functioning as subordinate clauses: Sitting in a chair, he watched TV.

Vocabulary List

annoy	effort	noisily	storm
argue	fulfill	profitable	talent
campaign	gallery	purchase	thrill
contest	geometry	require	toss
creak	hobby	shout	

Exercise 1   (A, pp. 282–83)

Write the correct form of the verb. Use the *-ing* form in the subject position.

(walk) It's good exercise ___to walk___ every day.

(walk) ___Walking___ every day is good exercise.

1. (study) It's necessary _____ to learn English.

2. (study) _____ is necessary to learn English.

3. (go) It's important _____ to class every day.

4. (eat) _____ spaghetti is fun.

5. (play) _____ tennis is good exercise.

6. (ride) It makes me tired _____ bicycles for a long time.

7. (ride) _____ bicycles makes me tired.

8. (drive) _____ that car isn't safe.

9. (drive) It isn't safe _____ that car.

10. (learn) _____ English is usually easy.

Lesson 28

Exercise 2 (A, pp. 282–83)
Read the two sentences, and then write a new sentence.
Practice the *-ing* form of the verb.

I play tennis. It's fun.

_____ **Playing tennis is fun.** _____

1. We drive our cars. It's necessary.

   _____

2. She learned to use chopsticks. It was fun.

   _____

3. I always do the homework. It's difficult.

   _____

4. They visited Europe. It was very exciting.

   _____

5. I read all the compositions. It was tiring.

   _____

Exercise 3 (B, pp. 283–84)
Write a new sentence which begins with an *-ing* verb phrase.

John was cleaning his room. He found his wallet.

__**Cleaning his room, John found his wallet.**_____

1. Mary is a secretary. She knows how to type.

   _____

2. George has a new car. He doesn't have to take a bus any more.

   _____

3. They were eating lunch. They saw us from their kitchen window.

   _____

4. I saw the picture. I thought about my cousin.

_____

5. She was waiting for the bus. She got tired.

_____

6. The boys were playing baseball. They lost the ball.

_____

7. I was wiping the table. I spilled hot water on myself.

_____

8. I was preparing dinner. I cut my finger.

_____

9. He was playing baseball. He tore his pants.

_____

10. They were speaking with their friends. They had a great time.

_____

Exercise 4   (B, pp. 284–85)
Write a new sentence which begins with *having* + past participle.

I ate dinner. Then I began to study.

Having eaten dinner, I began to study.

1. We played tennis. We took a shower and ate lunch.

_____

2. They called us. They called the other students.

_____

3. John did the work. He sat down to watch television.

_____

4. Mark worked last year. He went to France at Christmas.

_____

5. The children took the medicine. They felt much better.

_____

6. He ate dinner. He washed all the dishes.

_____

7. I finished my homework. I went to bed.

_____

8. I was sick for a week. I went to see the doctor today.

_____

9. He finished the test early. He started to look his answers over.

_____

10. She wrote some letters. She went to the post office to mail them.

_____

Exercise 5: Review Test
A. Write the correct verb form on the line.

1. (write) It's important _____ letters to your family and friends.

2. (drive) _____ a big car is expensive.

3. (play) It's fun _____ tennis.

4. (stay) _____ awake all night made me late for class.

5. (be) _____ on time is important.

B. Write a new sentence which begins with an *-ing* form of the verb or *having* + past participle.

1. We ate dinner. We ate dessert.

_____

2. We were watching television. We ate all of the popcorn.

_____

3. She is the teacher. She knows all the students' names.

_____

4. Mary wrote the verbs several times. She learned them quickly.

_____

Exercise 6: Review Test
Choose the correct answer. Put a circle around the letter of the answer.

1. _____ the test, I left the classroom.
   a) Finish
   b) Finished
   c) Finishing
   d) Having finished

2. It's necessary _____ to class.
   a) go
   b) goes
   c) to go
   d) going

3. _____ her car on Main Street, she had an accident.
   a) Drive
   b) To drive
   c) Driving
   d) Having driven

4. _____ that car is fun.
   a) Drive
   b) To drive
   c) Driving
   d) Having driven

5. _____ Chinese is very difficult.
   a) Learn
   b) Learned
   c) Learning
   d) Having learned

6. It makes us very happy _____ you.
   a) see
   b) to see
   c) seen
   d) have seen

7. It isn't very safe _____ that motorcycle.
   a) to drive
   b) driven
   c) driving
   d) drive

8. "Why do you enjoy tennis?"
   "_____ tennis is a lot of fun."
   a) Plays
   b) Played
   c) Playing
   d) Having play

9. "Did you see him when you were going to lunch?"
   "Yes, _____ ."
   a) he saw me going to lunch
   b) I saw him going to lunch
   c) going to lunch, he saw me
   d) going to lunch, I saw him

10. "Did he go to lunch after he had phoned you?"
    "Yes, _____ ."
    a) phoning me, he went to lunch
    b) having phoned me, he went to lunch
    c) phoning him, I went to lunch
    d) having phoned him, I went to lunch

Lesson 29

A. Conjunctions: *and, but, or,* and sentence connectors: *however, therefore, also,* etc.

B. Adverbial expressions of time and place in sentence initial position: At nine o'clock, we have class.

C. Summary statements: *in other words*

Vocabulary List

also	cotton	in fact	on the other hand
apply	elsewhere	in other words	over
appointment	farm	in spite of that	peach
as a matter of fact	field	in summary	refreshment
as a result	forest	intonation	rose
besides	furthermore	lawn	similarly
bowl	however	lie	still
briefly	in addition	lie down	therefore
carpenter	in a word	likewise	thus
cherry	in brief	moreover	to summarize
coast	in contrast	nevertheless	veto
consequently	indeed	on the contrary	yet
conversely			

Exercise 1   (A.1, pp. 286–87)
Put a comma where it is necessary.

John was sick, but he was happy.
John was sick but happy.

1. We like swimming and fishing.
2. I must go or I'll never wake up tomorrow.
3. We need eggs butter and milk.
4. They want Mary and John to go.
5. We ate fish but they had beef.
6. The food was delicious but expensive.
7. We need bread or crackers.
8. She went to the doctor but she's still sick.
9. She kept on singing and listening to the radio.
10. Mary ordered steak rice green beans and a dessert.
11. He likes reading and writing.
12. They went to North America and South America.

13. I did the work and I went to sleep.
14. Did you prefer the red blue or white shirts?
15. The tea was good but it was very sweet.

Exercise 2 (A.2, pp. 288–89)
Put the correct punctuation. Indicate which letters should be capitalized.

She played tennis, but she lost.
She played tennis. However, she lost.

1. We ran four miles therefore we were very tired.
2. The boys made a cake but it tasted horrible.
3. Mary was happy about the news however Sue was sad.
4. Mr. Smith likes baseball but I prefer football.
5. It was raining therefore we didn't have a picnic.

Exercise 3 (A.2, pp. 288–89)
Write *therefore, however,* or *also.* Add the correct punctuation.

I failed the test. **Therefore,** I was unhappy.

1. I'm on a diet. _____ I will not eat any bread.

2. She's sick. _____ she must go to class.

3. Paul has a test in the morning. _____ he has a test in the afternoon.

4. We like tennis. _____ we don't like basketball.

5. You're very short. _____ you can't reach the ceiling.

6. I was late today. _____ I was late twice last week.

7. She has a quarter and a nickel. _____ she has thirty cents.

8. We bought a new radio. _____ we don't like it very much.

9. The store is closed. _____ I can't buy the food until tomorrow.

10. Mike visited France. _____ he visited Germany and England.

Exercise 4 (A.2, pp. 289–90)
Read the first sentence, and then decide if the italicized word is similar to *but, and,* or *so.*

He didn't study. *However*, he passed the test.

He didn't study, __but__ he passed the test.

1. Paul was very sick. *Therefore*, he didn't attend class.

    Paul was very sick, _____ he didn't attend class.

2. She ate a sandwich. *Also*, she ate some ice cream.

    She ate a sandwich, _____ she ate some ice cream.

3. Bob won the prize. *As a result*, he was very happy.

    Bob won the prize, _____ he was very happy.

4. Going to the beach on a hot summer day is a lot of fun. *On the other hand*, getting too much sun is painful.

    Going to the beach on a hot summer day is a lot of fun, _____ getting too much sun is painful.

5. Mr. Smith bought a present for his daughter. *Likewise*, he bought a gift for his son.

    Mr. Smith bought a present for his daughter, _____ he bought a gift for his son.

6. That car costs a lot of money. *In spite of that*, Jack plans to buy it.

    That car costs a lot of money, _____ Jack plans to buy it.

7. We don't like ice cream because it's expensive. *In addition*, it's very fattening.

    We don't like ice cream because it's expensive _____ it's very fattening.

8. It was raining hard. *Thus*, we had to cancel the game.

    It was raining hard _____ we had to cancel the game.

9. Steve moved to another city. *Nevertheless*, we call each other at least once a week.

    Steve moved to another city, _____ we call each other at least once a week.

10. We went on vacation in Mexico because the plane ticket was cheap. *Moreover*, the hotels there were inexpensive.

    We went on vacation in Mexico because the plane ticket was cheap _____ the hotels there were inexpensive.

Exercise 5   (B, pp. 290–92)
Change the position of the time/place expression in the second sentence and add the word *there*.

The paper is on the desk. Envelopes are inside the drawer.

The paper is on the desk.
Inside the drawer there are envelopes.

We always eat lunch at noon. Grammar class is afterwards.

We always eat lunch at noon.
Afterwards there is grammar class.

1. The Atlantic is to the east of our country. The Pacific lies to the west.

_____

_____

2. Writing class is at eight o'clock. Reading class is immediately afterwards.

_____

_____

3. That station was playing good music last hour. Other good songs are on it now.

_____

_____

4. Canada is north of the United States. Mexico is south of the United States.

_____

_____

5. She watched a good movie at nine. The news was at eleven.

_____

_____

Exercise 6 (C, p. 293)
Write a statement which summarizes the situation. Begin your sentence with *in other words*.

He doesn't have a nickel or a dime. He doesn't have a dollar.

<u>In other words, he doesn't have any money.</u>

1. You don't think Paul is nice. He makes you unhappy and nervous.

_____

_____

2. Joe went to Norway during his last vacation. He wants to return as soon as possible.

_____

_____

3. Edward studies very hard. He seldom misses class, and he always makes good grades.

_____

_____

4. She watched television from six until midnight. Then, she listened to the radio and wrote some letters until it was time for breakfast.

_____

_____

5. Martha knows how to cook spaghetti, potatoes, and rice. She knows how to cook meat, fish, and seafood.

_____

_____

Exercise 7: Review Test
A. Add the correct punctuation.

1. I want cake coffee and a glass of milk.
2. She's working and he's studying.
3. I don't like fish. However I sometimes eat it.
4. I'm tired but happy.

B. Underline the correct answer.

1. He's hungry. (Therefore, Also), he's thirsty.
2. My car is broken, and I don't have any money for a taxi. (However, In other words), I must walk.
3. I like vegetables. (Therefore, However), I eat potatoes.
4. She has a high fever, and she feels dizzy. (Also, In other words), she's very sick.
5. We can write the letters now, (or, but) we can write them later.
6. They sent me a Christmas card. (Nevertheless, Likewise), I sent them a card.

C. Change the position of the time/place expression in the second sentence. Use the word *there*.

1. The post office is to the north. The bank is to the south.

   _____

   _____

2. The meeting begins at six. The party is at seven.

   _____

   _____

3. Ten people are eating in the cafeteria. Eight people are studying in the library.

   _____

   _____

Exercise 8: Review Test
Choose the correct answer. Put a circle around the letter of the answer.

1. They went to Austria, Greece, and England. _____ , they spent their vacation in Europe.
   a) But
   b) And
   c) However
   d) In other words
2. We ate dinner, _____ Alice wasn't hungry then.
   a) or
   b) and
   c) also
   d) but

361

3. They called Mary, _____ .

   a) Joe but Paul

   b) Joe, but Paul

   c) Joe and Paul

   d) Joe, and Paul

4. Mexico is to the south. _____ lies Canada.

   a) To the north is

   b) To the north there

   c) It to the north

   d) There to the north

5. We had a picnic, played some games, and went swimming. _____ we had a lot of fun.

   a) However

   b) However,

   c) In other words

   d) In other words,

6. I've already been to the park. I didn't enjoy it. _____ , I don't want to go there again.

   a) But

   b) And

   c) Therefore

   d) However

7. The weather was _____ .

   a) sunny but hot

   b) sunny, but hot

   c) sunny also hot

   d) sunny, also hot

8. Most cars are expensive. _____ , this car isn't.

   a) Also

   b) And

   c) However

   d) Therefore

9. It's raining very hard. _____ , we won't be able to have the picnic today.

   a) Or

   b) But

   c) However

   d) Therefore

10. Mr. Smith is very tall. His _____ is short.

   a) son, but,

   b) son, but

   c) son, however,

   d) son, however

Review Test 5 (Lessons 21–29)

Choose the best answer and put a circle around the letter of the correct answer.

1. We _____ Mary to go.
   a) saw
   b) heard
   c) told
   d) made

2. The teacher ____ me do the work.
   a) wanted
   b) told
   c) made
   d) found

3. I ____ the boy eating my sandwich.
   a) told
   b) found
   c) promised
   d) let

4. She _____ them find the answers.
   a) helped
   b) wanted
   c) advised
   d) observed

5. "Tom speaks so loudly."
   "Yes, but I wish he _____ ."
   a) doesn't
   b) didn't
   c) hadn't
   d) hasn't

6. "Did you go to the store?"
   "Yes, but I didn't know _____ ."
   a) what buy
   b) what to buy
   c) what buying
   d) what bought

7. "Did you forget the letters?"
   "I don't think I did, but I ____ ."
   a) might
   b) must
   c) might have
   d) must forgotten

8. "Are they in London?"
   "Yes, and I wish I ____ there, too."
   a) was
   b) were
   c) am
   d) had been

9. "Did you go to class?"
   "No, I didn't go, but I _____ ."
   a) must
   b) must have
   c) should
   d) should have

10. My car is wet. It _____ last night.
   a) must rain
   b) should rain
   c) must have rained
   d) should have rained

11. "Did you understand the class?"
   "No, but I wish I _____ it."
   a) did
   b) had
   c) understood
   d) had understood

12. "I failed my test."
   "You _____ harder last week."
   a) should study
   b) must study
   c) should have studied
   d) must have studied

13. "She went on vacation."
   "I wish she _____ ."
   a) doesn't go
   b) didn't go
   c) wouldn't gone
   d) hadn't gone

363

14. "Did you have an opportunity to eat lunch?"

"I _____ lunch, but I didn't."

a) could eat

b) must eat

c) could have eaten

d) must have eaten

15. He wasn't here, but he wishes he _____ .

a) did

b) was

c) were

d) had been

16. "What were they doing?"

"They might have _____ at the library."

a) studied

b) studying

c) been studied

d) been studying

17. She can't go, but she wishes she _____ .

a) can

b) did

c) could

d) had gone

18. "Why didn't she answer her phone?"

"Well, she might _____ in the shower."

a) be

b) being

c) have been

d) have being

19. We can't go _____ it is raining.

a) if

b) but

c) unless

d) in spite of

20. "Did the students finish their tests?"

"Yes, they _____ ."

a) must

b) must have

c) will

d) will have

21. "Why is the teacher happy?"

"John is _____ student."

a) such a good

b) a such good

c) so good

d) good so

22. "What did you do to your house?"

"I had my house _____ green."

a) paint

b) painted

c) to paint

d) painting

23. "Can he talk yet?"

"No, he's _____ to talk."

a) too young

b) for young

c) so young

d) such young

24. "Weren't you afraid?"

"Yes, I _____ ."

a) was

b) were

c) wasn't

d) weren't

25. "Isn't your father a doctor?"

"Yes, _____ ."

a) he is

b) he isn't

c) they are

d) they aren't

26. "Where were the boys?"

"We found them _____ ."

a) play

b) playing

c) to play

d) played

27. "She should be studying, _____ ?"

"Yes, she should."

a) should she

b) shouldn't she

c) ought she

d) oughtn't she

28. "Paul has had a cold, _____?"
"Yes, you're right."
a) has he
b) hasn't he
c) does he
d) doesn't he

29. "Do you like airplanes?"
"Yes, _____ is a good experience."
a) to fly
b) fly
c) flying
d) having flown

30. "They play very well, _____?"
"Yes, they are excellent players."
a) are they
b) aren't they
c) do they
d) don't they

31. They were happy _____ they passed the hard tests.
a) although
b) whether
c) because
d) regardless

32. "Did they go on vacation?"
"No, they stayed home _____ the bad weather."
a) unless
b) for
c) because of
d) in spite of

33. If John _____ lunch there, he will like it.
a) ate
b) eats
c) will eat
d) had eaten

34. If I'm sick tomorrow, I _____ the doctor.
a) call
b) called
c) will call
d) would call

35. We liked the movie.
Watching the movie, _____.
a) it was very good
b) we had a good time
c) it liked us a lot
d) it lasted two hours

36. I like all fruit. _____, I like apples.
a) And
b) But
c) Therefore
d) However

37. I found the food very good.
_____, John didn't like it.
a) Also
b) However
c) Therefore
d) In other words

38. _____ he didn't like it, John ate the food.
a) Regardless of
b) In spite of
c) Because
d) Although

39. If it rains, we _____.
a) wouldn't go
b) won't go
c) wouldn't have gone
d) hadn't gone

40. If we had gone, we _____ a good time.
a) had had
b) would have had
c) had been
d) would have been

41. He is _____ that he can reach the ceiling.
a) too tall
b) so tall
c) tall too
d) tall so

42. "How did you go to France?"
"We considered _____ by ship, but we flew."
a) go
b) to go
c) going
d) gone

43. We need tables, _____ lamps.
    a) chairs and
    b) chairs, and
    c) chairs also
    d) chairs, also

44. "They didn't listen to the teacher."
    "They ___ listened more carefully."
    a) must have
    b) should have
    c) must have been
    d) should have been

45. She lost her purse, and she couldn't find her keys. ___ , today has not been a good day for her.
    a) However
    b) In other words
    c) Also
    d) But

46. "Do you need any help?"
    "No, thank you. I'll do it ___ ."
    a) for myself
    b) by myself
    c) for me
    d) by me

47. "What did he do when the phone rang?"
    "He stopped _____ and answered the phone."
    a) eat
    b) ate
    c) to eat
    d) eating

48. "What will Ann do?"
    "She will _____ doing the work."
    a) let
    b) see
    c) avoid
    d) watch

49. They named _____ .
    a) Steve the new baby
    b) Steve he
    c) the new baby Steve
    d) he Steve

50. "What happened to your finger?"
    "I cut _____ ."
    a) me
    b) my
    c) myself
    d) me it

Review Test 6 (Lessons 21–29)

Choose the best answer and put a circle around the letter of the correct answer.

1. "I found the movie boring."
   " _____ , you wasted your
   money, didn't you?"
   a) However
   b) Likewise
   c) On the other hand
   d) In other words

2. "John looked tired in class."
   "Yes, he _____ have studied all night."
   a) should
   b) would
   c) must
   d) can

3. "He went home."
   "I wish he _____ here now to help us."
   a) was
   b) gone
   c) were
   d) went

4. "Are we going to eat at home?"
   "Yes, we are _____ you have better plans."
   a) unless
   b) however
   c) if
   d) and

5. "Has it been a long time since you played
   this game?"
   "Yes, I might have forgotten how _____ ."
   a) to play
   b) playing
   c) it plays
   d) played

6. "Did he receive the letter?"
   "If he _____ it, he would have told me."
   a) receive
   b) received
   c) had received
   d) would have received

7. "I need a car."
   "Maybe Tom will let you _____ his."
   a) use
   b) used
   c) using
   d) to use

8. These are _____ expensive apples
   that we can't buy any.
   a) such an
   b) such a
   c) such
   d) so

9. "I saw Joe a few minutes ago."
   "You _____ have seen him. He's
   out of town."
   a) wouldn't
   b) couldn't
   c) mustn't
   d) shouldn't

10. "Anne bought a book for
    _____ , didn't she?"
    "Yes, she did."
    a) sheself
    b) herself
    c) she
    d) her

11. "What was he doing?"
    "He might have been _____ television."
    a) watched
    b) watching
    c) watch
    d) watches

12. "Why didn't you go?"
    "It was _____ cold that we
    didn't want to go."
    a) too
    b) such
    c) so
    d) unless

367

13. "Did it rain last night?"

"It _____ . My car is wet."

a) should have

b) must have

c) might not

d) could not

14. "What did he tell the secretary to do?"

"He _____ her type a letter."

a) remembered

b) would like

c) had

d) wanted

15. "Are you hungry?"

"Yes, I'd like salad _____ meat."

a) and

b) , and

c) so

d) , so

16. I didn't study, but I wish I _____ .

a) do

b) did

c) had

d) would

17. "Are you going to the beach?"

"I'll go _____ the weather's nice."

a) unless

b) although

c) so

d) if

18. "He needs a new radio."

"He wishes he _____ enough money to buy one right now."

a) has

b) had

c) had had

d) would have

19. "She has a new car, _____ she?"

"No, she still has her old one."

a) hasn't

b) has

c) doesn't

d) does

20. "Why did you go?"

"Bob _____ going."

a) made us

b) insisted on

c) promised

d) wanted

21. "I didn't see that movie."

"I wish you _____ it."

a) had seen

b) were seen

c) saw

d) had

22. "What did you do when your leg began to hurt?"

"I stopped _____ ."

a) to play

b) playing

c) played

d) play

23. "Did you buy some fruit?"

"No, I didn't know how much _____ ."

a) to buy

b) buying

c) bought

d) buy

24. "She wore a raincoat yesterday, didn't she?"

"Yes, she wore one _____ it was raining."

a) regardless of

b) in spite of

c) because

d) although

25. "Isn't his name Robert?"

"Yes, but they call _____ ."

a) Bob to him

b) him to Bob

c) Bob him

d) him Bob

26. We have vocabulary class in the morning. _____ there is grammar class.

a) On the other hand

b) In the afternoon

c) In other words

d) Nevertheless

27. "Do you want the maid to clean your room?"
"Yes, I want it _____ as soon as possible."
a) to clean
b) cleaning
c) cleaned
d) cleans

28. "Did you hear her _____ ?"
"No, I didn't."
a) to sing
b) singing
c) sings
d) having sung

29. He didn't feel well. _____ , he went to work.
a) So
b) But
c) Therefore
d) However

30. "What did she do when she received the letter?"
"She started _____ ."
a) cry
b) cried
c) crying
d) cries

31. "Did he pass the test?"
"He failed the test _____ the questions on verbs."
a) regardless
b) because of
c) therefore
d) likewise

32. "What are you going to do?"
"If I had some money, I _____ a trip now."
a) would take
b) will take
c) take
d) took

33. "Where were you yesterday?"
"I was at work, but I wish I _____ there."
a) wasn't
b) weren't
c) hadn't been
d) wouldn't have been

34. _____ lunch, we took a walk.
a) Eaten
b) Eating
c) Having eaten
d) Having eating

35. "When can I call you?"
"Please call me _____ it's late."
a) because of
b) in spite of
c) whether or not
d) regardless

36. "Did they paint the white house?"
"Yes, they painted _____ ."
a) red the white house
b) the white house red
c) the red house white
d) white the red house

37. " _____ English is hard work, isn't it?"
"Yes, it is."
a) Having taught
b) To teaching
c) Teaching
d) To taught

38. "What will you do if it's raining?"
"We'll go to the park _____ the weather."
a) whether or not
b) however
c) regardless
d) in spite of

39. "John is here, _____ he?"
    "Yes, he is."
    a) isn't
    b) is
    c) doesn't
    d) does

40. "Will you help me?"
    "If I _____ here tomorrow,
    I'll be glad to help you."
    a) were
    b) am
    c) be
    d) will be

41. "I heard that he speaks fast."
    "I wish he _____ slowly."
    a) speaks
    b) speak
    c) spoke
    d) spoken

42. "He wasn't tired was he?"
    "No, he wasn't tired, _____ the
    distance that he had driven."
    a) regardless of
    b) in spite of
    c) because
    d) whether

43. "Can you cook?"
    "If I _____, I wouldn't eat out so much."
    a) had cooked
    b) would have
    c) could cook
    d) would cook

44. "I'm lost."
    "Don't worry. I know which road _____ ."
    a) taking
    b) to take
    c) having taken
    d) that we take

45. Mr. Smith is _____ busy man
    that he rarely takes a vacation.
    a) so
    b) too
    c) such a
    d) a such

46. "Did he go alone?"
    "Yes, he went _____ ."
    a) himself
    b) him
    c) by himself
    d) for himself

47. "Do you speak French?"
    "No, but I wish I _____ ."
    a) speak
    b) spoke
    c) do
    d) did

48. "Are you going to Chicago?"
    "Yes, I'm going _____ Peter
    goes with me or not."
    a) because
    b) whether
    c) regardless
    d) unless

49. "Mark broke his arm, _____ he?"
    "Yes, he had an accident."
    a) hadn't
    b) hasn't
    c) didn't
    d) doesn't

50. "Paul caught a bad cold."
    "He _____ have worn his coat yesterday."
    a) would
    b) should
    c) must
    d) was able

Answer Key

Lesson 1

Exercise 1, p. 1: I *am*, you *are*, he *is*, she *is*, it *is*, we *are*, you *are*, they *are*

Exercise 2, p. 2: 1. is 2. are 3. are 4. are 5. are 6. is 7. are 8. am 9. are 10. are

Exercise 3, p. 2: 1. are 2. is 3. am 4. is 5. is 6. is 7. are 8. is 9. is 10. are

Exercise 4, p. 3: 1. Is 2. Are 3. Is 4. Is 5. Are 6. Are 7. Are 8. Is 9. Are 10. Is

Exercise 5, p. 3: 1. Are 2. Is 3. Am 4. Are 5. Is 6. Is 7. Is 8. Are 9. Are 10. Are

Exercise 6, p. 3: 1. Are the dogs hungry? 2. Is the pen new? 3. Is my key on the table? 4. Are they from Honduras? 5. Are you sick today? 6. Is it cold in the room? 7. Are the green books heavy? 8. Is Bill thirsty? 9. Am I right? 10. Are we wrong?

Exercise 7, p. 4: 1. it 2. they 3. he 4. they 5. he 6. we 7. we 8. we 9. she 10. they 11. he 12. they 13. he (or, she) 14. they 15. it 16. they 17. he 18. she 19. she 20. they

Exercise 8, p. 5: 1. It 2. We 3. they 4. They 5. They 6. he 7. it 8. You 9. She 10. they

Exercise 9, p. 5: 1. S,. 2. S,. 3. Q,? 4. S,. 5. Q,? 6. Q,? 7. S,. 8. Q,? 9. S,. 10. Q,?

Exercise 10, p. 6: 1. it's 2. I'm 3. she's 4. they're 5. you're 6. Mike's 7. the key's 8. the boy's 9. he's 10. we're

Exercise 11, p. 6: 1. He's 2. They're 3. I'm 4. She's 5. It's 6. They're 7. They're 8. We're 9. Mary's 10. I'm 11. You're 12. She's 13. It's 14. They're 15. John's 16. You're 17. I'm 18. We're 19. You're 20. He's 21. Mary's 22. The book's 23. It's 24. I'm 25. The key's

Exercise 12, p. 7: 1. Yes, they are. 2. Yes, he is. 3. Yes, we are. (Yes, you are.) 4. Yes, he is. 5. Yes, I am. (Yes, we are.) 6. Yes, you are. 7. Yes, it is. 8. Yes, they are. 9. Yes, she is. 10. Yes, I am. (Yes, we are.)

Exercise 13, p. 7: 1. No, they aren't. 2. No, he isn't. 3. No, we aren't. 4. No, she isn't. 5. No, I'm not. (No, we aren't.) 6. No, we aren't. (No, you aren't.) 7. No, it isn't. 8. No, they aren't. 9. No, it isn't. 10. No, you aren't.

Exercise 14, p. 8: 1. Are you hungry?; Yes, I am. (Yes, we are.); No, I'm not. (No, we aren't.) 2. Are the boys cold?; Yes, they are.; No, they aren't. 3. Am I a good student?; Yes, you are.; No, you aren't. 4. Are they late for class?; Yes, they are.; No, they aren't. 5. Are the books on the table?; Yes, they are.; No, they aren't.

Exercise 15, p. 9: 1. No, it isn't. It's green. 2. No, they aren't. They're closed. 3. No, I'm not. I'm a student. 4. No, she isn't. She's from the United States. 5. No, it isn't. It's easy.

Exercise 16, p. 9: 1. — 2. an 3. — 4. a 5. a 6. a 7. a 8. — 9. an 10. —

Exercise 17, p. 10: 1. The boys are hungry. 2. They are sick now. 3. We are busy in class. 4. The shoes are black. 5. Are the books closed? 6. Are we late for class? 7. They are teachers. 8. You are students. 9. The cats are black. 10. They are good students.

Exercise 18, p. 10: A. 1. am 2. is 3. are 4. are 5. are 6. Are B. 1. We're here. 2. You're students. 3. They're busy now. 4. They're books. C. 1. Are the books green? Yes, they are. 2. Is the watch new? No, it isn't. 3. Are you tall? Yes, I am. (Yes, we are.) D. 1. a 2. a 3. an 4. — 5. —

Exercise 19, p. 11: 1. *a*) 2. *c*) 3. *c*) 4. *c*) 5. *b*) 6. *c*) 7. *d*) 8. *c*) 9. *a*) 10. *a*)

Lesson 2

Exercise 1, p. 13: 7. I speak 8. you speak 9. he speaks 10. she speaks 11. we speak 12. they speak 13. I have 14. you have 15. he has 16. she has 17. we have 18. they have 19. I practice 20. you practice 21. he practices 22. she practices 23. we practice 24. they practice 25. I study 26. you study 27. he studies 28. she studies 29. we study 30. they study 31. I do 32. you do 33. he does 34. she does 35. we do 36. they do

Exercise 2, p. 14: 1. begins 2. drink 3. have 4. pronounces 5. work 6. arrives 7. comes 8. eats 9. leave 10. sing 11. is 12. go 13. are 14. speaks 15. arrives 16. study 17. has 18. likes 19. teach 20. have

Exercise 3, p. 15: 1. arrive 2. begin 3. come 4. drinks 5. eat 6. has 7. leaves 8. pronounce 9. sing 10. works 11. is 12. like 13. have 14. is 15. speaks 16. lives 17. practice 18. eats 19. are 20. studies

Exercise 4, p. 17: 7. do I speak 8. do you speak 9. does he speak 10. does she speak 11. do we speak 12. do they speak 13. do I have 14. do you have 15. does he have 16. does she have 17. do we have 18. do they have 19. do I practice 20. do you practice 21. does he practice 22. does she practice 23. do we practice 24. do they practice 25. do I study 26. do you study 27. does he study 28. does she study 29. do we study 30. do they study 31. do I do 32. do you do 33. does he do 34. does she do 35. do we do 36. do they do

Exercise 5, p. 18: 1. do they drink 2. do I have 3. do we work 4. do they teach 5. do you sing 6. does he drink 7. do you leave 8. do we study 9. does she speak 10. does Bill eat 11. does he work 12. does she study 13. do you like 14. do you have 15. does he go 16. do they like 17. does he have 18. do we go 19. do you live 20. does John have

Exercise 6, p. 19: 1. Do they sing well? 2. Does she come late every day? 3. Do they have ten books? 4. Does Paul have a new watch? 5. Does Mary arrive at 9:00 A.M.?

Exercise 7, p. 19: 1. He eats; Does he eat 2. He has; Does he have 3. She drinks; Does she drink 4. Bob studies; Does Bob study 5. Mark speaks; Does Mark speak

Exercise 8, p. 20: 1. Yes, they do. 2. Yes, it does. 3. Yes, they do. 4. Yes, she does. 5. Yes, he does. 6. Yes, I do. (Yes, we do.) 7. Yes, she does. 8. Yes, he does. 9. Yes, they do. 10. Yes, you do.

Exercise 9, p. 21: 1. No, it doesn't. 2. No, they don't. 3. No, they don't. 4. No, it doesn't. 5. No, he doesn't. 6. No, she doesn't. 7. No, I don't. (No, we don't.) 8. No, you don't. 9. No, we don't. 10. No, it doesn't.

Exercise 10, p. 22: 1. Yes, I do. 2. No, he doesn't. 3. Yes, they do. 4. Yes, she does. 5. Yes, we do. 6. No, they don't. 7. Yes, she does. 8. Yes, they do. 9. No, he doesn't. 10. No, she doesn't.

Exercise 11, p. 22: 1. Are 2. Do 3. Is 4. Am 5. Does 6. Is 7. Does 8. Does 9. Are 10. Is 11. Do 12. Am 13. Are 14. Do 15. Are 16. Is 17. Is 18. Does 19. Is 20. Do

Exercise 12, p. 23: 1. Do 2. Are 3. Do 4. Is 5. Does 6. Do 7. Does 8. Is 9. Does 10. Is 11. Are 12. Does 13. Does 14. Is 15. Do 16. Are 17. Am 18. Do 19. Are 20. Do

Exercise 13, p. 23: 1. Yes, they are. 2. No, he isn't. 3. Yes, they do. 4. No, they aren't. 5. Yes, he does. 6. Yes, it is. 7. No, I don't. 8. Yes, we are. 9. Yes, she does. 10. No, it isn't. 11. Yes, they do. 12. No, I don't. 13. Yes, it is. 14. No, they aren't. 15. Yes, I do. 16. Yes, I am. 17. Yes, I am. 18. Yes, we are. 19. Yes, I do. 20. Yes, I do. 21. Yes, they do. 22. No, they aren't. 23. Yes, you are. 24. Yes, I am. 25. Yes, I do.

Exercise 14, p. 24: 1. No, it isn't. 2. No, I'm not. 3. No, it isn't. 4. Yes, I do. 5. Yes, I do. 6. Yes, they are. 7. No, you aren't. 8. Yes, I am. 9. Yes, he does. 10. No, he doesn't. 11. No, it isn't. 12. No, they aren't. 13. Yes, he does. 14. No, it isn't. 15. Yes, we do. 16. No, it isn't. 17. Yes, I do. 18. Yes, it is. 19. Yes, I do. 20. Yes, you are. 21. Yes, we are. 22. No, it isn't. 23. No, he doesn't. 24. Yes, it is. 25. Yes, they do.

Exercise 15, p. 26: 2. usually 3. often 4. sometimes 5. seldom 6. never

Exercise 16, p. 26: 1. often has 2. never eat 3. seldom study 4. sometimes drink 5. often drinks

Exercise 17, p. 27: 1. I sometimes study grammar at night. 2. He usually studies vocabulary. 3. We always practice pronunciation. 4. They seldom write letters to their parents. 5. You always have coffee for breakfast. 6. Jack often comes to class late. 7. Mary never sings. 8. We seldom speak Spanish in class. 9. They often study at night. 10. I never eat toast.

Exercise 18, p. 28: 1. am always 2. are never 3. is usually 4. are often 5. are seldom

Exercise 19, p. 28: 1. The class is always at 8 A.M. 2. The letters are seldom long. 3. He is usually hungry. 4. We are seldom at home in the morning. 5. Bill is never absent. 6. They're seldom in class. 7. I'm always well. 8. Mary's often happy. 9. The teacher is sometimes busy in the afternoon. 10. She is never sick.

Exercise 20, p. 29: 1. is never 2. always eat 3. never study 4. is sometimes 5. seldom drinks 6. always arrive 7. is always 8. seldom speak 9. never go 10. are seldom 11. is usually 12. always has 13. is always 14. is often 15. never studies

Exercise 21, p. 29: 1. Is the man often in class? 2. Do they usually work in the afternoon? 3. Does he often study grammar? 4. Are you often in the library? 5. Are pencils always yellow? 6. Do we always write our homework? 7. Are they usually on time? 8. Do they usually drink milk? 9. Does she always eat a sandwich for lunch? 10. Is she sometimes late?

Exercise 22, p. 30: 1. Are they ever at home in the morning? 2. Do they ever eat hamburgers for dinner? 3. Do you ever sing in class? 4. Am I ever wrong? 5. Do we ever have toast for breakfast?

Exercise 23, p. 30: 1. No, never. 2. Yes, usually. 3. Yes, always. 4. Yes, sometimes. 5. Yes, often.

Exercise 24, p. 31: A. 1. Do you eat toast? Yes, I do. 2. Are they sick? No, they aren't. 3. Does he always arrive late? Yes, he does. 4. Am I usually right? No, you aren't. B. 1. We always eat lunch in the kitchen. 2. They are usually in class. 3. I sometimes write letters. 4. You never understand the lesson. 5. He is seldom late. C. 1. Are you ever in the library? Yes, usually. 2. Do we ever eat lunch at noon? No, never. D. 1. is always 2. begins 3. Do 4. Are 5. usually eat 6. write 7. always do

Exercise 25, p. 32: 1. *a*) 2. *c*) 3. *d*) 4. *a*) 5. *c*) 6. *c*) 7. *d*) 8. *d*) 9. *c*) 10. *b*)

Lesson 3

Exercise 1, p. 33: 1. place 2. place 3. time 4. place 5. time 6. frequency 7. time 8. time 9. frequency 10. place

Exercise 2, p. 34: 1. C 2. X 3. X 4. C 5. C

Exercise 3, p. 34: 1. We eat lunch in a restaurant at noon. 2. They have class at the university at 10 A.M. 3. I have coffee there before class. 4. He studies in the library every night. 5. She practices pronunciation in the laboratory every day. 6. They go to class every day. 7. You drink milk at the table in the morning. 8. You write letters in the library at night. 9. She studies in class every day. 10. He comes to class every day.

Exercise 4, p. 35: 1. They teach Spanish in my school every day. 2. Mary usually understands the lessons in class. 3. He goes to the office at 7:00 A.M. every day. 4. They eat breakfast at 8:30 in the morning. 5. I have coffee in the kitchen in the morning. 6. The girl is always in class in the morning. 7. I seldom do my homework in my room. 8. He comes to class at noon every day. 9. He lives in a big house on Main Street in Atlanta. 10. John usually plays baseball at 4:00 P.M.

Exercise 5, p. 36: 1. am 2. are 3. is 4. is 5. is 6. are 7. are 8. was 9. were 10. was 11. was 12. was 13. were 14. were

Exercise 6, p. 37: 1. was 2. were 3. were 4. were 5. was

Exercise 7, p. 37: 1. was 2. Were 3. was 4. was 5. Was 6. was 7. were 8. Was 9. was 10. were

Exercise 8, p. 38: 1. Were you hungry? Yes, I was. (Yes, we were.) No, I wasn't. (No, we weren't.) 2. Were the boys cold? Yes, they were. No, they weren't. 3. Was I wrong? Yes, you were. No, you weren't. 4. Were they late for class? Yes, they were. No, they weren't. 5. Was Mary in the kitchen? Yes, she was. No, she wasn't.

Exercise 9, p. 39: 1. work 2. work 3. works 4. works 5. works 6. work 7. work 8. worked 9. worked 10. worked 11. worked 12. worked 13. worked 14. worked

Exercise 10, p. 39: 1. he studied 2. she listened 3. they attended 4. I was 5. you presented 6. he learned 7. you talked 8. she was 9. you arrived 10. he waited 11. I repeated 12. I worked 13. he worked 14. they studied 15. you liked

Exercise 11, p. 40: 1. Did we practice writing? Yes, we did. No, we didn't. 2. Did I study the right lesson? Yes, you did. No, you didn't. 3. Did he ask the question? Yes, he did. No, he didn't. 4. Did Mary and John like the book? Yes, they did. No, they didn't. 5. Did he wait for Pat? Yes, he did. No, he didn't. 6. Did they want to go home? Yes, they did. No, they didn't. 7. Did she repeat the words? Yes, she did. No, she didn't. 8. Did the student arrive late? Yes, he did. No, he didn't. 9. Did Mr. Miller work there for two years? Yes, he did. No, he didn't. 10. Did the cat like the milk? Yes, it did. No, it didn't.

Exercise 12, p. 42: 1. have 2. was 3. do 4. Did 5. Were 6. worked 7. practice 8. were 9. worked 10. was 11. does 12. was 13. listened 14. does 15. Did

Exercise 13, p. 42: 1. Were they here? Yes, they were. 2. Was John hungry? No, he wasn't. 3. Did they speak English? Yes, they did. 4. Were the boys here? No, they weren't. 5. Did John have a book? Yes, he did. 6. Was the book green? Yes, it was. 7. Did you like the book? No, I didn't. 8. Were you and John hungry? Yes, we were. 9. Did Mary have a car? Yes, she did. 10. Was the car blue? No, it wasn't. 11. Did the boys study? Yes, they did. 12. Did you understand the lesson? No, I didn't. 13. Was the test easy? Yes, it was. 14. Were the tests easy? No, they weren't. 15. Did you need a pencil? Yes, I did. 16. Were you hungry? Yes, I was. 17. Were you a student? Yes, I was. 18. Were you students? Yes, we were. 19. Did you have a pen? No, I didn't. 20. Did you have a nickel? Yes, I did. 21. Did John and Mary like the sandwich? Yes, they did. 22. Were they in class? No, they weren't. 23. Was I a good teacher? Yes, you were. 24. Were you a good student? Yes, I was. 25. Did you study at night? Yes, I did.

Exercise 14, p. 43: 1. Was your father the president? No, he wasn't. 2. Were you the president? No, I wasn't. 3. Was the man hungry? No, he wasn't. 4. Did you like the movie? Yes, I did. 5. Did you speak English? Yes, I did. 6. Were the girls here? Yes, they were. 7. Was I right? No, you weren't. 8. Were you right? Yes, I was. (Yes, we were.) 9. Did the man have a pencil? Yes, he did. 10. Did Mr. Miller write long letters? No, he didn't. 11. Was the pencil green? No, it wasn't. 12. Were the books heavy? No, they weren't. 13. Did the teacher have a pencil? Yes, he did. 14. Was the vocabulary class difficult? No, it wasn't. 15. Did we have a green grammar book? Yes, we did. 16. Was the book blue? No, it wasn't. 17. Did you like the book? Yes, I did. 18. Was the watch new? Yes, it was. 19. Did you like the watch? Yes, I did. 20. Were John and I good students? Yes, you were. 21. Were you and I good students? Yes, we were. 22. Was the test difficult? No, it wasn't. 23. Did John like bread? No, he didn't. 24. Was the test easy? Yes, it was. 25. Did Paul, Mary, and John have a car? No, they didn't.

Exercise 15, p. 45: A. 1. We study English in class every day. 2. He goes to the bank at 7:00 A.M. every day. 3. I was in the library at 8:00 last night. B. 1. I watched 2. you studied 3. he worked 4. they practiced 5. she was 6. we were C. 1. Did the man listen to the radio? Yes, he did. No, he didn't. 2. Did he play tennis yesterday? Yes, he did. No, he didn't. 3. Did you practice the verbs yesterday? Yes, I did. (Yes, we did.) No, I didn't. (No, we didn't.) 4. Did Mary and Matt arrive at noon? Yes, they did. No, they didn't. D. 1. was 2. walked 3. pronounced 4. Did 5. Is 6. listen 7. Did 8. Is 9. Do 10. Do

Exercise 16, p. 46: 1. *c*) 2. *a*) 3. *b*) 4. *d*) 5. *d*) 6. *a*) 7. *d*) 8. *c*) 9. *b*) 10. *c*)

Lesson 4

Exercise 1, p. 48: 1. Does John study history? Yes, he does. What does John study? History. 2. Do we like hamburgers? Yes, we do. What do we like? Hamburgers. 3. Do you write letters? Yes, I do. What do you write? Letters. 4. Do they eat soup for lunch? Yes, they do. What do they eat for lunch? Soup. 5. Did we like grammar class? Yes, we did. What did we like? Grammar class. 6. Does Mark write letters every day? Yes, he does. What does Mark write every day? Letters. 7. Did Paul study French? Yes, he did. What did he study? French. 8. Did she pronounce the word? Yes, she did. What did she pronounce? The word. 9. Did the student learn the lesson? Yes, he did. What did the student learn? The lesson. 10. Did the teacher present the vocabulary? Yes, he did. What did the teacher present? The vocabulary.

Exercise 2, p. 51: 1. What does large mean? It means big. 2. What does tiny mean? It means very small. 3. What does rarely mean? It means seldom. 4. What does noon mean? It means twelve o'clock in the day. 5. What does hard mean? It means difficult. 6. What does unhappy mean? It means sad (or not happy). 7. What does week mean? It means seven days. 8. What does dozen mean? It means twelve. 9. What does excellent mean? It means very good. 10. What does smart mean? It means intelligent.

Exercise 3, p. 52: 1. Does Mary study at night? Yes, she does. When does Mary study? At night. 2. Do we

eat at noon? Yes, we do. When do we eat? At noon.
3. Did John arrive yesterday? Yes, he did. When did
John arrive? Yesterday. 4. Did they practice on
Monday? Yes, they did. When did they practice? On
Monday. 5. Does she have class in the afternoon? Yes,
she does. When does she have class? In the afternoon.
Exercise 4, p. 53: 1. When did Mary study? Every
day. 2. When did she work? Yesterday. 3. When do
you eat breakfast? At 10 o'clock. 4. When does he
arrive? In the afternoon. 5. When does John have
class? At 2 P.M.
Exercise 5, p. 54: 1. Did you learn French in France?
Yes, I did. (Yes, we did.) Where did you learn French?
In France. 2. Does she study at home? Yes, she does.
Where does she study? At home. 3. Do they play
tennis in the park? Yes, they do. Where do they play
tennis? In the park. 4. Did Sam study in the library?
Yes, he did. Where did Sam study? In the library.
5. Does Ruth live in Texas? Yes, she does. Where does
Ruth live? In Texas.
Exercise 6, p. 55: 1. Where do we study? In the
library. 2. Where does Mary have class? In room four.
3. Where did John and Sam live? In New York.
4. Where did you practice English? In the laboratory.
5. Where do you eat lunch? In the kitchen.
Exercise 7, p. 56: 1. Who visited Mr. Miller? Mary
did. 2. Who asked Mark? He did. 3. Who helped Alan
with the homework? Joe did. 4. Who telephoned Paul?
The girl did. 5. Who plays tennis with John? Ann
does. 6. Who knows Jack well? You do. 7. Who
understands Mary? Bill does. 8. Who waited for Greg?
We did. 9. Who listened to the doctor? She did.
10. Who works with Pat? Rick and Sue do.
Exercise 8, p. 57: 1. Whom did Mary visit? Mr. Miller.
2. Whom did he ask? Mark. 3. Whom did Joe help
with the homework? Alan. 4. Whom did the girl
telephone? Paul. 5. Whom does Ann play tennis with?
John. 6. Whom do you know well? Jack. 7. Whom
does Bill understand? Mary. 8. Whom did we wait for?
Greg. 9. Whom did she listen to? The doctor.
10. Whom do Rick and Sue work with? Pat.
Exercise 9, p. 59: 1. Who visited Martha yesterday?
Whom did Jane visit yesterday? 2. Who studies with
Matt? Whom does Anne study with? 3. Who studies
with Matt in the evening? Whom do Anne and Bob
study with in the evening? 4. Who plays tennis with
Anne and Matt every day? Whom do John and Martha
play tennis with every day? 5. Who waited for all the
students? Whom did the teacher wait for?
Exercise 10, p. 60: 1. Whom 2. Who 3. Who 4. Who
5. Whom 6. Whom 7. Who 8. Who 9. Who
10. Whom
Exercise 11, p. 60: 1. When does she arrive? 2. Where
did Mary learn French? 3. Whom did she ask? 4. Who
wants a new car? 5. What does Jane have?
Exercise 12, p. 61: 1. *a)* Who studied English in
England? *b)* What did Susan study in England?
c) Where did Susan study English? 2. *a)* Who
practices tennis in the park? *b)* What does Joe practice
in the park? *c)* Where does Joe practice tennis?
3. *a)* Who usually studies history with Peter? *b)* What

does Mike usually study with Peter? *c)* Whom does
Mike usually study history with?
Exercise 13, p. 61: 1. Who 2. Whom 3. Whom
4. Who 5. Where 6. When 7. Who 8. Where
9. When 10. When
Exercise 14, p. 62: 1. When is he usually hungry?
2. Where is she now? 3. When is Mark tired? 4. Who
is in New York? 5. Where is the book? 6. What is on
the table? 7. Who was late to class yesterday?
8. When is he absent? 9. Who is a teacher? 10. What
is he?
Exercise 15, p. 62: 1. *a)* Who is in class now?
b) Where is Mary now? *c)* When is Mary in class?
2. *a)* What is in Florida? *b)* Where is the school?
3. *a)* Who is always hungry at noon? *b)* When is
Mrs. Jones always hungry? 4. *a)* Who is the
president? *b)* What is Peter?
Exercise 16, p. 63: 1. What do they do in the library?
2. What does Joe do at noon? 3. What did she do last
night? 4. What does Bob do at night? 5. What does
she do after dinner? 6. What did Paul and Peter do in
France? 7. What did they do at noon? 8. What do you
do at 9 o'clock? 9. What do we do every morning?
10. What do they do at night?
Exercise 17, p. 63: 1. Whom did John wait for?
2. Whom did the students listen to? 3. Whom does he
give presents to? 4. When does she arrive? 5. What
did he look for? 6. Where are they from? 7. What do
you always watch in the afternoon? 8. Whom do the
students write letters to? 9. Who has class at 9 A.M.?
10. What do you listen to every evening?
Exercise 18, p. 64: 1. work 2. work 3. works
4. works 5. work 6. work 7. am working 8. are
working 9. is working 10. is working 11. are working
12. are working
Exercise 19, p. 65: 1. is studying 2. is teaching 3. am
writing 4. are watching 5. are eating 6. am using 7. is
walking 8. is looking 9. are doing 10. is looking
Exercise 20, p. 65: 1. you are reading 2. X 3. I am
studying 4. X 5. X 6. you are working 7. X 8. X
9. we are writing 10. X 11. X 12. X 13. I am
drinking 14. X 15. she is playing 16. she is eating
17. I am writing 18. we are walking 19. they are
studying 20. X
Exercise 21, p. 66: 1. are eating 2. likes 3. have
4. am 5. see 6. is writing 7. are watching 8. is going
9. has 10. am listening
Exercise 22, p. 66: 1. Are they speaking Japanese? Yes,
they are. 2. Is Martha writing a letter? No, she isn't.
3. Is the teacher teaching lesson 6? No, he isn't.
4. Are the students studying? Yes, they are. 5. Is Patti
eating lunch? Yes, she is.
Exercise 23, p. 67: 1. *a)* Who is talking to Paul?
b) Whom is Mary talking to? 2. *a)* Who likes coffee
and tea? *b)* What do they like? 3. *a)* Who is studying
English in Canada? *b)* What are my sisters studying in
Canada? *c)* Where are my sisters studying English?
4. *a)* Who is drinking tea in the kitchen? *b)* What is
she drinking in the kitchen? *c)* Where is she drinking
tea?
Exercise 24, p. 68: 1. Where 2. Who 3. When

4. Whom 5. What 6. What 7. Where 8. What
9. Whom 10. Who 11. When 12. What 13. What
14. Where 15. Whom 16. What 17. Who 18. Who
19. Where 20. When 21. What 22. Who 23. Who
24. When 25. What

Exercise 25, p. 70: 1. is walking 2. have 3. opened
4. rained 5. play 6. repeats 7. need 8. are studying
9. are going 10. is working 11. likes 12. isn't 13. is
14. is playing 15. aren't

Exercise 26, p. 71: 1. It's a wall clock. 2. They're red
pencils. 3. It's a big dog. 4. I'm an intelligent student.
5. It's a gold watch. 6. They're grammar books. 7. It's
an apple tree. 8. She's a French teacher. 9. He's a
good man. 10. It's a car factory.

Exercise 27, p. 72: 1. It's a bottle. 2. It's a tree.
3. It's a garden. 4. It's a flower. 5. It's a station.
6. It's a watch. 7. It's a pocket. 8. It's a magazine.

Exercise 28, p. 72: A. 1. *a*) Who arrived late every
day? *b*) What did Paul do every day? *c*) When did
Paul arrive late? 2. *a*) What was on the table?
b) Where was the book? 3. *a*) Who is explaining the
lesson to the class? *b*) What is the teacher explaining
to the class? *c*) Whom is the teacher explaining the
lesson to? 4. *a*) What does dozen mean? 5. *a*) Who is
playing tennis now? *b*) What are they doing now?
c) When are they playing tennis? B. 1. Is the man
waiting for the bus? Yes, he is. 2. Are they eating
lunch now? No, they aren't. C. 1. is reading 2. reads
3. prefer 4. sees 5. need D. 1. It's a small watch.
2. They're good books. 3. It's an apple tree. 4. It's an
expensive car. 5. It's a car factory.

Exercise 29, p. 74: 1. *b*) 2. *d*) 3. *b*) 4. *d*) 5. *b*) 6. *b*)
7. *c*) 8. *b*) 9. *b*) 10. *b*)

Lesson 5

Exercise 1, p. 76: 1. work 2. work 3. works
4. works 5. works 6. work 7. work 8. worked
9. worked 10. worked 11. worked 12. worked
13. worked 14. worked 15. am going to work 16. are
going to work 17. is going to work 18. is going to
work 19. is going to work 20. are going to work
21. are going to work

Exercise 2, p. 77: 1. I am going to study 2. she is
going to read 3. they are going to do 4. he is going to
eat 5. he is going to eat 6. we are going to go 7. I am
going to study 8. she is going to study 9. he is going to
work 10. they are going to visit

Exercise 3, p. 78: 1. am going to work 2. is going to
go 3. are going to eat 4. are going to study 5. is going
to write 6. are going to go 7. are going to read 8. are
going to play 9. are going to buy 10. are going to visit

Exercise 4, p. 79: 1. No, I'm going to eat the cake
tomorrow. 2. No, we're going to study all of the
lessons tomorrow. 3. No, Jane's going to speak with
Paul tomorrow. 4. No, John and Sue are going to go to
New York tomorrow. 5. No, Mark is going to do the
homework tomorrow.

Exercise 5, p. 79: 1. Are the students going to study
history? Yes, they are. What are the students going to
study? History. 2. Is Rick going to write a letter

tomorrow? No, he isn't. Who is going to write a letter
tomorrow? Rick is. 3. Are Judy and Jane going to play
tennis tomorrow? No, they aren't. Who is going to play
tennis tomorrow? Judy and Jane are. 4. Are we going
to study math tomorrow afternoon? Yes, we are. What
are we going to do tomorrow afternoon? Study math.
5. Is Mrs. Sanders going to call Joe? Yes, she is. Whom
is Mrs. Sanders going to call? Joe. 6. Are Bob and Bill
going to go to Florida? No, they aren't. Where are Bob
and Bill going to go? To Florida. 7. Is the party going
to begin at seven o'clock? Yes, it is. When is the party
going to begin? At seven o'clock.

Exercise 6, p. 81: 1. I'm not 2. they don't 3. it
wasn't 4. he isn't 5. we don't 6. I didn't 7. you
aren't 8. I don't 9. I wasn't 10. you didn't 11. it
doesn't 12. he didn't 13. you weren't 14. she isn't
15. they weren't 16. you don't 17. she didn't 18. we
aren't 19. he wasn't 20. it didn't 21. he doesn't
22. we didn't 23. they aren't 24. they didn't 25. we
weren't 26. she doesn't 27. she wasn't

Exercise 7, p. 82: 1. He doesn't work hard. 2. They
aren't studying. 3. He didn't study French. 4. I'm not
hungry now. 5. They aren't writing letters. 6. You
don't have all your books. 7. She doesn't have all her
books. 8. He wasn't sick. 9. He doesn't speak
French. 10. They didn't arrive late. 11. I'm not going
to write two letters. 12. You didn't like the movie.
13. She doesn't play tennis. 14. They weren't hungry.
15. Mr. Smith doesn't teach German. 16. They don't
do the work on time. 17. He doesn't do the work on
time. 18. They didn't do the work on time. 19. He
didn't do the work on time. 20. He isn't going to do
the work on time.

Exercise 8, p. 83: 1. He didn't play tennis. 2. He isn't
playing tennis. 3. She isn't going to call Paul. 4. He
doesn't like toast with butter. 5. He didn't like the
book. 6. I'm not tired. 7. He doesn't have a new car.
8. I don't do my work all of the time. 9. I didn't do my
work last week. 10. I'm not doing my work. 11. I'm
not going to do my work tomorrow. 12. They don't
have my keys. 13. We weren't very tired. 14. Mike
doesn't know all the answers. 15. Mike doesn't study
at night. 16. The student from Mexico wasn't absent
yesterday. 17. She didn't study last night. 18. She isn't
going to study tomorrow. 19. Pat doesn't write well.
20. They weren't late to class today.

Exercise 9, p. 84: 1. He isn't always sick. 2. He
doesn't usually study. 3. I'm not often late. 4. I don't
always arrive on time. 5. The students don't usually
read well. 6. She doesn't always do her work. 7. Mark
doesn't always arrive late. 8. Mark didn't always arrive
late. 9. They aren't usually early. 10. He didn't always
do his work on time.

Exercise 10, p. 84: The negative adverbs are:
2. seldom, 4. rarely, 7. never

Exercise 11, p. 84: 1. She doesn't usually arrive on
time. 2. She seldom arrives on time. 3. She doesn't
always arrive on time. 4. She rarely arrives on time.
5. She never arrives on time. 6. She doesn't often
arrive on time.

Exercise 12, p. 85: 1. They don't usually study at

night. 2. They aren't always at home. 3. negative
4. They don't always do the work. 5. negative
Exercise 13, p. 85: 1. any 2. some 3. some 4. any
5. some 6. any 7. some or any 8. any 9. any
10. some or any
Exercise 14, p. 86: 1. some 2. any 3. some/any
4. some/any 5. some 6. some/any 7. some/any
8. any 9. some 10. some
Exercise 15, p. 86: 1. Yes, he does. No, he doesn't.
Yes, he has some. No, he doesn't have any. 2. Yes,
they are. No, they aren't. Yes, they are going to buy
some. No, they aren't going to buy any. 3. Yes, I do.
No, I don't. Yes, I have some. No, I don't have any.
4. Yes, I do. No, I don't. Yes, I want some. No, I don't
want any.
Exercise 16, p. 87: 1. played 2. are going to study
3. are going to be 4. attends 5. need 6. are listening
7. assisted 8. is raining 9. did 10. visit
Exercise 17, p. 87: 1. is studying 2. studied 3. studies
4. am going to study 5. did 6. do 7. are doing 8. is
going to do 9. needed 10. are going to need 11. need
12. need 13. am 14. was 15. am going to be 16. am
17. Do you work 18. Are you working 19. Did you
work 20. Are you going to work 21. Is it going to rain
22. Did it rain 23. Does it rain 24. Is it raining
Exercise 18, p. 89: A. 1. Is George going to study
Spanish next year? 2. Who is going to study Spanish
next year? 3. What is George going to study next
year? 4. When is George going to study Spanish?
B. 1. Paul isn't here. 2. He doesn't usually study
hard. 3. She wasn't absent. 4. We didn't play for one
hour. 5. She doesn't smoke most of the time.
C. 1. I'm not 2. I wasn't 3. they aren't 4. it isn't
5. you weren't D. 1. some 2. any 3. some/any
4. some/any 5. any
Exercise 19, p. 90: 1. *b*) 2. *a*) 3. *c*) 4. *c*) 5. *b*) 6. *b*)
7. *b*) 8. *b*) 9. *c*) 10. *d*)

Lesson 6

Exercise 1, p. 91: 1. The apple. 2. The radio. 3. The
car. 4. The spoon. 5. The new house. 6. The glass of
water. 7. The television. 8. The shoes. 9. The apple.
10. The coffee.
Exercise 2, p. 92: 1. — Mr. Smith is *a* teacher. 2. —
John is studying — architecture. 3. *The* University of
California is on — College Street in—Los Angeles.
4. I bought *a* comb and *a* pen yesterday. *The* comb is
black, and *the* pen is green. 5. Do you prefer—
American history or *the* history of—France? 6. —
Mrs. Miller bought *a* newspaper and *a* watch. She was
reading *the* newspaper last night. 7. — Spanish is *a*
popular language. 8. — John likes—coffee. 9. I prefer
the music of—Mexico, but she likes—French music.
10. — Doctor Allen is from *the* Netherlands. He has *a*
new office here. 11. — Mrs. Allen is *a* good nurse.
12. I live in—Bogotá. It is *the* capital of—Colombia.
13. We visited *the* Atlantic Ocean, but we didn't visit
the Mississippi River. 14. — Harvard University is in
the United States. 15. Last summer we visited—
Switzerland,—Egypt,—South Africa, and *the* Soviet
Union. 16. Ann: "Do you like—oranges?" Sam: "Yes,

but I prefer—apples." 17. *The* Hawaiian Islands are in
the Pacific Ocean. 18. Peter is from *the* Dominican
Republic. 19. He studied—English,—algebra, and *the*
architecture of—Greece this semester. 20. —Argentina
is in—South America. 21. *The* Orinoco River is in—
Venezuela. 22. *The* United States is in—North
America. 23. *The* people in Switzerland speak—
French,— German, and— Italian. 24. I eat—salad
for—lunch every day. 25. Sue: "How was lunch?" Pat:
"*The* salad was excellent."
Exercise 3, p. 94: 1. I like—coffee for—breakfast.
2. *The* United States is a large country. 3. Did you ever
see *the* Amazon River? 4. He speaks—Japanese and—
Chinese. 5. Who visited *the* Soviet Union? 6. She
studied—American history. 7. Did you study—history
last semester? 8. Did you study *the* history of—Greece
last semester? 9. — Professor Jones teaches —
mathematics. 10. Matt doesn't like — tea.
Exercise 4, p. 94: 1. I like— hamburgers. 2. Do you
like—tea? 3. Did you ever visit—Argentina? 4. We
study—English in school. 5. — Greek architecture is
interesting. 6. Joe is studying — music. 7. He likes
the music of Mozart. 8. I'm going to see — Canada.
9. — Dr. Borman is a busy man. 10. *The* Netherlands
is in — Europe.
Exercise 5, p. 95: 1. C 2. C 3. NC 4. C 5. NC
6. NC 7. C 8. NC 9. NC 10. C 11. C 12. NC
13. C 14. NC 15. C
Exercise 6, p. 95: 1. some 2. a 3. some 4. some
5. an 6. a 7. some 8. a 9. some 10. some 11. some
12. some 13. some 14. a 15. some 16. a 17. a
18. some 19. a 20. a 21. some 22. some 23. some
24. a 25. a 26. a 27. some 28. some 29. an 30. some
Exercise 7, p. 96: 1. some 2. some 3. a 4. some
5. the 6. — 7. an 8. some 9. some 10. a 11. some
12. a 13. the 14. — 15. some 16. an 17. the 18. an
19. a 20. some 21. — 22. the 23. some 24. some
25. —
Exercise 8, p. 97: 1. I need three pieces of bread.
2. She wants two glasses of orange juice. 3. He wants
two slices of cake. 4. They are going to buy five
pounds of sugar. 5. You need three tubes of
toothpaste. 6. I need two sheets of paper.
7. Mr. Smith wants a cup of coffee.
Exercise 9, p. 98: 1. a few 2. a few 3. a little 4. a
few 5. a few 6. a little 7. a few 8. a little 9. a little
10. a little 11. a little 12. a little 13. a little 14. a
little 15. a few 16. a little 17. a little 18. a few 19. a
little 20. a little
Exercise 10, p. 98: 1. much 2. much 3. many
4. much 5. much 6. many 7. many 8. many 9. much
10. much 11. many 12. much 13. many 14. many
15. many 16. much 17. much 18. much 19. much
20. many
Exercise 11, p. 99: 1. a little 2. a lot of 3. a little 4. a
few 5. a lot of 6. a lot of 7. a little 8. a few 9. a lot
of 10. a lot of
Exercise 12, p. 100: 1. much, a lot of 2. many, a lot of
3. many, a lot of 4. much, a lot of 5. much, a lot of
Exercise 13, p. 101: 1. much, a lot of 2. a little
3. many, a lot of 4. many, a lot of 5. a few
Exercise 14, p. 101: 1. many 2. a little 3. a lot of 4. a

lot of 5. a few 6. a lot of 7. much 8. a lot of 9. a little 10. much

Exercise 15, p. 102: 1. How much ink do you want? A little. 2. How many bottles of ink do you want? A few. 3. How many apples do you want? A few. 4. How much orange juice do you want? A little. 5. How much coffee do you want? A little. 6. How many books do you want? A few. 7. How much money do you want? A little. 8. How much homework do you want? A little. 9. How many stamps do you want? A few. 10. How much furniture do you want? A little.

Exercise 16, p. 103: 1. not many 2. not much 3. not all 4. not any or none

Exercise 17, p. 103: 1. No, not much of the class was interesting. 2. No, not many of the students are excellent. 3. No, none of the teachers are excellent. 4. No, not all of the girls are going to New York. 5. No, none of the stories are very good. 6. No, not much of the food is delicious. 7. No, not many of the tests in the class were good.

Exercise 18, p. 104: 1. This 2. Those 3. These 4. That 5. This 6. These 7. this 8. Those 9. that 10. these 11. those 12. Those 13. Those 14. This 15. That

Exercise 19, p. 104: 1. her 2. his 3. their 4. my 5. your 6. our 7. their 8. his 9. her 10. its

Exercise 20, p. 105: 1. his 2. her 3. his 4. his 5. our 6. their 7. her 8. her 9. your 10. our 11. my 12. your 13. our 14. their 15. my

Exercise 21, p. 106: A. 1. — Mr. Jones studies — English in *the* United States. 2. I bought *a* pencil and *a* newspaper. I use *the* pencil to write letters and I read *the* newspaper. 3. *The* Netherlands and — Germany are in — Europe. 4. Mary is going to study — Greek philosophy and *the* philosophy of — Rome. 5. Would you like *some* oranges? 6. Would you like *an* orange? 7. Would you like *the* orange on the table? 8. Do you like — oranges? B. 1. I need two sheets of paper. 2. I want two slices of bread. C. 1. a little 2. many/a lot of 3. many/a lot of 4. a few D. 1. these 2. those 3. this 4. that E. 1. my 2. your 3. their 4. her 5. his

Exercise 22, p. 107: 1. *c)* 2. *d)* 3. *c)* 4. *b)* 5. *b)* 6. *c)* 7. *c)* 8. *c)* 9. *b)* 10. *c)*

Lesson 7

Exercise 1, p. 109: 1. Please write your name. 2. Please go to the bank. 3. Please give me a sheet of paper. 4. Please lend me a dollar.

Exercise 2, p. 110: 1. Would you please read page 95. 2. Would you please close the window. 3. Would you please pass me the salt. 4. Would you please come in.

Exercise 3, p. 110: 1. Don't sleep late. 2. Don't forget your ticket. 3. Don't eat my lunch. 4. Don't call me tonight. 5. Don't arrive late.

Exercise 4, p. 110: 1. Let's leave soon. 2. Let's sing some songs. 3. Let's go to a movie. 4. Let's do our homework. 5. Let's eat lunch now.

Exercise 5, p. 111: 1. shelf 2. loaf 3. knives 4. wives 5. child 6. women 7. businessman 8. — 9. men 10. feet 11. — 12. sheep 13. fish 14. — 15. teeth 16. policeman 17. mice 18. gentlemen

Exercise 6, p. 112: 1. is 2. children 3. knives 4. are 5. are 6. are 7. feet 8. teeth 9. loaves 10. is 11. arrive 12. men 13. These 14. are 15. have

Exercise 7, p. 112: 1. one 2. it 3. some 4. one 5. some 6. one 7. one 8. some 9. It 10. one

Exercise 8, p. 113: 1. another one 2. the other one 3. the other one 4. another one 5. The other one 6. another one 7. The other one 8. another one 9. the other one 10. the other one

Exercise 9, p. 113: 1. another one, the other one 2. the other one 3. the other one 4. others 5. the others 6. the other one 7. others 8. others 9. the other one 10. the other one 11. others 12. Another one 13. the other one 14. another one 15. others

Exercise 10, p. 114: 1. others 2. Another one 3. others 4. the other one 5. the others

Exercise 11, p. 115: 1. I 2. you 3. he 4. she 5. it 6. we 7. they 8. me 9. you 10. him 11. her 12. it 13. us 14. them 15. my 16. your 17. his 18. her 19. its 20. our 21. their

Exercise 12, p. 115: 1. She, her 2. He, them 3. He, them 4. She, them 5. They, it 6. We, you 7. he, his, him 8. they, their, them 9. we, our, us 10. We, it

Exercise 13, p. 116: 1. We 2. their 3. her 4. I, it 5. him 6. her 7. it, him 8. My 9. I 10. them 11. She, her 12. his, him 13. he, them 14. me 15. I, it 16. them 17. It 18. me 19. His 20. It

Exercise 14, p. 116: A. 1. Please pass the sugar. 2. Would you please pass the sugar. 3. Let's have a party. 4. Please don't speak loudly. B. 1. men 2. knives 3. children 4. mice 5. sheep 6. feet C. 1. are 2. is 3. are D. 1. one 2. another one 3. others 4. some 5. it 6. other E. 1. She, them 2. It 3. them 4. He, her 5. you 6. you, your, you

Exercise 15, p. 118: 1. *b)* 2. *b)* 3. *b)* 4. *b)* 5. *a)* 6. *c)* 7. *b)* 8. *c)* 9. *b)* 10. *c)*

Lesson 8

Exercise 1, p. 119: 1. Susan writes a letter to Sam. 2. I always read the newspaper to my brother. 3. We show our gift to the class. 4. She teaches new words to the students. 5. Please tell the good news to Mary. 6. I'm going to sell my bicycle to Bob. 7. I usually lend my car to Paul. 8. Did she bring an apple to the teacher? 9. Would you please take the food to your father. 10. He passed the salt to me.

Exercise 2, p. 120: 1. I teach Bill the lesson. 2. You showed Mr. Smith the map. 3. He brings my family the newspaper. 4. Please lend John the money. 5. Did you write your sister a long letter? 6. I sold Bill my car. 7. Pass your father the glass. 8. She is going to read me the letter. 9. Take Mrs. Jones the money. 10. I never tell my father lies.

Exercise 3, p. 120: 1. *a),b)* 2. *a),b)* 3. *a),b)* 4. *a),b)* 5. *a),b)*

Exercise 4, p. 121: 1. He's going to ask the teacher a question. 2. They charged Mr. Smith twenty dollars. 3. She saved Joe ten cents. 4. We asked the man the time of day. 5. Santa Claus wished the child Merry Christmas. 6. The bicycle cost me fifty dollars. 7. The store charged them ten dollars for a new shirt.

Exercise 5, p. 121: 1. *b*) 2. *b*) 3. *b*) 4. *b*) 5. *b*)

Exercise 6, p. 122: 1. She explained the vocabulary to the students. 2. Mary reported the news to the women. 3. We suggested that restaurant to them. 4. I introduced Susan to Mike. 5. I described my trip to my family. 6. Bill mentioned the idea to the men. 7. I spoke English to Mr. Jones. 8. He proved his age to the girl. 9. The teacher repeated the answers to the class. 10. I always say "hello" to Jane.

Exercise 7, p. 123: 1. *a*) 2. *a*) 3. *a*) 4. *a*) 5. *a*)

Exercise 8, p. 123: 1. *ab*) 2. *b*) 3. *a*) 4. *ab*) 5. *ab*) 6. *b*) 7. *ab*) 8. *ab*) 9. *a*) 10. *a*) 11. *ab*) 12. *b*) 13. *ab*) 14. *a*) 15. *a*) 16. *b*) 17. *a*) 18. *ab*) 19. *ab*) 20. *ab*) 21. *a*) 22. *ab*) 23. *ab*) 24. *b*) 25. *a*)

Exercise 9, p. 124: 1. I'm going to get some water for John. 2. She found the newspaper for Mr. Miller. 3. She made a cake for the girl. 4. The teacher got a test for the student. 5. My brother did a favor for me.

Exercise 10, p. 125: 1. I made the students some tea. 2. Mr. Smith bought his wife a dress. 3. He found me a pencil. 4. He did me a favor. 5. They got me a ticket.

Exercise 11, p. 125: 1. *a*),*b*) 2. *a*),*b*) 3. *a*),*b*) 4. *a*),*b*) 5. *a*),*b*)

Exercise 12, p. 125: 1. The doctor prescribed the medicine for me. 2. She cashed the check for Mike. 3. The teacher pronounced the word for the students. 4. He closed the window for the girl. 5. Martha did the homework for Bill. 6. The teacher answered the question for the boy. 7. The teacher changed the test grade for the student.

Exercise 13, p. 126: 1. *a*) 2. *a*) 3. *a*) 4. *a*) 5. *a*) 6. *a*) 7. *a*) 8. *a*)

Exercise 14, p. 127: 1. *a*) 2. *a*) 3. *ab*) 4. *a*) 5. *ab*) 6. *ab*) 7. *a*) 8. *a*) 9. *ab*) 10. *ab*) 11. *a*) 12. *a*) 13. *ab*)

Exercise 15, p. 127: 1. to me 2. for me 3. me 4. for me 5. to me 6. me 7. to me 8. to me 9. me 10. to me 11. for me 12. me 13. to me 14. for me 15. to me 16. me 17. me 18. me 19. for me 20. me 21. for me 22. for me 23. to me 24. for me 25. for me

Exercise 16, p. 129: 1. explained 2. made 3. show 4. sends 5. pass 6. pronounced 7. take 8. sent 9. bring 10. get 11. lend 12. found 13. tells 14. wished 15. mentioned 16. give

Exercise 17, p. 130: 1. drank 2. gave 3. became 4. read 5. began 6. got 7. saw 8. wore 9. took 10. sat 11. woke 12. broke 13. ate 14. knew 15. spoke 16. forgot 17. met 18. tore 19. came 20. wrote 21. chose

Exercise 18, p. 130: 1. gave 2. come 3. took 4. forget 5. break ·6. was 7. began 8. give 9. ate 10. got

Exercise 19, p. 131: 1. Yes, he chose a car. 2. No, they didn't break the glass. 3. No, she didn't begin the work. 4. Yes, I saw the movie. 5. No, I didn't forget your book.

Exercise 20, p. 131: 1. left 2. did 3. understood 4. sent 5. had 6. stood 7. felt 8. spent 9. made 10. put 11. slept 12. cost 13. lent 14. meant 15. cut 16. heard 17. brought 18. taught 19. told 20. bought 21. thought 22. said

Exercise 21, p. 132: 1. had 2. bought 3. hear 4. sent 5. cut 6. made 7. tell 8. said 9. felt 10. sleep

Exercise 22, p. 133: 1. They ate steak. 2. You told me yes. 3. Robert made tea. 4. I slept six hours. 5. She brought one book.

Exercise 23, p. 133: 1. broke 2. brought 3. ate 4. did 5. woke 6. cut 7. attended 8. felt 9. drank 10. sent 11. spoke 12. slept 13. wanted 14. knew 15. meant 16. wore 17. were 18. bought 19. studied 20. chose 21. went 22. put 23. made 24. got 25. began 26. had 27. gave 28. thought 29. sat 30. spent 31. said 32. read 33. was 34. saw 35. met 36. left 37. worked 38. tore 39. took 40. taught 41. told 42. cost 43. understood 44. became 45. wrote 46. forgot 47. heard 48. came 49. lent 50. stood

Exercise 24, p. 134: A. 1. She cashed a check for me. 2. I did a favor for the boys. I did the boys a favor. 3. He announced the schedule to us. 4. Mr. Jones bought a present for Bill. Mr. Jones bought Bill a present. 5. The shirt cost him six dollars. B. 1. to me 2. me 3. for me 4. me 5. for me 6. to me 7. for me 8. me 9. to me 10. for me C. 1. brought 2. told 3. bought 4. read 5. spent 6. slept 7. meant 8. found 9. gave 10. saw 11. chose 12. heard 13. cut 14. taught 15. drank

Exercise 25, p. 136: 1. *c*) 2. *c*) 3. *b*) 4. *c*) 5. *d*) 6. *d*) 7. *b*) 8. *a*) 9. *d*) 10. *b*)

Lesson 9

Exercise 1, p. 137: 1. quietly 2. wisely 3. clearly 4. fast 5. sadly 6. easily 7. silently 8. sincerely 9. badly 10. hard 11. loudly 12. slowly 13. carefully 14. well 15. beautifully 16. promptly 17. really 18. poorly 19. rapidly 20. suddenly

Exercise 2, p. 138: 1. correctly 2. carefully 3. fast 4. well 5. beautifully 6. hard 7. carefully 8. sincerely 9. quickly 10. well

Exercise 3, p. 138: 1. an excellent writer 2. a slow eater 3. fast readers 4. a careful driver 5. good singers 6. a hard worker 7. a clear speaker 8. a rapid swimmer 9. a good adviser 10. good workers

Exercise 4, p. 139: 1. correctly 2. easy 3. carefully 4. quiet 5. silently 6. loud 7. rapidly 8. careful 9. clear 10. sincere 11. sad 12. quickly 13. wise 14. slow 15. beautiful

Exercise 5, p. 139: 1. The students pronounced the words correctly yesterday. 2. She always cooks dinner rapidly. 3. He called the store immediately. 4. She always drives carefully at night. 5. He spoke to me sincerely last night. 6. I never eat fast at home. 7. He is going to read the lesson carefully. 8. He is a careful worker at the bank. 9. The good students always arrive punctually. 10. Steven spoke English well a year ago.

Exercise 6, p. 140: 1. The quiet lady is reading. 2. The student from Colombia has a blue shirt. 3. The store on Green Street sells shoes. 4. The boy from Canada speaks English and French. 5. The question about verbs is difficult. 6. That short story is very good. 7. The chair near the door is old. 8. The lady with blond hair is a nurse. 9. Those students from Canada are intelligent. 10. The book about tennis is very good. **Exercise 7, p. 141:** 1. Who talked to Mary last night? When did they talk to Mary? Whom did they talk to last night? 2. Who visited Jack in Miami last month? Whom did she visit in Miami last month? Where did she visit Jack last month? 3. How much did that blue shirt cost him? Which shirt cost him ten dollars? 4. When did Mike eat two hamburgers? How many hamburgers did Mike eat at noon? What did Mike eat at noon? 5. Who walked six miles this morning? How far did Tim walk this morning? 6. Who was a teacher in New York in 1977? What was Mr. Smith in New York in 1977? When was Mr. Smith a teacher in New York? 7. What did they give to him? Whom did they give a present to?

Exercise 8, p. 142: 1. Who saw Bill yesterday? Whom did we see yesterday? When did we see Bill? 2. What cost ten dollars? How much did that book cost? 3. Who bought two pens for Jill? How many pens did he buy for Jill? Whom did he buy two pens for? 4. What did George do in Brazil? Where did George study Portuguese? 5. How much did the girls spend at the store? Where did the girls spend twenty dollars?

Exercise 9, p. 143: A. 1. fast 2. wisely 3. easily 4. hard 5. sincerely 6. well B. 1. well 2. carefully C. 1. careful 2. slow D. 1. Please read the questions carefully. 2. They always read slowly in class. E. 1. That store on State Street is expensive. 2. That student from Brazil studies a lot. F. 1. *a)* Who bought two shirts for his father yesterday? *b)* How many shirts did John buy for his father yesterday? *c)* Whom did John buy two shirts for yesterday? *d)* When did John buy two shirts for his father? 2. *a)* Who spent five dollars in the store? *b)* Where did Bill spend five dollars? *c)* How much did Bill spend in the store?

Exercise 10, p. 144: 1. *a)* 2. *a)* 3. *b)* 4. *b)* 5. *c)* 6. *c)* 7. *d)* 8. *b)* 9. *c)* 10. *a)*

Review Test 1: Lessons 1–9, pp. 146–49

1. *b)* 2. *b)* 3. *d)* 4. *b)* 5. *d)* 6. *c)* 7. *d)* 8. *c)* 9. *c)* 10. *a)* 11. *c)* 12. *b)* 13. *d)* 14. *a)* 15. *b)* 16. *c)* 17. *b)* 18. *a)* 19. *b)* 20. *b)* 21. *b)* 22. *d)* 23. *c)* 24. *c)* 25. *d)* 26. *c)* 27. *b)* 28. *b)* 29. *c)* 30. *d)* 31. *b)* 32. *b)* 33. *c)* 34. *c)* 35. *c)* 36. *d)* 37. *a)* 38. *c)* 39. *c)* 40. *b)* 41. *b)* 42. *b)* 43. *b)* 44. *d)* 45. *a)* 46. *c)* 47. *a)* 48. *b)* 49. *a)* 50. *d)*

Review Test 2: Lessons 1–9, pp. 150–53

1. *d)* 2. *b)* 3. *a)* 4. *c)* 5. *b)* 6. *b)* 7. *d)* 8. *a)* 9. *b)* 10. *d)* 11. *c)* 12. *d)* 13. *c)* 14. *b)* 15. *c)* 16. *c)* 17. *b)* 18. *d)* 19. *b)* 20. *c)* 21. *c)* 22. *b)* 23. *c)* 24. *d)* 25. *c)* 26. *c)* 27. *b)* 28. *b)* 29. *b)* 30. *c)* 31. *a)* 32. *a)* 33. *b)* 34. *d)* 35. *c)* 36. *b)* 37. *c)* 38. *c)* 39. *c)* 40. *a)* 41. *b)* 42. *d)* 43. *d)* 44. *c)* 45. *a)* 46. *c)* 47. *c)* 48. *a)* 49. *d)* 50. *c)*

Lesson 11

Exercise 1, p. 154: 7. I can play 8. you can play 9. he can play 10. she can play 11. we can play 12. they can play 13. I should study 14. you should study 15. he should study 16. she should study 17. we should study 18. they should study 19. I must be 20. you must be 21. he must be 22. she must be 23. we must be 24. they must be 25. I might have 26. you might have 27. he might have 28. she might have 29. we might have 30. they might have 31. I may use 32. you may use 33. he may use 34. she may use 35. we may use 36. they may use

Exercise 2, p. 155: 1. must 2. might 3. should 4. can 5. will 6. must 7. may 8. could 9. should 10. might

Exercise 3, p. 156: 1. can 2. will 3. must 4. might 5. must 6. May 7. must 8. should 9. might 10. will 11. must 12. can 13. could 14. must 15. must

Exercise 4, p. 157: 1. can drive 2. must get 3. can type 4. could play 5. may use 6. might receive 7. will arrive 8. must be 9. must take 10. must have 11. can speak and write 12. can run 13. should have 14. can sing 15. will leave

Exercise 5, p. 158: 1. aren't able to 2. won't 3. couldn't 4. can't 5. might not 6. mustn't 7. isn't going to 8. may not 9. aren't able to 10. won't 11. don't have to 12. doesn't have to 13. can't 14. shouldn't 15. shouldn't

Exercise 6, p. 159: 1. Will Paul arrive in a few minutes? Yes, he will. 2. Should Mark study grammar now? Yes, he should. 3. Might they be at home now? No, they might not. 4. Could he get up late every day? No, he couldn't. 5. May I smoke in this room? No, you may not. 6. Can your mother cook very well? Yes, she can. 7. Must every student do his homework? Yes, he must. 8. May we help you? Yes, you may. 9. Can you speak Spanish? No, I can't. 10. Should you go to bed early? Yes, I should.

Exercise 7, p. 161: 1. Who could play tennis every day? What could they play every day? When could they play tennis? 2. What must we study tonight? When must we study vocabulary? 3. Who should be here around nine o'clock? Where should she be around nine o'clock? When should she be here? 4. Who will see Mary tonight? Whom will Henry see tonight? When will Henry see Mary? 5. Which man might have five chairs for sale? How many chairs might that man have for sale?

Exercise 8, p. 162: 1. Who should listen to the radio more often? What should he listen to more often? 2. Who might arrive tonight? When might the girls arrive? 3. Where must Mr. and Mrs. Jones be tomorrow morning? When must Mr. and Mrs. Jones be here? 4. Who shouldn't play with matches? What shouldn't children play with? 5. Who will talk to the doctor at the hospital? Whom will you talk to at the hospital? Where will you talk to the doctor?

Exercise 9, p. 163: 1. Who speaks English? What does Martha speak? 2. Who arrived at noon? When did they arrive? 3. Whom did she see at school? Where did she see Joe? 4. Who can play tennis very well? What can they play very well? 5. Who has a new car? 10. What does Bob have?

Exercise 10, p. 163: 1. Who had a history test yesterday? Which test did Paul have yesterday? 2. Who will drive four hundred miles tonight? How many miles will they drive tonight? 3. What should everyone send to the sick boy? Whom should everyone send a card to? 4. What cost him twenty dollars? How much did this new shirt cost him? 5. Who will take a history test tomorrow? What will the students take tomorrow?

Exercise 11, p. 164: 1. and Suzy is too. 2. and they will too 3. and she does too 4. and Mr. Todd does too 5. and she is too 6. and they did too 7. and he might too 8. and Mike does too 9. and he should too 10. and I was too

Exercise 12, p. 165: 1. and John won't either 2. and the reading book isn't either 3. and I didn't either 4. and Peter couldn't either 5. and Jane might not either 6. and he wasn't either 7. and we don't either 8. and he didn't either 9. and Mr. Jones isn't either 10. and I'm not either

Exercise 13, p. 166: 1. but my sister does 2. but she isn't 3. but Jane will 4. but Mr. Art doesn't 5. but your brother can 6. but her husband was 7. but she could 8. but my sister did 9. but their friends won't 10. but I never do

Exercise 14, p. 167: 1. but they don't 2. and we should too 3. and he couldn't either 4. and she did too 5. and John and Mary weren't either 6. but her brother will 7. and my sister is too 8. but I am not 9. and she does too 10. and she does too

Exercise 15, p. 168: 1. might not 2. don't either 3. do too 4. is too 5. will 6. wasn't 7. didn't 8. couldn't either 9. didn't 10. doesn't either 11. will too 12. won't 13. could 14. didn't either 15. does

Exercise 16, p. 169: A. 1. should 2. will 3. must 4. might 5. may 6. can 7. must 8. must 9. could B. 1. I could play football. 2. She will do the work. 3. It might rain. 4. She must have two brothers. C. 1. John isn't very hungry now, and Mary isn't either. 2. They will come by bus, but my brother won't. 3. They had to study yesterday, and we did too. 4. Sally speaks French, and Paul does too. 5. This man couldn't go with us, and that man couldn't either.

Exercise 17, p. 170: 1. *b)* 2. *b)* 3. *b)* 4. *d)* 5. *c)* 6. *b)* 7. *b)* 8. *c)* 9. *d)* 10. *b)*

Lesson 12

Exercise 1, p. 171: 1. ask for it 2. hand it in 3. put it on 4. take it off 5. listen to it 6. speak to you 7. wake you up 8. think of you 9. wait for you 10. call on you 11. talk to us 12. pick us up 13. wait for us 14. listen to us 15. look for us 16. look at them 17. throw them away 18. give them back 19. hand them out 20. look for them 21. leave me out 22. think of me 23. call me up 24. call on me 25. pick me up

Exercise 2, p. 172: 1. Look for them 2. Think of it. 3. Turn them on. 4. Look it over. 5. Talk to him.

6. Pick it up. 7. Put them on. 8. Ask for him. 9. Wait for it. 10. Put it out. 11. listen to it. 12. throw it away. 13. handed them out. 14. handed them in. 15. looking for it.

Exercise 3, p. 173: 1. he looked them up 2. he (she) gives them back 3. I didn't wake him (her) up 4. he won't look at them 5. I can't think of it 6. he turned them off 7. he waited for her 8. they may take them off 9. he didn't talk to her 10. she put it up

Exercise 4, p. 174: 1. Why did Matt go to the store? In order to buy some fruit. To buy some fruit. For some fruit. 2. Why did Peter leave the room? In order to look for a chair. To look for a chair. For a chair. 3. Why did he have to study a lot? In order to pass the test. To pass the test. For the test. 4. Why will Patty go home? In order to get her homework. To get her homework. For her homework.

Exercise 5, p. 175: 1. to 2. to 3. for 4. to 5. for 6. to 7. for 8. to 9. for 10. to 11. for 12. to 13. to 14. to 15. to 16. for 17. for 18. for 19. to 20. for

Exercise 6, p. 176: 1. by 2. by 3. with 4. with 5. by 6. with 7. by 8. by 9. with 10. with 11. by 12. with 13. with 14. with 15. by 16. by 17. with 18. by 19. with 20. by

Exercise 7, p. 177: 1. slowly 2. well 3. fast 4. rapidly 5. beautifully 6. hard 7. carefully 8. promptly 9. sincerely 10. well

Exercise 8, p. 178: 1. by running 2. by working 3. by writing 4. by listening 5. by walking 6. by reading 7. by using 8. by following 9. by mixing 10. by repeating

Exericse 9, p. 179: 1. How 2. How 3. Why 4. How 5. Why 6. How 7. How 8. How 9. Why 10. Why 11. How 12. How 13. How 14. Why 15. How

Exercise 10, p. 179: 1. How did he answer? With a smile. 2. Why did they call? To ask a question. 3. How did we learn French? By practicing every day. 4. How did she arrive? By bus. 5. Why did Kay go to the bank? For some money. 6. Why did she come? To learn English. 7. Why did we call? To get some information. 8. How did he cut the apple? With a knife. 9. How are they communicating? By phone. 10. How should they go? With a group.

Exercise 11, p. 181: A. 1. them off 2. at it 3. them back 4. it down B. 1. Why did she go to the store? For some bread. 2. How did they cook the meat? By frying it. 3. Why did he write a letter? To get some information. 4. How did she come home? By bus. 5. How does he prefer to write? With a pencil. C. 1. by 2. with 3. by 4. to 5. for 6. with 7. by 8. up 9. down 10. up

Exercise 12, p. 182: 1. *c)* 2. *b)* 3. *b)* 4. *b)* 5. *c)* 6. *a)* 7. *d)* 8. *a)* 9. *c)* 10. *c)*

Lesson 13

Exercise 1, p. 184: 1. like to swim 2. might be 3. hopes to be 4. trying to learn 5. will arrive 6. intends to work 7. might need 8. planning to go 9. promises to come 10. may pick up 11. could speak 12. needs to write 13. decided to go 14. agrees to pay

15. expect to arrive 16. will try to learn 17. needs to try to learn to speak 18. should promise to help 19. must want to go 20. need to agree to do

Exercise 2, p. 185: 1. but he had to 2. but they plan to 3. but I am hoping to 4. but they might 5. but she has to 6. but we need to 7. but it must 8. but he didn't intend to 9. but he would like to 10. but he should 11. but I hoped to 12. but she wanted to 13. but she has to 14. but he shouldn't 15. but he doesn't want to

Exercise 3, p. 186: 1. The boys don't want to eat now. 2. John didn't plan to study for the examination. 3. You aren't trying to learn English rapidly. 4. She doesn't prefer to drink water. 5. I don't need to eat more at night.

Exercise 4, p. 187: 1. She is trying not to talk loudly. 2. We prefer not to drink that beer. 3. I tried not to sleep in class. 4. Tom and Sue agree not to do the work. 5. Frank decided not to go with me.

Exercise 5, p. 187: 1. my brother to fix 2. Mr. Brown to help 3. the students to bring 4. George to go 5. me to use 6. us to clean 7. Mr. and Mrs. Jones to come 8. me to write 9. you to look 10. the children to do

Exercise 6, p. 188: 1. The teacher told Joe to be quiet. 2. Mr. Max asked Mark to mail the letters. 3. She wanted Paul to go to the store. 4. They invited me to play tennis. 5. George would like me to eat lunch with him. 6. Jack told me to call him up. 7. He expects me to pick him up. 8. They need Bob to carry the box. 9. I want you to go to the bank. 10. Fran asked me to erase the blackboard.

Exercise 7, p. 189: 1. Books can be interesting to read. 2. Dogs are beautiful to watch. 3. This lesson is easy for me to understand. 4. English words are difficult to pronounce. 5. These pants are very comfortable to wear. 6. This medicine is important for you to take. 7. This song is very pretty to listen to. 8. This cake was easy to make. 9. These words are difficult to spell. 10. The book will be easy for us to read. 11. Cigarettes are bad for you to smoke. 12. Hamburgers are not expensive to eat. 13. That recipe is hard to follow. 14. This record is nice to listen to. 15. That movie is not interesting to watch.

Exercise 8, p. 190: 1. enough 2. too 3. enough 4. too 5. enough 6. too 7. enough 8. too 9. enough 10. too 11. too 12. too 13. enough 14. too 15. too 16. too 17. enough 18. enough 19. enough 20. too

Exercise 9, p. 192: 1. James is too sick to go on the trip. 2. I'm tall enough to reach the ceiling. 3. Peter is rich enough to buy a new car. 4. It is warm enough for the children to go swimming. 5. That man is strong enough to pick up this box. 6. The car is cheap enough for her to buy. 7. This hat is too large for me to wear. 8. You're happy enough to forget all your problems. 9. We were too sick to go to class. 10. Those books are too heavy for the boys to carry. 11. The window is low enough for him to reach. 12. Randy is hungry enough to eat four sandwiches. 13. James is too short to reach the faucet. 14. The food is too hot for us to eat. 15. The dog is too dirty for us to keep in the house.

Exercise 10, p. 193: A. 1. We will learn to speak English. 2. John doesn't study, but he should. 3. I want Mary to open the window. 4. They promised not to arrive early. 5. The doctor ordered me to rest. 6. They might arrive late. 7. I didn't get a letter, but I would like to. 8. She is going to try to do the homework. 9. We would like Rosemary to be here. 10. We didn't get a letter, but we wanted to.
B. 1. John is too young to vote. 2. Books are interesting to read. 3. It is too cold for us to go swimming. 4. The table is too heavy for you to pick up. 5. Long words are difficult to pronounce. 6. That shirt is too expensive for me to buy. C. 1. are 2. is 3. is 4. is 5. is

Exercise 11, p. 195: 1. *c*) 2. *c*) 3. *d*) 4. *c*) 5. *b*) 6. *d*) 7. *b*) 8. *d*) 9. *c*) 10. *c*)

Lesson 14

Exercise 1, p. 196: 1. It's 10:45. 2. It was 10:30. 3. It's March 6. 4. It was March 1. 5. It's raining. (or, It's rainy.) 6. It's Monday. 7. It will be Tuesday. 8. It's Mr. Prince. 9. It's August. 10. It was Mary.

Exercise 2, p. 197: 1. It is 1,100 miles from New Orleans to Washington. 2. It is 2 miles from here to the store. 3. It's 7 hours from here to Miami. 4. It is 1 block to the post office. 5. It is 200 miles from New York to Boston.

Exercise 3, p. 198: 1. It is easy to understand this lesson. 2. It is difficult to pronounce English sounds. 3. It is comfortable to wear these pants. 4. It is good for you to take this medicine. 5. It is expensive to call long distance. 6. It was difficult to make that cake. 7. It is bad for your health to smoke cigarettes. 8. It will be easy for us to read the book. 9. It must be fun to play tennis. 10. It is not expensive to eat hamburgers.

Exercise 4, p. 198: 1. "Thank you" is polite to say. It is polite to say "thank you." 2. A motorcycle can be dangerous to drive. It can be dangerous to drive a motorcycle. 3. These words are difficult to spell. It is difficult to spell these words. 4. Those shoes were very practical to buy. It was very practical to buy those shoes. 5. Big houses are very expensive to live in. It is very expensive to live in big houses.

Exercise 5, p. 199: 1. will be 2. were 3. are 4. was 5. is 6. are 7. was 8. will be 9. were 10. are

Exercise 6, p. 200: 1. There is an apple in the refrigerator now. 2. There was a test in history class yesterday. 3. There are many students studying English now. 4. There were a few books on the desk a few minutes ago. 5. There is a lot of bread on the table now.

Exercise 7, p. 200: 1. *a*) 2. *a*) 3. *b*) 4. *a*) 5. *a*) 6. *a*) 7. *b*) 8. *a*) 9. *a*) 10. *b*)

Exercise 8, p. 201: 1. John's pencil 2. the child's toy 3. the top of the table 4. the cover of the box 5. the man's car 6. the lady's ring 7. the ladies' rings 8. today's newspaper 9. Mr. Smith's tie 10. the men's cars 11. the girl's book 12. the girls' books 13. the children's toys 14. the ladies' purses 15. the point of the pencil 16. Ned's house 17. Tom's car 18. the end of the movie 19. the students' test papers 20. the beginning of the story

Exericse 9, p. 202: 1. John's book 2. Today's newspaper 3. The cover of the book 4. Mike's car 5. yesterday's homework 6. Jack's story 7. Sue's party 8. The children's cat 9. The boys' father 10. The secretary's work

Exercise 10, p. 202: 1. ours 2. ours 3. hers 4. theirs 5. yours 6. his 7. mine 8. yours 9. hers 10. its

Exercise 11, p. 203: 1. mine 2. mine 3. his 4. hers 5. yours 6. theirs 7. his 8. his 9. ours 10. mine

Exercise 12, p. 203: 1. and mine does too 2. and ours is too 3. and hers are too 4. and theirs did too 5. and hers was too 6. and his did too 7. and Paul's might too 8. and ours did too 9. and yours can too 10. and mine was too

Exercise 13, p. 204: 1. Whose pencil is this? Steve's. 2. Whose car cost ten thousand dollars? Mine. 3. Whose father owns this grocery store? Matt's. 4. Whose car would she like to have? Mine. 5. Whose pencil is John using? Steve's. 6. Whose father did we meet? Jack's. 7. Whose letter was on the table this morning? Hers. 8. Whose letter did they want to read? Paul's. 9. Whose test did the teacher correct first? George's. 10. Whose dog ran away? Mark's.

Exercise 14, p. 206: 1. a red one 2. two red ones 3. two 4. one 5. a red one 6. a good red one 7. mine 8. my green one 9. his 10. his green ones 11. some 12. a new one 13. a few 14. this old one 15. theirs 16. your old one 17. theirs 18. theirs 19. their green ones 20. many difficult ones 21. many 22. several good ones 23. these green ones 24. a cheap one 25. an expensive one 26. some 27. some yellow ones 28. a few 29. a few red ones 30. a nice one

Exercise 15, p. 207: (Some answers in this exercise may vary.) 1. sweet ones 2. his 3. green ones 4. ones 5. his 6. small ones 7. red ones 8. a small one 9. that one 10. a late one

Exercise 16, p. 208: A. 1. It is hot. 2. It is May. 3. It is Rick. 4. It is 1,300 miles from New York to Miami. B. 1. It is easy to write letters. 2. It is good to know English. 3. It can be fun to play baseball. C. 1. will be 2. was 3. are D. 1. Mr. Miller's car 2. a week's vacation 3. the top of the table 4. his 5. theirs E. 1. Whose father speaks English and Spanish? 2. Whose father did we visit yesterday? F. 1. yes 2. yes 3. yes 4. no 5. no 6. yes 7. no 8. no 9. no 10. yes

Exercise 17, p. 209: 1. c) 2. c) 3. d) 4. d) 5. c) 6. c) 7. c) 8. c) 9. c) 10. c)

Lesson 15

Exercise 1, p. 211: 1. like 2. different from 3. the same as 4. like 5. the same as 6. like 7. the same as 8. the same as 9. like 10. different from

Exercise 2, p. 212: 1. Your watch is like mine. 2. My shirt is the same as yours. 3. This house is different from that one. 4. My sister is like yours. 5. My uncle's address is the same as my aunt's. 6. Mary's

purse is different from Jane's. 7. Your age is the same as mine. 8. Her dog is like mine. 9. Your passport is different from hers. 10. This restaurant is different from that one.

Exercise 3, p. 213: 1. price 2. thickness 3. speed 4. width 5. distance 6. depth 7. height 8. height 9. hardness 10. length

Exercise 4, p. 214: 1. price 2. old 3. thick 4. fast 5. size 6. length 7. heavy 8. depth 9. hard 10. height 11. age 12. depth 13. deep 14. wide 15. length

Exercise 5, p. 214: 1. many, much 2. many 3. many 4. much, many 5. much, many 6. many, much 7. much, many 8. many 9. much, many 10. many, much

Exercise 6, p. 216: 1. Joe doesn't swim as well as Paul. 2. Peter can't run as fast as John. 3. Mr. Smith works as hard as his wife. 4. George doesn't cook as well as Mary. 5. Ann swims as quickly as Jan.

Exercise 7, p. 217: 1. Bill is the same height as Joe. Bill is as tall as Joe. 2. I ate as many sandwiches as Joe. I ate as much as Joe. 3. Peter isn't the same age as Joe. Peter isn't as old as Joe. 4. Mark drank as many glasses of milk as Nancy. Mark drank as much milk as Nancy. 5. This steak is the same thickness as that one. This steak is as thick as that one.

Exercise 8, p. 218: The correct comparative forms are: 1, 2, 3, 5, 6, 10

Exercise 9, p. 218: 1. taller 2. more expensive 3. better 4. more carefully 5. older 6. worse 7. more intelligent 8. longer 9. more delicious 10. heavier

Exercise 10, p. 219: 1. more quickly than 2. happier than 3. as old as 4. more difficult than 5. as good as

Exercise 11, p. 220: The correct superlative forms are: 1, 3, 4, 5, 8, 9, 10

Exercise 12, p. 220: 1. taller, the tallest 2. more careful, the most careful 3. better, the best 4. nicer, the nicest 5. more intelligent, the most intelligent 6. faster, the fastest 7. more slowly, the most slowly 8. more rapidly, the most rapidly 9. worse, the worst 10. more quickly, the most quickly

Exercise 13, p. 221: 1. taller 2. the best 3. happier, the happiest 4. more interesting 5. more difficult, the most difficult 6. the prettiest 7. nice, nicer 8. the worst 9. easy 10. cold

Exercise 14, p. 221: 1. more 2. more 3. more 4. the most 5. more, the most 6. more, the most 7. more 8. more 9. the most 10. the most

Exercise 15, p. 222: A. 1. height 2. age 3. size 4. thickness 5. length B. 1. more careful, the most careful 2. taller, the tallest 3. better, the best 4. faster, the fastest 5. more quickly, the most quickly 6. busier, the busiest C. 1. weight 2. tall 3. best 4. worst 5. tallest

Exercise 16, p. 223: 1. c) 2. c) 3. b) 4. b) 5. a) 6. b) 7. c) 8. d) 9. b) 10. a)

Lesson 16

Exercise 1, p. 225: 1. I think (that) a book is more expensive. 2. I learned (that) taller was correct. 3. I know (that) 2+2=4 is correct. 4. I think (that) a car is heavier. 5. I think (that) Alaska is the biggest state in the United States. 6. I think (that) kitchen is more difficult to pronounce. (or I think (that) chicken is more difficult to pronounce.) 7. I think (that) a cat is faster. 8. I think (that) a plane ticket is more expensive. 9. I think (that) fried chicken is better for a picnic. 10. I think (that) toast is easier to cook.

Exercise 2, p. 226: 1. Does Beth know who answered the phone? 2. Does Ron know whom John called? 3. Can he explain why his tests were so bad? 4. Did George know when the party was? 5. Did she ask who was coming to the party? 6. Would the teacher like to know what time it is? 7. Did Pedro explain where his country is? 8. Will Rob tell us whose books he has? 9. Will the teacher tell us which answer is correct? 10. Did Bill tell you where the party was?

Exercise 3, p. 227: 1. why Greg was late 2. which shirt she prefers 3. where the new television is 4. what the boy's name is 5. whose keys he found 6. whom they called 7. what time it is 8. how far the post office is 9. where he went 10. what this word means 11. where he is from 12. who that girl in the red dress is 13. what he lost 14. what Pete ate 15. when we have a test 16. what her phone number is 17. how many students passed the test 18. how he went to France 19. why he went to France 20. how much he spent

Exercise 4, p. 230: 1. what they speak (or which they speak) 2. how far the post office is 3. how Paul went to France 4. when I have grammar class 5. who can drive a car 6. when the party begins 7. whose book this is 8. where the Smiths will go 9. what the new boy's father is 10. how much that new car costs

Exercise 5, p. 231: 1. if she baked some bread 2. if George went to the doctor 3. if he likes ice cream 4. if they are going home now 5. if I am in the right room 6. if you are in the right room 7. if their baby was born in December 8. if the new student bought his books 9. if they will arrive soon 10. if we can go to Florida

Exercise 6, p. 232: 1. (✔) 2. We'll ask where they are going. 3. (✔) 4.(✔) 5. (✔) 6. You must ask how much a ticket costs. 7. He didn't say why he wasn't there. 8. (✔) 9. (✔) 10. Do you know what time it is?

Exercise 7, p. 233: A. 1. I think (that) a car is heavier. 2. I believe (that) a diamond is more expensive. 3. I think (that) chocolate is sweeter. 4. I suppose (that) a man is stronger. B. 1. when Joe called 2. how far New York is 3. how John is coming 4. when they were here 5. who that lady is 6. if they understand English 7. if Joe called last night

Exercise 8, p. 234: 1. c) 2. a) 3. c) 4. c) 5. b) 6. a) 7. c) 8. a) 9. c) 10. a)

Lesson 17

Exercise 1, p. 235: 1. This is the letter that was in my book. 2. This is the letter that John wrote. 3. We read the book that discusses Kennedy. 4. We read the book that Peter owns. 5. They ate the food that was in the refrigerator. 6. They ate the food that I cooked. 7. Did

you find the pen that was on the floor? 8. Did you find the pen that I needed? 9. That is the car that costs four thousand dollars. 10. That is the car that we saw yesterday. 11. Does Mary have the pen that writes green? 12. Does Mary have the pen that John gave to her? 13. This is the television that was on sale. 14. This is the television that I bought. 15. Did you watch the movie that was on television last night? 16. Did you watch the movie that we watched? 17. I know the girl that has a new green car. 18. I know the girl that you know. 19. We helped the man that had a car accident. 20. We helped the man that you know.

Exercise 2, p. 237: 1. that is on Main Street 2. that has a broken arm 3. that sent her a letter 4. that is riding a red bicycle 5. that we saw 6. that she bought 7. that I wrote 8. that Mary made 9. that had thirty questions 10. that Mrs. Jones made

Exercise 3, p. 238: 1. John ate the cake that Mary baked 2. the cake that John ate was delicious 3. I know the student that speaks German 4. the store that we called closed at nine o'clock 5. I spoke to the doctor that Mary spoke to 6. I looked at the book that the boys bought 7. the book that the boys bought cost a lot 8. the teacher liked the story that Phil wrote 9. the story that Phil wrote was very interesting 10. I liked the rice that she cooked

Exercise 4, p. 239: 1. whose house is on State Street 2. whose house is on State Street is our friend 3. whose car we rode in yesterday 4. whose test grade was poor 5. whose tests are extremely difficult only teaches in the morning 6. whose father always says "hello" to us 7. whose mother was on television last night is always late to class 8. whose notes we would like to borrow studies every night 9. whose uniform is almost always dirty was excellent in last night's game 10. whose father owns several stores

Exercise 5, p. 240: 1. c) 2. a) 3. b) 4. b) 5. b)

Exercise 6, p. 241: 1. (that is) 2. (who was) 3. (that was) 4. (that is) 5. (who is) 6. (that is) 7. (who is) 8. (which is) 9. (who is) 10. (who is)

Exercise 7, p. 241: 1. for 2. for 3. during 4. for 5. for 6. for 7. during 8. during 9. for 10. for

Exercise 8, p. 242: 1. I wrote letters during my vacation. 2. I had the flu for two weeks. 3. He talked to me for twenty minutes. 4. She studied grammar during the morning. 5. They stayed with me for a few days.

Exercise 9, p. 242: 1. when 2. while 3. when 4. while 5. when 6. while 7. when 8. while 9. while 10. when

Exercise 10, p. 243: 1. Bill lost his book while he was walking to school. Bill was walking to school when he lost his book. 2. Susan called while I was getting ready to eat. I was getting ready to eat when Susan called. 3. His pen ran out of ink while he was writing a letter. He was writing a letter when his pen ran out of ink. 4. Kay received a telephone call while she was cooking dinner. Kay was cooking dinner when she received a telephone call. 5. Tom found a dollar bill while he was cleaning under the sofa. Tom was cleaning under the sofa when he found a dollar bill.

Exercise 11, p. 244: 1. after 2. after 3. after 4. until 5. After

Exercise 12, p. 244: 1. After we studied, we ate dinner. 2. Until they arrived, she was studying. 3. After I got his letter, I called John up. 4. Before the party begins, you should put the food on the table. 5. Before Ken did his other homework, he studied grammar.

Exercise 13, p. 245: 1. Afterwards 2. After 3. After 4. after 5. after 6. Afterwards 7. after 8. After 9. Afterwards 10. afterwards

Exercise 14, p. 245: A. 1. the man who wrote a book (or, the man that wrote a book) 2. the man whom Mary and John know (or, the man that Mary and John know) 3. the cake that Mary baked was delicious (or, the cake which Mary baked was delicious) 4. the cake that was on the table was delicious (or, the cake which was on the table was delicious) 5. to the boy whose mother is my teacher 6. whose mother is our teacher lent us his bicycle B. 1. was reading while Mary was writing 2. my dinner before I did my homework 3. my homework before I ate my dinner 4. grammar until 7:30 5. was eating when the telephone rang 6. rang while he was eating

Exercise 15, p. 247: 1. *a*) 2. *a*) 3. *d*) 4. *c*) 5. *d*) 6. *d*) 7. *a*) 8. *d*) 9. *c*) 10. *d*)

Lesson 18

Exercise 1, p. 248: 1. work 2. work 3. works 4. works 5. works 6. work 7. work 8. worked 9. worked 10. worked 11. worked 12. worked 13. worked 14. worked 15. have worked 16. have worked 17. has worked 18. has worked 19. has worked 20. have worked 21. have worked

Exercise 2, p. 249: The possible answers are: 2, 6, 7, 8, 10

Exercise 3, p. 249: 1. worked 2. have talked 3. answered 4. ate 5. have read 6. ate 7. have bought 8. studied 9. Did you work 10. Have you studied

Exercise 4, p. 250: 1. called 2. worked 3. was, were 4. had 5. has wanted 6. have played 7. visited 8. listened 9. Did . . . call 10. Has . . . wanted 11. Did . . . work 12. Did . . . visit 13. opened 14. have answered 15. Did . . . answer

Exercise 5, p. 251: 1. has been, was 2. lived, have lived 3. ate, has eaten 4. flew, has flown 5. read, has read 6. have had, had 7. went, have gone 8. have written, wrote 9. saw, have . . . seen 10. worked, has worked

Exercise 6, p. 252: 1. since 2. for 3. since 4. for 5. since 6. since 7. since 8. for 9. since 10. since

Exercise 7, p. 252: 1. Mr. Brown has worked at the bank since May. 2. Peter has had a big car for two months. 3. I have been in class for ten minutes. 4. Paul and I have known you since last week. 5. I have gone to high school for two years. 6. She hasn't spoken Spanish in class since last week. 7. We have liked television since our radio broke. 8. They have heard that noise for an hour. 9. I have known his name since last week. 10. I have liked tennis for a few years.

Exercise 8, p. 253: 1. yes 2. yes 3. no 4. yes 5. yes 6. no 7. no 8. yes 9. yes 10. no 11. yes 12. yes 13. yes 14. no 15. no 16. no 17. no 18. yes 19. no 20. yes 21. no 22. no 23. yes 24. no 25. yes

Exercise 9, p. 254: 1. am working 2. are working 3. is working 4. is working 5. is working 6. are working 7. are working 8. have been working 9. have been working 10. has been working 11. has been working 12. has been working 13. have been working 14. have been working

Exercise 10, p. 255: 1. has been reading 2. have been eating 3. has been studying 4. has been making 5. have been writing 6. has been talking 7. haven't been studying 8. has been working 9. has been boiling 10. has been knocking

Exercise 11, p. 256: 1. worked 2. worked 3. worked 4. worked 5. worked 6. worked 7. worked 8. had worked 9. had worked 10. had worked 11. had worked 12. had worked 13. had worked 14. had worked

Exercise 12, p. 256: 1. had worked, called 2. called, had worked 3. arrived, had had 4. had lived, moved 5. had saved, was 6. had been, answered 7. understood, had explained 8. had been, weren't 9. said, had been 10. knew, had been

Exercise 13, p. 257: 1. he has 2. they haven't 3. she had 4. I haven't 5. she has 6. I haven't 7. we have 8. it hadn't 9. you have 10. they haven't

Exercise 14, p. 258: 1. read, read, read 2. sleep, slept, slept 3. choose, chose, chosen 4. leave, left, left 5. lend, lent, lent 6. speak, spoke, spoken 7. build, built, built 8. know, knew, known 9. sing, sang, sung 10. fly, flew, flown 11. make, made, made 12. understand, understood, understood 13. give, gave, given 14. come, came, come 15. fall, fell, fallen 16. meet, met, met 17. lose, lost, lost 18. cost, cost, cost 19. drink, drank, drunk 20. take, took, taken 21. cut, cut, cut 22. begin, began, begun 23. wring, wrung, wrung 24. find, found, found 25. run, ran, run 26. win, won, won 27. get, got, gotten 28. think, thought, thought 29. forget, forgot, forgotten 30. buy, bought, bought

Exercise 15, p. 259: 1. write, wrote, written 2. sit, sat, sat 3. sell, sold, sold 4. show, showed, shown 5. see, saw, seen 6. bite, bit, bitten 7. teach, taught, taught 8. break, broke, broken 9. grow, grew, grown 10. bring, brought, brought 11. freeze, froze, frozen 12. send, sent, sent 13. drive, drove, driven 14. be, was/were, been 15. do, did, done 16. tell, told, told 17. spend, spent, spent 18. ring, rang, rung 19. have, had, had 20. eat, ate, eaten

Exercise 16, p. 260: 1. sink, sank, sunk 2. feed, fed, fed 3. put, put, put 4. shrink, shrank, shrunk 5. hang, hung, hung 6. set, set, set 7. wear, wore, worn 8. shoot, shot, shot 9. swing, swung, swung 10. tear, tore, torn 11. catch, caught, caught 12. fight, fought, fought 13. lie, lay, lain 14. keep, kept, kept 15. wake, woke, woken 16. throw, threw, thrown 17. let, let, let 18. bend, bent, bent 19. hide, hid, hidden 20. slide, slid, slid 21. blow, blew, blown 22. hurt, hurt, hurt

23. ride, rode, ridden 24. lead, led, led 25. say, said, said 26. bleed, bled, bled 27. strike, struck, struck 28. feel, felt, felt 29. swear, swore, sworn 30. mean, meant, meant

Exercise 17, p. 262: 1. have worked 2. did 3. wrote, hasn't written 4. watched 5. had moved 6. lost, hasn't lost 7. had eaten 8. hasn't had, had 9. has told 10. began, has begun 11. bought, haven't bought 12. gave 13. has spoken 14. didn't drink 15. had studied

Exercise 18, p. 263: 1. had baked 2. has lived 3. lived 4. had lived 5. told 6. came 7. wrote 8. have had 9. was 10. have seen

Exercise 19, p. 263: A. 1. John has spoken French for two years. 2. We have been studying since ten o'clock. 3. I have had a cold for a month. (or, I have had a cold since last month.) 4. She has been learning English since June. B. 1. went, gone 2. did, done 3. began, begun 4. ate, eaten 5. studied, studied 6. sent, sent 7. gave, given 8. wrote, written 9. broke, broken 10. found, found C. 1. went 2. has been 3. did, had studied 4. talked 5. saw

Exercise 20, p. 264: 1. *b)* 2. *c)* 3. *d)* 4. *a)* 5. *a)* 6. *b)* 7. *c)* 8. *b)* 9. *d)* 10. *d)*

Lesson 19

Exercise 1, p. 266: A. 1. write 2. write 3. writes 4. writes 5. write 6. write 7. are written 8. are written 9. are written 10. is written 11. are written 12. is written 13. wrote 14. wrote 15. wrote 16. wrote 17. wrote 18. wrote 19. were written 20. were written 21. were written 22. was written 23. were written 24. was written 25. am writing 26. are writing 27. is writing 28. is writing 29. are writing 30. are writing 31. are being written 32. are being written 33. are being written 34. is being written 35. are being written 36. is being written 37. am going to write 38. are going to write 39. is going to write 40. is going to write 41. are going to write 42. are going to write 43. are going to be written 44. are going to be written 45. are going to be written 46. is going to be written 47. are going to be written 48. is going to be written 49. will write 50. will write 51. will write 52. should write 53. should write 54. should write 55. will be written 56. will be written 57. will be written 58. should be written 59. should be written 60. should be written 61. have written 62. have written 63. has written 64. has written 65. have written 66. have written 67. have been written 68. have been written 69. have been written 70. has been written 71. have been written 72. has been written

Exercise 2, p. 270: 1. is going to be done 2. have to be written 3. are cleaned 4. should be eaten 5. has been done 6. was painted 7. had been called, were called 8. will be given 9. were found 10. are being cooked

Exercise 3, p. 271: 1. Tonight's dinner is being made by Mary. 2. The grammar and vocabulary tests will be given by Mr. Smith. 3. Many new laws were made by the president. 4. The dishes are washed by Susan every night. 5. That car was bought by my brother a long time ago. 6. The work must be done by all of the people. 7. Mrs. Smith has been telephoned by Susan. 8. Our test papers will be graded by the grammar teacher. 9. Those letters should be written by the secretary immediately. 10. The police have to be called by someone immediately.

Exercise 4, p. 272: 1. were signed 2. watched 3. has studied 4. shouldn't use 5. saw 6. has sharpened 7. is being built 8. are going to bring 9. was written 10. is making

Exercise 5, p. 272: 1. any more 2. still 3. any more 4. still 5. still 6. any more 7. any more 8. any more 9. any more 10. still

Exercise 6, p. 273: 1. We can't speak French any more. 2. They still don't have a telephone. 3. I am still sick. 4. Joe is still working here. 5. She isn't hungry any more.

Exercise 7, p. 274: 1. already 2. yet 3. yet 4. yet 5. yet 6. already 7. already 8. already 9. already 10. already

Exercise 8, p. 275: 1. The weather is already very hot. 2. The bus hasn't come yet. 3. John has already eaten lunch. 4. We have already bought our Christmas gifts. 5. The store is already closed.

Exercise 9, p. 276: 1. already 2. still 3. yet 4. any more 5. already, yet 6. yet 7. still 8. already 9. yet 10. already

Exercise 10, p. 277: 1. boring, bored 2. frightened, frightening 3. surprised, surprising 4. entertaining, entertained 5. disappointed, disappointing

Exercise 11, p. 277: 1. shocked 2. disgusted 3. disgusting 4. confusing 5. interesting, interested 6. convincing 7. frightened 8. exciting 9. boring 10. confused 11. bored 12. surprised 13. worried 14. interesting 15. amazing

Exercise 12, p. 278: 1. of 2. at 3. with 4. about 5. to 6. of 7. with 8. with (or, in) 9. to 10. in

Exercise 13, p. 279: 1. John was surprised at making the best grade. 2. Mike is tired of eating hamburgers all of the time. 3. George is unhappy about not having a car. 4. They are interested in learning English. 5. I am worried about spending too much money. 6. David is accustomed to waking up at six in the morning. 7. Bill and Frank are bored with going to the park every Sunday. 8. Maria is used to eating American food now. 9. Mr. Jones is not in favor of paying a lot of taxes. 10. Mark is excited about going to Europe.

Exercise 14, p. 280: 1. am used to reading 2. are used to reading 3. is used to reading 4. is used to reading 5. are used to reading 6. are used to reading 7. used to read 8. used to read 9. used to read 10. used to read 11. used to read 12. used to read

Exercise 15, p. 280: 1. is used to eating, used to eat 2. is used to attending, used to attend (or, used to have) 3. used to cook, is used to eating 4. used to be 5. used to eat

Exercise 16, p. 281: A. 1. was made 2. was seen 3. be sold 4. being built 5. do B. 1. still 2. yet 3. already 4. any more 5. yet C. 1. disappointed 2. tired 3. exciting 4. disgusting D. 1. at 2. to 3. about 4. to 5. about

Exercise 17, p. 282: 1. *c)* 2. *d)* 3. *b)* 4. *b)* 5. *d)*
6. *c)* 7. *b)* 8. *d)* 9. *c)* 10. *d)*

Review Test 3: Lessons 11–19, pp. 284–87

1. *d)* 2. *a)* 3. *c)* 4. *c)* 5. *a)* 6. *d)* 7. *c)* 8. *c)* 9. *d)*
10. *d)* 11. *b)* 12. *b)* 13. *c)* 14. *d)* 15. *d)* 16. *b)*
17. *c)* 18. *d)* 19. *c)* 20. *d)* 21. *c)* 22. *c)* 23. *c)*
24. *c)* 25. *a)* 26. *b)* 27. *d)* 28. *d)* 29. *a)* 30. *b)*
31. *b)* 32. *d)* 33. *d)* 34. *d)* 35. *c)* 36. *d)* 37. *d)*
38. *b)* 39. *a)* 40. *d)* 41. *d)* 42. *c)* 43. *c)* 44. *d)*
45. *c)* 46. *c)* 47. *c)* 48. *c)* 49. *b)* 50. *d)*

Review Test 4: Lessons 11–19, pp. 288–91

1. *d)* 2. *c)* 3. *b)* 4. *a)* 5. *b)* 6. *c)* 7. *c)* 8. *c)* 9. *c)*
10. *c)* 11. *d)* 12. *c)* 13. *c)* 14. *a)* 15. *a)* 16. *d)*
17. *b)* 18. *c)* 19. *b)* 20. *c)* 21. *b)* 22. *c)* 23. *b)*
24. *a)* 25. *c)* 26. *a)* 27. *d)* 28. *d)* 29. *b)* 30. *c)*
31. *c)* 32. *c)* 33. *a)* 34. *b)* 35. *a)* 36. *c)* 37. *b)*
38. *a)* 39. *d)* 40. *a)* 41. *b)* 42. *b)* 43. *b)* 44. *c)*
45. *a)* 46. *a)* 47. *d)* 48. *c)* 49. *b)* 50. *b)*

Lesson 21

Exercise 1, p. 292: 1. to help 2. play 3. ring, to answer 4. to go 5. use 6. to use 7. sing 8. make 9. shake 10. make, eat 11. type 12. to help 13. go 14. learn (or, to learn) 15. to borrow

Exercise 2, p. 293: 1. — 2. to 3. to 4. — 5. — 6. to 7. — 8. — 9. to 10. to (or, —) 11. to 12. — 13. to 14. — 15. to 16. — 17. to 18. — 19. to 20. — 21. — 22. to 23. to 24. — 25. —

Exercise 3, p. 294: 1. wanted 2. knew 3. would arrive 4. spoke 5. spoke 6. had 7. could 8. would talk 9. were 10. could

Exercise 4, p. 295: 1. would, easy 2. were well 3. ate slowly 4. were open 5. were right 6. were present 7. lived, country 8. were Friday 9. gave easy 10. were cheap

Exercise 5, p. 296: 1. didn't cost 2. didn't work 3. didn't have 4. didn't have 5. didn't begin 6. didn't speak 7. didn't have 8. wouldn't 9. didn't need 10. didn't use

Exercise 6, p. 297: 1. were 2. weren't 3. were 4. weren't 5. spoke 6. didn't speak 7. didn't have 8. didn't eat 9. didn't have 10. didn't work 11. were 12. were 13. had 14. understood 15. wrote 16. were 17. liked 18. spoke 19. didn't speak 20. knew

Exercise 7, p. 298: 1. were 2. wouldn't 3. were 4. weren't 5. could 6. did 7. didn't 8. didn't 9. did 10. did 11. didn't 12. didn't 13. did 14. could 15. would

Exercise 8, p. 298: 1. what to do 2. when to leave 3. whom to invite 4. when to arrive 5. how long to stay 6. how to get 7. how much to send 8. how much to make 9. how to cook 10. which to buy

Exercise 9, p. 299: A. 1. to help, study/to study 2. to go 3. drive 4. go B. 1. spoke 2. weren't 3. would 4. didn't have 5. were C. 1. when to arrive 2. how much to bring 3. whom to invite 4. what to do

Exercise 10, p. 300: 1. *b)* 2. *c)* 3. *a)* 4. *b)* 5. *b)* 6. *c)* 7. *c)* 8. *d)* 9. *a)* 10. *b)*

Lesson 22

Exercise 1, p. 302: 1. should 2. must 3. could 4. might 5. must 6. must 7. should 8. might 9. must 10. must 11. should 12. shouldn't 13. shouldn't 14. must not 15. couldn't 16. might 17. might not 18. must 19. could 20. might

Exercise 2, p. 304: 1. John might be a good student. 2. He must have been a good tennis player. 3. Mary should have studied for the test. 4. Mary should study for the test. 5. They could have eaten lunch. 6. Paul must like hamburgers. 7. We might have spent too much money. 8. George must have eaten all of the bread. 9. They could have been here yesterday. 10. It might have rained last night.

Exercise 3, p. 305: 1. It might have been raining last night. 2. She must have been studying for a long time. 3. John couldn't have been studying. 4. He should have gone to class every day. 5. Paul must not have been doing all of the homework. 6. He should have been saving his money. 7. Ben might have been eating dinner when I called. 8. He must have been eating dinner when I called. 9. Sam should have been studying last night. 10. You couldn't have been talking to Tim at noon.

Exercise 4, p. 306: 1. Jane must have been mailing a letter. 2. She should have been wearing a coat. 3. I could have helped the new students from France. 4. I could have been studying last night. 5. Mark should have gone to the bank.

Exercise 5, p. 306: 1. she might have 2. she might have been 3. they couldn't have been 4. they couldn't have 5. he should have 6. I should have been 7. I could have 8. you shouldn't have 9. he should have 10. he should have been

Exercise 6, p. 307: 1. but they might have 2. but she must have 3. but we could have 4. but they couldn't have been 5. but he could have been

Exercise 7, p. 308: 1. hadn't cost 2. had known 3. hadn't arrived 4. hadn't spoken 5. had spoken 6. had had 7. had been 8. had helped 9. hadn't been 10. hadn't been

Exercise 8, p. 308: 1. had been easy 2. had been well 3. had eaten dinner slowly 4. had been open 5. had written the correct answer 6. had driven slowly 7. had arrived early 8. had explained the words slowly 9. had been easy 10. had been cheap

Exercise 9, p. 309: 1. he could 2. they did 3. I had been 4. she had been 5. she were 6. they hadn't 7. she weren't 8. he had been 9. I hadn't 10. I did 11. we didn't 12. he hadn't 13. they would 14. she had 15. we hadn't been 16. we hadn't been 17. we weren't 18. he didn't 19. he hadn't 20. they could

Exercise 10, p. 310: A. 1. should 2. must 3. couldn't 4. might 5. could 6. should B. 1. should have 2. couldn't have 3. must have been C. 1. they had 2. we had been 3. she hadn't 4. it had been

Exercise 11, p. 311: 1. *d)* 2. *c)* 3. *d)* 4. *c)* 5. *d)* 6. *c)* 7. *a)* 8. *c)* 9. *a)* 10. *c)*

Lesson 23

Exercise 1, p. 312: 1. if 2. unless 3. unless 4. if 5. if 6. unless 7. if 8. unless 9. if 10. unless 11. if

12. unless 13. If 14. Unless 15. Unless

Exercise 2, p. 313: 1. They will do the work unless they go to the party. 2. He can't learn English unless he studies. 3. We will call off the party if the rain doesn't stop. 4. She can't buy a new car unless she gets a job. 5. I won't study if it isn't necessary.

Exercise 3, p. 313: 1. because 2. although 3. because 4. because 5. because 6. although 7. although 8. because 9. because 10. because 11. Because 12. Because 13. Because 14. Although 15. Because

Exercise 4, p. 314: 1. We don't like the summer because it's too hot. 2. They aren't going to buy the car although they have enough money. 3. She's very tall although all of her brothers are short. 4. She's very tall because both of her parents are tall. 5. My watch was expensive because it is made of gold.

Exercise 5, p. 315: 1. whether it's raining or not 2. whether or not she has a test 3. whether Paul comes or not 4. whether or not I help them 5. if I find my keys 6. whether or not he looks them over 7. if he cooks steak 8. whether or not it is cheap 9. if it's interesting 10. if he gets a stamp

Exercise 6, p. 315: 1. because 2. because of 3. because 4. because of 5. because 6. Because 7. Because of 8. Because of 9. because of 10. Because

Exercise 7, p. 316: 1. although 2. although 3. in spite of 4. Although 5. although 6. in spite of 7. although 8. in spite of 9. in spite of 10. Although

Exercise 8, p. 316: 1. regardless of 2. regardless of 3. whether or not 4. Whether or not 5. Regardless of 6. regardless of 7. whether or not 8. whether or not 9. regardless of 10. Regardless of

Exercise 9, p. 317: 1. although 2. in spite of 3. regardless of 4. although 5. regardless of 6. in spite of 7. although 8. although 9. regardless of 10. in spite of

Exercise 10, p. 318: 1. regardless of the price 2. because of the rain 3. regardless of the length 4. in spite of the bad grade 5. in spite of the price

Exercise 11, p. 318: 1. because 2. because of 3. in spite of 4. although 5. whether or not 6. regardless of 7. because 8. in spite of 9. regardless of 10. because 11. whether or not 12. because of 13. although 14. whether or not 15. because of 16. Regardless of 17. although 18. although 19. in spite of 20. Because of

Exercise 12, p. 319: 1. if 2. because 3. unless 4. although 5. if 6. if 7. whether or not 8. because 9. because 10. whether or not 11. regardless of 12. although 13. in spite of 14. if 15. if 16. although 17. if 18. whether or not 19. in spite of 20. although

Exercise 13, p. 320: 1. *b*) 2. *a*) 3. *b*) 4. *c*) 5. *a*) 6. *c*) 7. *b*) 8. *b*) 9. *d*) 10. *b*)

Lesson 24

Exercise 1, p. 321: 1. gets, will buy 2. got, would buy 3. had gotten, would have bought 4. comes, will be 5. came, would be 6. had come, would have been 7. has, will take 8. had, would take 9. had had, would have taken 10. will make, works 11. would make, worked 12. would have made, had worked 13. studies,

will pass 14. studied, would pass 15. had studied, would have passed 16. will do, am 17. would do, were 18. would have done, had been

Exercise 2, p. 322: 1. study, will pass 2. pass, will enter 3. enter, will be 4. am, will have 5. have, will make 6. make, will receive 7. receive, will get

Exercise 3, p. 323: 1. received, would put 2. put, would have 3. had, would take 4. took, would go 5. went, would visit 6. visited, would have 7. had, would stay

Exercise 4, p. 323: 1. had gone, would have known 2. had known, would have done 3. had done, would have written 4. had written, would have been 5. had been, would have liked 6. had liked, would have gotten 7. had gotten, would have been

Exercise 5, p. 324: (Answers may vary.) 1. If the ticket is expensive, I won't buy it. 2. If I have a test, I will study. 3. If they had invited me, I would have gone to their party. 4. If I went to Switzerland, I would buy a watch. 5. If I hadn't drunk water, I would have drunk tea. 6. If I had studied last night, I would have studied history. 7. If someone tells me "Thank you," I will say "You're welcome." 8. If I lived in France, I would speak French. 9. If my car has a flat tire, I will change it. 10. If I hadn't had enough money, I would have borrowed some from you.

Exercise 6, p. 325: 1. get 2. were 3. had done 4. would have eaten 5. hear 6. would go 7. would play 8. will wear 9. will need 10. were

Exercise 7, p. 325: 1. are 2. eat 3. had done 4. had had 5. gets 6. had written 7. will cook 8. would have called 9. were 10. would lend

Exercise 8, p. 326: 1. have 2. would buy 3. had eaten 4. is, will be 5. had seen 6. worked 7. would have written 8. had run 9. plays 10. were 11. would call 12. would have gone 13. will read 14. would have studied 15. had flown

Exercise 9, p. 327: 1. *c*) 2. *a*) 3. *d*) 4. *a*) 5. *b*) 6. *c*) 7. *c*) 8. *b*) 9. *c*) 10. *c*)

Lesson 25

Exercise 1, p. 328: 1. such a beautiful baby 2. such a cold day 3. such an expensive car 4. such a tall boy 5. such heavy books 6. such an interesting movie 7. such ugly cats 8. such an interesting person 9. such a pretty watch 10. such an unhappy person

Exercise 2, p. 328: 1. so dirty 2. so expensive 3. so cold 4. so good 5. so delicious 6. so heavy 7. so intelligent 8. so pretty 9. so heavy 10. so nice

Exercise 3, p. 329: 1. such a 2. such a 3. so 4. so 5. such 6. so 7. such a 8. so 9. such a 10. such

Exercise 4, p. 330: 1. The weather is so cold that there is ice on our car. This is such cold weather that there is ice on our car. 2. This car is so expensive that we can't buy it. This is such an expensive car that we can't buy it. 3. This lesson is so easy that everyone understands it. This is such an easy lesson that everyone understands it. 4. Mark and Henry are so nice that everyone likes them. Mark and Henry are such nice people that everyone likes them. 5. The restaurant was so good that we want to return as soon as possible.

This was such a good restaurant that we want to return as soon as possible.

Exercise 5, p. 330: 1. Isn't she going to France? 2. Don't they work in the bank? 3. Didn't he have a cold during the vacation? 4. Wasn't it raining when you arrived? 5. Doesn't he speak French? 6. Hasn't he been in Austria? 7. Hadn't they already done their work? 8. Didn't you eat dinner with John? 9. Hasn't it been snowing since Monday? 10. Shouldn't we clean our room now?

Exercise 6, p. 331: 1. I was 2. I wasn't 3. he did 4. they don't 5. they aren't 6. she is 7. he can 8. there isn't 9. she does 10. she can't

Exercise 7, p. 332: 1. can't you? Yes, I can. 2. aren't we? Yes, we are. 3. do they? No, they don't. 4. can we? No, we can't. (or, No, you can't.) 5. isn't she? Yes, she is. 6. is it? No, it isn't. 7. did he? No, he didn't. 8. could she? No, she couldn't. 9. doesn't he? Yes, he does. 10. will she? No, she won't. 11. didn't he? Yes, he did. 12. are you? No, I'm not. 13. won't she? Yes, she will. 14. didn't she? Yes, she did. 15. didn't I? Yes, you did. 16. has he? No, he hasn't. 17. had she? No, she hadn't. 18. is there? No, there isn't. 19. shouldn't they? Yes, they should. 20. should they? No, they shouldn't.

Exercise 8, p. 333: A. 1. so 2. so 3. such a 4. so 5. so 6. such an B. 1. Didn't she go to France? 2. Aren't they here? 3. Isn't it hot in here? 4. Doesn't she have a car now? C. 1. isn't she? Yes, she is. 2. didn't they? Yes, they did 3. hasn't it? Yes, it has. 4. did he? No, he didn't. 5. were we? No, we weren't. (or, No, you weren't.) 6. won't he? Yes, he will.

Exercise 9, p. 334: 1. *c*) 2. *b*) 3. *a*) 4. *a*) 5. *b*) 6. *b*) 7. *c*) 8. *c*) 9. *c*) 10. *a*)

Lesson 26

Exercise 1, p. 336: 1. myself 2. yourself 3. himself 4. herself 5. itself 6. ourselves 7. yourselves 8. themselves 9. himself 10. themselves

Exercise 2, p. 336: 1. a chair for herself, herself a chair 2. a car for myself, myself a car 3. a short story for himself, himself a short story 4. some aspirin for himself, himself some aspirin 5. some skirts for themselves, themselves some skirts 6. a piece of pie for ourselves, ourselves a piece of pie 7. a glass of milk for himself, himself a glass of milk 8. some fish for ourselves, ourselves some fish 9. some eggs for themselves, themselves some eggs 10. a sweater for herself, herself a sweater

Exercise 3, p. 338: 1. yourself (or, yourselves) 2. themselves 3. himself 4. ourselves 5. herself 6. myself 7. himself 8. ourselves 9. yourself 10. himself

Exercise 4, p. 338: 1. by himself 2. by themselves 3. by myself 4. by herself 5. by myself 6. by themselves 7. by yourself (or, by yourselves) 8. by yourself 9. by ourselves 10. by himself

Exercise 5, p. 339: 1. *a*) 2. *c*) 3. *a*) 4. *b*) 5. *a*) 6. *c*) 7. *b*) 8. *a*) 9. *b*) 10. *a*) 11. *c*) 12. *a*)

Exercise 6, p. 340: 1. to cook, cooking 2. going 3. to study, studying 4. to eat, eating 5. smoking 6. eating 7. moving 8. to see 9. working 10. to write

Exercise 7, p. 340: 1. go, to go 2. to eat 3. writing 4. to stay, staying 5. swimming, swimming 6. to play, playing 7. to play 8. smoking 9. reading 10. speaking

Exercise 8, p. 341: 1. to see 2. to do 3. thinking 4. to watch 5. listening 6. play 7. move (or, moving) 8. singing 9. going 10. eating 11. working 12. eating 13. to learn, learning 14. to have 15. taking

Exercise 9, p. 342: A. 1. *c*) 2. *b*) 3. *a*) 4. *a*) B. 1. myself 2. himself 3. herself 4. himself 5. ourselves C. 1. writing 2. help 3. going 4. eating 5. play

Exercise 10, p. 343: 1. *c*) 2. *d*) 3. *a*) 4. *c*) 5. *b*) 6. *d*) 7. *c*) 8. *c*) 9. *c*) 10. *a*)

Lesson 27

Exercise 1, p. 344: 1. Bob as our new leader 2. their new baby Paul 3. Edward king (or, Edward the king) 4. Joseph Joe 5. Mark as the winner

Exercise 2, p. 345: 1. I call baby dogs puppies. 2. I call people from Japan Japanese. 3. The Americans elected (the name of the president) as president in the last election. 4. I call people from Spain Spaniards. 5. The coach selected (a person's name) as the best player.

Exercise 3, p. 345: 1. his car fixed 2. the curtain closed 3. her hair short 4. my house sold 5. my picture taken 6. my potatoes fried 7. our beds made 8. my car repaired 9. my soup hot 10. my room cleaned 11. my house painted 12. my clothes washed 13. his bread toasted 14. my mistakes corrected 15. her steak well-done

Exercise 4, p. 347: 1. me swimming 2. the cat eating its food 3. John copying my homework 4. the girls singing 5. our brother sleeping on the sofa 6. her face getting hot and turning red 7. the cake burning in the oven 8. us leaving school 9. her son studying in his room 10. the dog barking all night

Exercise 5, p. 348: 1. to stop, smoking 2. try, to catch, stealing 3. having, arrive 4. watching, play (or, playing) 5. to consider, letting, use 6. to do 7. try, to avoid, eating 8. to cook, cooking 9. promise, to help 10. trying (or, to try), to call 11. to watch, land, take (or, landing, taking) 12. to go, to try, to buy 13. studying, to study (or, studying) 14. driving, traveling 15. let, watch 16. to eat 17. smell, burning 18. remember (or, to remember) 19. to avoid, driving 20. getting, sleep

Exercise 6, p. 349: A. 1. The people elected Jackson president. 2. I like my soup hot. 3. Mary swept the floor clean. 4. I want the floor cleaned. 5. She cut her hair short. 6. The man painted the room pink. 7. I want the dishes washed. 8. They saw us taking the money. 9. He heard her singing a song. 10. John found them studying grammar. B. 1. frying 2. cleaned 3. toasted 4. sold

Exercise 7, p. 350: 1. *a*) 2. *d*) 3. *c*) 4. *a*) 5. *b*) 6. *c*) 7. *d*) 8. *c*) 9. *a*) 10. *a*)

Lesson 28

Exercise 1, p. 351: 1. to study 2. Studying 3. to go 4. Eating 5. Playing 6. to ride 7. Riding 8. Driving 9. to drive 10. Learning

Exercise 2, p. 352: 1. Driving our cars is necessary. 2. Learning to use chopsticks was fun. 3. Doing the homework is always difficult. 4. Visiting Europe was very exciting. 5. Reading all the compositions was tiring.

Exercise 3, p. 352: 1. Being a secretary, Mary knows how to type. 2. Having a new car, George doesn't have to take a bus any more. 3. Eating lunch, they saw us from their kitchen window. 4. Seeing the picture, I thought about my cousin. 5. Waiting for the bus, she got tired. 6. Playing baseball, the boys lost the ball. 7. Wiping the table, I spilled hot water on myself. 8. Preparing dinner, I cut my finger. 9. Playing baseball, he tore his pants. 10. Speaking with their friends, they had a great time.

Exercise 4, p. 353: 1. Having played tennis, we took a shower and ate lunch. 2. Having called us, they called the other students. 3. Having done the work, John sat down to watch television. 4. Having worked last year, Mark went to France at Christmas. 5. Having taken the medicine, the children felt much better. 6. Having eaten dinner, he washed all the dishes. 7. Having finished my homework, I went to bed. 8. Having been sick for a week, I went to see the doctor today. 9. Having finished the test early, he started to look his answers over. 10. Having written some letters, she went to the post office to mail them.

Exercise 5, p. 354: A. 1. to write 2. Driving 3. to play 4. Staying 5. Being B. 1. Having eaten dinner, we ate dessert. 2. Watching television, we ate all of the popcorn. 3. Being the teacher, she knows all the students' names. 4. Writing the verbs several times, she learned them quickly.

Exercise 6, p. 355: 1. d) 2. c) 3. c) 4. c) 5. c) 6. b) 7. a) 8. c) 9. d) 10. b)

Lesson 29

Exercise 1, p. 356: 1. no comma 2. go, or 3. eggs, butter, and 4. no comma 5. fish, but 6. no comma 7. no comma 8. doctor, but 9. no comma 10. steak, rice, green beans, and 11. no comma 12. no comma 13. work, and 14. red, blue, or 15. good, but

Exercise 2, p. 357: 1. miles. Therefore, we 2. cake, but 3. news. However, Sue 4. baseball, but 5. raining. Therefore, we

Exercise 3, p. 357: 1. Therefore, 2. However, 3. Also, 4. However, 5. Therefore, 6. Also, 7. Therefore, 8. However, 9. Therefore, 10. Also,

Exercise 4, p. 358: 1. so 2. and 3. so 4. but 5. and 6. but 7. and 8. so 9. but 10. and

Exercise 5, p. 359: 1. The Atlantic is to the east of our country. To the west there lies the Pacific. 2. Writing class is at eight o'clock. Immediately afterwards there is reading class. 3. That station was playing good music last hour. Now there are other good songs on it. 4. Canada is north of the United States. South of the United States there is Mexico. 5. She watched a good movie at nine. At eleven there was the news.

Exercise 6, p. 360: (Answers may vary) 1. In other words, you don't like Paul very much. 2. In other words, Joe had a good time in Norway. 3. In other words, he is a very good student. 4. In other words, she didn't sleep last night. 5. In other words, Martha is a very good cook.

Exercise 7, p. 360: A. 1. cake, coffee, and 2. working, and 3. However, I 4. no comma B. 1. Also 2. In other words 3. Therefore 4. In other words 5. or 6. Likewise C. 1. The post office is to the north. To the south there is the bank. 2. The meeting begins at six. At seven there is the party. 3. Ten people are eating in the cafeteria. In the library there are eight people studying.

Exercise 8, p. 361: 1. d) 2. d) 3. d) 4. b) 5. d) 6. c) 7. a) 8. c) 9. d) 10. c)

Review Test 5: Lessons 21–29, pp. 363–66

1. c) 2. c) 3. b) 4. a) 5. b) 6. b) 7. c) 8. b) 9. d) 10. c) 11. d) 12. c) 13. d) 14. c) 15. d) 16. d) 17. c) 18. c) 19. a) 20. b) 21. a) 22. b) 23. a) 24. a) 25. a) 26. b) 27. b) 28. b) 29. c) 30. d) 31. c) 32. c) 33. b) 34. c) 35. b) 36. c) 37. b) 38. d) 39. b) 40. b) 41. b) 42. c) 43. b) 44. b) 45. b) 46. b) 47. d) 48. c) 49. c) 50. c)

Review Test 6: Lessons 21–29, pp. 367–70

1. d) 2. c) 3. c) 4. a) 5. a) 6. c) 7. a) 8. c) 9. b) 10. b) 11. b) 12. c) 13. b) 14. c) 15. a) 16. c) 17. d) 18. b) 19. c) 20. b) 21. a) 22. b) 23. a) 24. c) 25. d) 26. b) 27. c) 28. b) 29. d) 30. c) 31. b) 32. a) 33. c) 34. c) 35. c) 36. b) 37. c) 38. d) 39. a) 40. b) 41. c) 42. b) 43. c) 44. b) 45. c) 46. c) 47. d) 48. b) 49. c) 50. b)

Index